LIONS OF ENGLAND

To Anne, Clare, Ceri, Anna,
Louisa and Sofia.

PETER JACKSON

Lions of England

MAINSTREAM
PUBLISHING

EDINBURGH AND LONDON

First published in Great Britain in 2005 by
MAINSTREAM PUBLISHING COMPANY
(EDINBURGH) LTD
7 Albany Street
Edinburgh EH1 3UG

ISBN 1 84018 379 9

A catalogue record for this book is available
from the British Library

Typeset in Galliard and Gill Sans

Printed in Great Britain by
Clays Ltd, St Ives plc

ACKNOWLEDGEMENTS

THIS BOOK WOULD NOT HAVE BEEN POSSIBLE WITHOUT THOSE WHO GAVE UNSTINTINGLY of their time, especially the following interviewees:

Lady Noeline Aarvold, James Aarvold, the late Jeff Butterfield, Barbara Butterfield, Cliff Morgan, Dickie Jeeps, the late Peter Jackson, his son Martin Jackson, John Butler of Coventry RFC, John Pullin, David Duckham, Fran Cotton, Roger Uttley, Peter Wheeler, Ray Williams (formerly coaching organiser and secretary of the Welsh Rugby Union), Mike Burton, ex-RFU secretary Tony Hallett, Tommy David, Tony Ward, Sir Clive Woodward, Ray Gravell, Rodney O'Donnell, Henry and Sue Guscott, Jeremy Guscott, Martin Johnson, John Albert from King Country, Dean Richards, Rob Andrew, Jim Telfer, Scott Gibbs, Jason Leonard, Vincenzo and Eileen Dallaglio, Lawrence Dallaglio, Jason Robinson and Eric Hawley, the scout who set him off on the road to fame at Wigan Rugby League Football Club.

Other sources include the following: Sir Winston Churchill's *Their Finest Hour*, *Lions Down Under: The British Isles Rugby Tour of Australia and New Zealand, 1959* by Vivian Jenkins; *Bill Beaumont: The Autobiography*, Willie John McBride's *Willie John: The Story of My Life*, *My Autobiography* by Will Carling; Sir Clive Woodward's *Winning!*; Sir Terry McLean's *The Lion Tamers*, Kyran Bracken's *Behind the Scrum*; and *The History of the British & Irish Lions* by Clem Thomas.

I am indebted to the *Daily Mail*, and their sports pictures editor Brendan Monks, for providing the photographs, to Bill Campbell of Mainstream for his unfailing patience, to my editor Paul Murphy for making sense of it all and to Graeme Blaikie for putting it together.

To Tom Park, the late editor of the long defunct *Derry Standard*, for giving a pesky schoolboy the chance to start following a journalistic dream.

To colleagues and competitors alike for their camaraderie on the long haul from Rotherham to Rotorua and Bracknell to Brakpan. To Alastair Hignell of BBC Five Live, whose indomitable spirit to pursue his broadcasting career as normal in the face of adversity requires courage of truly lion-like proportions.

And, most of all, to Anne for her support-cum-understanding, even if it never went quite as far as appreciating why the obsession with a strange-shaped ball should wreak almost as much havoc with the summer social calendar as with the non-existent winter one . . .

CONTENTS

PROLOGUE

THIS BOOK HAS TAKEN SOME FIVE YEARS TO COMPILE INSTEAD OF TWO, WHICH ONLY goes to show what can happen when trying to locate out-of-the-way places from a geographically challenged perspective. For one afflicted not so much with a poor sense of direction as none at all, knowing where to go is one thing, how to get there another entirely. On their voyages of discovery, Marco Polo, Vasco da Gama and Christopher Columbus never had to contend with a bewildering array of speed limits or the fearful knowledge that they were but one camera flash away from being put in dry dock for six months with twelve penalty points.

A natural inclination to take a wrong turn caused infinitely more delays to the project than the professional demands of covering World Cups, Lions tours, Six Nations championships, European Cups and Premiership Grand Finals. That I have not once turned up at the wrong stadium on the wrong day is truly the eighth wonder of the world. Finding a house on a specific street or a farm far from the madding crowd has consistently proved difficult. Getting from A to B has rarely been negotiated without succumbing to the magnetic attraction of visiting C, D and E and, on really bad days, X, Y and Z as well.

The first journey on the spoor of the Lions of England was a case in point. My namesake, *the* Peter Jackson of Coventry, Warwickshire, England and the Lions, went to inordinate trouble to

9

give detailed directions to his home in the Birmingham suburb of Castle Bromwich, which he finished off with a reassuringly cheery, 'You can't miss it.' One false move on the motorway maze turned a two-hour journey into a confusing tour of the entire West Midlands, without the foggiest idea of where I had come from or where I was going.

It marked the start of a broad detour along the highways and byways of the country: through the villages of Buckinghamshire to deepest Suffolk; from the Peak District to the leafy lanes of Surrey and the one-way system through the metropolis of Leeds. Some of the places were so far off the beaten track as to be identified only by a tiny speck on the map, like Aust, a hamlet almost hidden beneath the Severn Bridge.

The idea of presenting a career profile of the more colourful English Lions caused endless, non-motorway hours agonizing over who to put in and who to leave out. The choice is entirely a subjective one, an attempt to span the three-quarters of a century when the BIRUTT (British Isles Rugby Union Touring Team) evolved from what sounded like an acronym for a Middle East capital into a sporting institution enjoying universal recognition as the Lions.

Lions of England, like *Lions of Wales* published some seven years ago, is not intended to be a definitive work on the subject, merely an attempt to do justice to some extraordinary people. My regret – more so than getting lost in the search to track them down – is that, unlike Sir Clive Woodward with the 2005 Lions in New Zealand, I have been unable to include everyone, well, almost everyone.

You do not have to be English to appreciate that each and every one of the chosen few offers a fascinating example of what drives a rugby player to succeed, often against heavy odds. Their success has left the sport all the richer and their impact has contributed to its booming popularity. Indeed, several of those featured in this book played major roles in the greatest English sporting achievement for almost 40 years: the World Cup victory in November 2003. It could even be argued that it was the greatest of all time: that beating West Germany at Wembley – even with 'der Kaiser' Franz Beckenbauer in their side – was a piece of Black Forest gateau compared to being asked to overcome Australia in Australia.

The book is an appreciation of a rare breed of extraordinary players whose backgrounds span the social spectrum. It is also an attempt to explain what set them apart and understand what made them tick, to capture the men behind the deeds and suggest, respectfully, that they are all worthy of a place in the pantheon. Each and every one has a fascinating story to tell. They all epitomize the famous lines from Rudyard Kipling's *If*: 'If you can meet with Triumph and Disaster / And treat those two impostors just the same.'

A journey that began enmeshed by Spaghetti Junction ended back at the scene of England's triumph in Sydney, not because I took the wrong plane – as opposed to the wrong motorway – but because it offered me a few days' refuge from a battered Lions tour on the other side of the Tasman Sea in which to meet the five-year deadline. With a lot of help from my friends along the way, putting me back on the right road, we got there in the end, and this is the result. Whether you think it was all worthwhile, dear reader, is for you to decide.

A man can be as great as he wants to be. If you believe in yourself and have the courage, the determination, the dedication, the competitive drive and if you are willing to sacrifice the little things in life and pay the price for the things that are worthwhile, it can be done.

Vince Lombardi, American football coach

I

THE VIKING

THE ANCIENT WHALING PORT OF TØNSBERG LIES ON THE WESTERN BANK OF THE Oslofjord, some 60 miles south of the capital. Founded by the Vikings in the ninth century, the oldest town in Norway provides a safe haven for the whaling fleet operating in the oceans of the Arctic and Antarctic. Apart from its sawmills and imposing fortifications, the maritime centre has another claim to fame that few, if any, of its 38,000 inhabitants would have the faintest clue about. Tønsberg was the ancestral home of a distinguished gentleman of England whose life spanned every decade of the last century. A true Corinthian from an era when sport was played for the love of the game and not much else, Sir Carl Aarvold might have leapt out of the celluloid of *Chariots of Fire* as effortlessly as his Scottish contemporary, and fellow international three-quarter, Eric Liddell. Just as the Flying Scot made his debut in the Five Nations during the '20s at the age of 20, so Aarvold did likewise a few years later, and, while he never quite got round to emulating Liddell's feat of winning an Olympic track gold, the English Lion blazed a trail wherever he went and whatever he did, weaving his family name into the rich tapestry of two strange bedfellows: Twickenham and the Old Bailey.

None of it would have been possible had Ole Aarvold not decided to do what thousands of seafaring Norwegians had done down the centuries and pushed the boat out: in his case rather a long way –

13

down the fjord into the Skagerrak, and on a course almost due west across the North Sea to England. The director of a shipping line, he had spotted a gap in the market of what was then a largely uncomplicated travel industry where everything either moved by boat or train or didn't move at all.

Accompanied by his wife Majen, Aarvold sailed into Hartlepool in 1902, at a time when the Wright brothers, Orville and Wilbur, were still building their heavier-than-air flying machine, and Henry Ford was working on his big idea for the combustion engine. By the following year, the Wrights were airborne, Ford had founded the first automobile factory and Aarvold had begun the business which would keep him in England for the rest of his life.

Carl, one of three sons, was born in Durham on 7 June 1907, which happened to be the year Billy Williams bought his famous cabbage patch at Twickenham. The ten and a quarter acres of land on a market garden site near the Thames cost £5,572 12s 6d, and, even if Williams could never have envisaged what it would become a century later, he at least had the foresight to provide the Rugby Football Union (RFU) with a fixed abode at a time when they were shuttling matches between the Crystal Palace, Richmond, Blackheath and the provinces.

Meanwhile, at Durham School, the teenaged Aarvold was being taught a brand of football that they would never have understood across the sea at Tønsberg. The dashing young fellow proved such a natural at the game of rugby that within two years of arriving at Cambridge University he was playing for England. He was only 20, and this was not any old England, but the Grand Slam winning team of 1928 led by Ronald Cove-Smith, following Wavell Wakefield's retirement the previous year.

That year they went one better and won five matches in a single season for the first time, starting with the Waratahs of New South Wales, who were, in effect, Australia. Over the course of the next ten weeks, they beat Wales in Swansea and Ireland in Dublin, before finishing up at Headquarters with wins over France and Scotland to secure the Grand Slam. Aarvold finished the following season on the right wing, scoring two of England's four tries in Paris, before skipping the 1930 championship to further his law career.

Aarvold had by then established himself among the best in the four home countries, gaining selection for the British Isles' tour of New Zealand at the end of that season, despite having missed the entire Five Nations tournament that, then as now, acted as a series of trial matches for the ultimate honour of travelling to the far side of the world.

Like his father before him, the young Aarvold sailed off on an adventure that would introduce the world to a new breed of rugby player: the Lion, so-called because each jersey bore the triple-lion motif, and, for those who failed to notice, the honorary team manager, James Baxter, made a point of sporting a silver lion lapel badge.

The two conditions for selection were a sufficient level of ability on the field and sufficient financial clout off it to provide a lump sum of £80 of spending money. One was no good without the other, which left nobody in much doubt as to the elitist nature of the early Lions. Having endured the general strike of 1926 and the depression which followed, not many working-class lads could stump up for a dinner jacket, which was considered de rigueur for the trip, let alone the 80 quid. Egalitarianism was not a word on many lips when the Lions gathered for a pre-departure dinner at the Savoy attended by the future King George VI. They set sail from Southampton the following day, 11 April, on the MV *Rangitata*, and, compared to the vast numbers dispatched 75 years later, it could be safely said that the Lions had never run a tighter ship.

While the 2005 team took an official entourage of more than seventy for eleven matches, the 1930 pioneers made do with just thirty: twenty-nine players, as opposed to forty-five, and a management team of one, compared to nearly thirty. While the 2005 touring team played a grand total of eleven matches, their predecessors played almost three times as many without once sending for a replacement, which was just as well because it would have taken him six weeks to get there.

There were no coaches, no doctors, no physiotherapists, no dietitians, no psychologists, no management consultants, no peripheral-vision coaches. There wasn't even a kit technician, the highfalutin description given nowadays to the baggage man. 'And there were no journalists,' as the Welsh nonagenarian Harry Bowcott, Aarvold's centre partner and the oldest twentieth-century Lion to reach the twenty-first, gleefully pointed out during a recent reminiscence. 'There was nobody to send word back to London that we'd been naughty boys. We had the place to ourselves.'

In truth, nobody would have been particularly interested. They were never going to be waiting on tenterhooks in the back streets of Derby or anywhere else for news about an event from the other side of the world that barely rated more than a passing mention. Sheffield Wednesday had won the First Division, Arsenal the FA Cup and the British sporting public were busy keeping track of Don Bradman on the first of his three tours with the Australian cricket team.

In New Zealand, the Lions drew crowds on such a massive scale that the country had never seen anything like it before. Five weeks after weighing anchor and sailing down the Solent, the *Rangitata* hove into view in Wellington harbour at ten o'clock in the morning, whereupon the New Zealand government steamer *Janie Seddon* took New Zealand RFU officials to meet the tourists and welcome them.

The best of British and Irish rugby disembarked on the Pipitea Wharf, which had been decorated for the occasion, and walked smack into an issue that would appear not to have occurred to anyone at Twickenham or anywhere else for that matter. Why, when they knew that the All Blacks would be playing in, er, all black, had the Lions chosen to play in navy blue?

Baxter explained that dark-blue jerseys had been worn by the British teams in South Africa in 1924 and in Argentina in 1927. Dark blue was the colour of 'Great Britain's rugby representatives' and that was that: take it or leave it. There is nothing in the history books to suggest that Mr Baxter – 'Bim' to his friends – regretted travelling 12,000 miles without a change strip or that he would order the players to travel another 12,000 miles back again to collect one.

Had he been so inclined, he could have sent word to the nearest outfitters and had them knock up a set of jerseys in pink and white. The Lions did take sufficient notice to change their colours for the next tour, from blue to red, on the assumption that there would be no more clashes unless, by some mysterious quirk, they were confined to home and obliged to tour Wales.

It wouldn't have been so bad had they come equipped in a light shade of Cambridge blue. Instead, the blue they chose could scarcely have been any closer to black, as Harry Bowcott remembered only too well. 'It became a topic of discussion every time we played,' he said some years before his death in 2004 at the age of 97. 'Everywhere we went, they were telling us that we would have to change for the Test matches but we couldn't change. We had no other jersey to change into. Nothing could have been more stupid, but it went on and on until after the first Test. We couldn't understand it. In the end they had to change. They weren't at all happy about it.'

The New Zealanders put the matter before a special meeting of their management committee, and it was decided that the New Zealand team would play in white jerseys with a silver fern on a black shield, plus the usual black shorts and black socks with two white bands. Even in all white, the All Blacks prevailed against a Lions team whom the historians acclaimed as containing 'some truly great players amongst the backs of whom the shining lights were the brilliant centre Carl Aarvold and the mercurial fly-half Roger Spong'.

Almost half a century later, Aarvold was still regarded by those lucky enough to have seen him in action as one of the greatest midfield backs ever to play in New Zealand. Elegant was the adjective most often used to capture the essence of a player whose four Varsity matches for Cambridge from 1925 to 1928 resulted in four wins for the Light Blues, Aarvold appearing in the first three in different positions – at centre, full-back and wing.

Well above average height by pre-war standards at 6 ft 2 in., he cut a dashing figure as one of the taller members of a squad, which would have been positively lightweight compared to the behemoths of the modern game. The tallest player, the uncapped English flanker John Hodgson, stood at 6 ft 3½ in., and only one player topped 16 st.: the Irish back-row forward George Beamish, a Battle of Britain pilot who was knighted towards the end of a distinguished career with the Royal Air Force.

Sixteen of the party were English of whom three were never capped: Bradford full-back G. Bonner, the Redruth three-quarter R. Jennings and the second-row forward, H. C. S. Jones of Manchester. Of all the young Lions in a hurry on that tour, James Reeve showed the All Blacks the quickest pair of feet to score the first try of the Test series. The 21-year-old Harlequin went on to become a barrister by profession, like Aarvold, only to lose his life in a road accident six years after returning from New Zealand. By contrast, Tony Novis, the Blackheath wing who replaced him for the second Test before Reeve reclaimed his place for the remainder of the series, lived to the age of 91.

A career soldier who doubled up as the Lions' on-deck trainer during the long voyage from Southampton, Lieutenant Colonel Novis was an outstanding all-round sportsman, making light of his short stature, which he attributed to the scarcity of food as a boy growing up during the First World War. A universally popular figure who was born in India, where his father served as a surgeon, Novis was described in one obituary as 'gentle, courteous, unassuming, good-humoured and sociable'.

He was also a war hero, winning the Military Cross at the Battle of Sidi Barrani in North Africa in December 1940 as part of the campaign under General Archibald Wavell that ended with the Allies taking 130,000 Italian prisoners. Novis's citation described how he was ordered to take his company forward over open ground, under enemy fire, and silence the Italian guns. Ordered to advance again, Novis – later wounded in the hand and neck by shrapnel – stormed a machine-gun post with three other men.

As a Lion, he topped the try chart on that tour of Australasia with twelve in New Zealand and four more in Australia. He sat out the first Test against the All Blacks when a try from each wing – one from Reeve of Harlequins on the left and another from Jack Morley from Newport on the right – gave the Lions a flying start to the four-Test series in Dunedin. As well as some stylish backs, they had a forward of gigantic proportion, the Welshman Ivor Jones, whose towering deeds during that tour earned him the ultimate soubriquet of 'The King'.

Jones, who spent a lifetime in the service of Welsh rugby in a variety of roles including chairman of selectors and president, was the nearest thing to a one-man team: he proved this in the second Test by taking over at scrum-half. A goal-kicking number 8 way ahead of his time, he would have been a superstar in today's celebrity-obsessed society, and at Carisbrook on a sleeting winter's day in July 1930 he engineered the decisive act of that opening Test, breaking clear on the Lions' ten-yard line, running almost half the length of the pitch and drawing the legendary George Nepia before putting Morley over for the try.

The rain and snow, which made it 'almost impossible' to distinguish one player from another during the traditional curtain-raiser, had forced spectators to huddle on the terraces under groundsheets in the hours before kick-off. As conditions worsened, some left before kick-off rather than risk hypothermia, and yet almost 30,000 braved the elements, a record crowd paying record receipts of £4,200.

At the end of the game, the crowd reportedly gave 'the visitors a fine reception and accepted the home team's defeat in the right spirit'. Their generosity would probably have been stretched beyond breaking point had the Lions not lost one half of their English half-back partnership during the first match of the tour. Wilfred Sobey of Old Millhillians was the Gareth Edwards of his day and Spong the best fly-half of his generation. As Bowcott said, 'If it hadn't been for poor Sobey, I think we'd have seen them off over the four matches.'

A fortnight after the first Test, the Lions lost the second in Christchurch, despite Aarvold scoring both tries. The visitors had captured the imagination of the New Zealand public as never before. Saturday, 5 July dawned 'cold and raw with the prospect of heavy rain', and yet they were queuing outside the gates of Lancaster Park before 7 a.m. By 9.30 a.m. when the ground was opened, several hundred had assembled; special trains brought thousands from all over the South Island, and the city's taxi drivers declared they had never known a day like it.

Without Sobey, the Lions had answered the emergency by converting the Wanderers centre Paul Murray to scrum-half. The Irish doctor's initiative set up the first Lions try, enabling Morley, in the words of one reporter, 'to beat Oliver before handing on to Aarvold. The flying centre ran across in the corner and was halfway to the posts when he dotted down. [Doug] Prentice goaled to give the tourists the lead.'

The All Blacks replied with a try of their own to nose ahead 8–5 moments before the tourists suffered a crippling blow: Murray broke a collarbone. Jones took over at scrum-half and proceeded to attempt to show that 14 men could beat 15. A second converted try stretched the Kiwis further clear at 13–5 only for the Lions to create a second of their own finished off by Aarvold in what was acclaimed at the time as the finest seen at Lancaster Park.

Jones made it possible by unhinging the All Black defence. One newspaper's blow-by-blow account recorded what happened next:

> Jones broke from a ruck in midfield and passed to Aarvold. Tony Novis (the left wing) came up in support but Aarvold clapped on the pace and shot between Lucas and Hart. As the British centre raced away, Hart dived at him and managed to touch his heels, but Aarvold kept his feet and ended a 40-yard run with a try under the posts.

The series, all-square with two down and two to go, had captured the imagination of the New Zealand public like never before. Newspapers across the country reacted to the clamour by devoting more column inches on a daily basis. One reported on the Thursday, fully 48 hours before the third Test at Eden Park, that, 'Thousands from outlying districts left their homes to ensure their arrival in Auckland in time.'

On match day, special trains from all over the North Island converged on the city carrying thousands more. They began queuing at 6.30 a.m. and 92 extra tram cars were pressed into service, shuttling an estimated 10,000 from the city centre to Eden Park. Forty thousand were inside by kick-off, the largest crowd for any match in the country's sporting history.

The entrepreneurial spirit flourished outside the ground. Makeshift stands erected in the backyards of houses overlooking part of the stadium, from elevated ground behind one end, allowed a few thousand more to watch. They did so despite attempts by the Eden Park authorities to spoil their view. A canvas screen erected to do just that was given short shrift and its framework used as a stand.

New Zealand critics had been quick to acknowledge that 'the Britishers had tons of pace on the wing' in singling out the Light Blues of Cambridge in the dark blue of the Lions: Aarvold and Bowcott. The Anglo-Welsh centre pairing scored a try each at Eden Park, Bowcott in the first half, Aarvold in the second, only for the Lions to lose 15–10. That they had, by all accounts, the best back on the field in Spong the Old Millhillian merely underlined the loss of his half-back partner and fellow Old Millhillian, the luckless Sobey.

Local historians praised the Lions, not only for their box-office appeal and 'venturesome approach to the game' but for 'accepting their victories modestly and their defeats without excuses. They did not resort to dirty play, nor did they complain about referees. The only sour note of the tour was sounded by the manager when he made scathing remarks about New Zealand wing-forwards, but he mellowed as the tour progressed.'

Far from mellowing, James 'Bim' Baxter blew his top at the official dinner on the night of the final Test. His target was none other than the All Black captain himself, Cliff Porter, by some distance the most controversial wing-forward of his generation. New Zealand operated a seven-man scrum: a 2–3–2 formation which consisted of two hookers in the front row, a lock bound by a man on either side in the second row and two wing-forwards at the rear.

Instead of acting as the eighth forward, Porter fed the ball into the scrum as an auxiliary scrum-half, which left him free to strike as 'the rover', either in support of his own backs or to hound Spong on the opposition put-in or whenever one of his dual hookers lost a strike against the head. Baxter, President of the RFU three years earlier, former England international, Olympic yachting silver medallist and past captain of the Royal Liverpool Golf Club, was offended by the tactic. He spoke out at the earliest available opportunity, after the opening match of the tour at Wanganui, attacking the detached wing-forward as 'the wolf of the game'.

'There is one thing I dislike,' he said. 'That is your wing-forward play. I am sure the gentleman who had the misfortune to play there, if he looked into his own heart, did not like it either. I won't say he is on the borderline. He is over it and must be discouraged. He causes irritation to both sets of forwards. It is contrary to the spirit of rugby football.'

Baxter's opposite number, the All Blacks' team manager Ted McKenzie, bit his tongue but could only contain himself for so long. He let fly at the official dinner after the third Test, flinging Baxter's words back in his face. 'Once Mr Baxter called him a cheat,' McKenzie said, referring to Porter and warming to his task with a cutting dose of sarcasm. 'I appreciate Mr Baxter's remarks, particularly as they were made by a man so high in the game. And I feel I might reply by criticising certain aspects of the British side's play. Shepherding the player with the ball so that he can't be tackled has been common with the British team. I hope it is not intentional, but it appears to have been deliberately studied. Jersey holding – pulling the jersey of an opponent after he has released the ball – is also common and an offence against the rules of the game.'

At that juncture, Aarvold tried to protest in his capacity as the acting Lions captain but was slapped down by the irate McKenzie: 'I am speaking now, Mr Aarvold, not you. I will not pretend our players are perfect. They may also on occasions be guilty of lapses in this respect, but I will say that the British team is a fine enough side to win matches without resorting to obstruction and similar tactics which may, or may not, be intentional. But I must say that some of the instances of obstruction appeared to have been deliberately studied.'

After what the distinguished New Zealand journalist Terry McLean described as 'an astonishing outburst', McKenzie sat down to an embarrassed silence. Baxter refused to comment, preferring to keep his powder dry until the end of the Test series, which Porter, the rogue rover, clinched in emphatic style, scoring two of the six tries in a 22–8 home win – 34–10 in today's currency. The match settled one argument but escalated another. While Porter had the last word on the field, Baxter made sure he had the last word off it.

'The rules under which we play are laid down by the International Board,' he told guests at the after-match dinner, 'and in our opinion [they] are good enough for the average young man to play under. We don't intend to alter them one jot. Those who don't want to play under them can stay outside.'

Within two years the two-man front row had been outlawed and New Zealand brought into line on the scrummage offside law. By then Aarvold had been made England captain, the *Daily Mail* paying suitable tribute to the appointment of a 'tall, slim young man who looks built for speed and is. Somehow, in the roughest match, he always manages to keep his fair hair unruffled. This is in accordance with his temperament.'

He led his country in seven successive internationals, starting with a defeat against Scotland at Murrayfield in March 1931 and finishing with another versus Wales at Twickenham in January 1933. In between, he had the presence of mind and linguistic skills to avert a diplomatic incident in Paris at the dinner following England's one-point defeat at Stade Colombes, a contretemps provoked, it seemed, by the distinguished Harlequin Adrian Stoop in his role as RFU president.

He regaled his French guests with a recollection of the English tries at the Parc des Princes in 1906, all nine of them. Not surprisingly, it went down like the proverbial lead balloon. 'As it was being translated, the glances conveyed the atmosphere,' the late E. W. Swanton wrote in the *Daily Telegraph*. He continued:

> The English, these men who have ostracised us, are they human?
>
> Happily, the night was saved by a young man down from Cambridge University, Carl Aarvold. Speaking in French, he thanked the home team for a sporting match. He said he enjoyed playing against France and hoped to be doing so again. Uproarious applause, and an elementary lesson in public relations . . .

Knowing what to say to the opposition and how to say it was one thing. Knowing every single member of his own team, at a time of chop and change, was another matter entirely. A chance encounter on the train journey to Edinburgh for his first match as captain illustrates the gloriously casual, splendidly amateurish approach of the time.

Aarvold, a man of humour and style who became a raconteur of some repute, had been minding his own business, as the train rattled north from King's Cross, when he passed the time of day with a fellow traveller. According to family sources, the conversation went something like this:

> Stranger: Are you going to Edinburgh on business?
> Aarvold: No, not really. I'm going to play a game of rugby.
> Stranger: That's a bit of a coincidence. So am I.
> Aarvold: Really? Who are you playing for?
> Stranger: I'm playing for England against Scotland.
> Aarvold: Good heavens. You're never going to believe this but . . .

None of the family is certain as to the stranger's identity, although he was thought to have been Tom Knowles, the Birkenhead Park fly-half who won his first and last cap in that match. Remember, rugby football in those days commanded precious little in the way of column inches in national newspapers. Television had not been invented, there were no specialist sports stations to be had on radio and therefore no earthly reason why one England player should know what another looked like unless he had bumped into him regularly on the club circuit.

Squad training was as alien to the ethos of the pure amateur game in the early '30s as other harbingers of professionalism like sponsorship. That the English captain and the English fly-half had not only never met but did not recognise each other, hard to believe by the modern standards of professionalism, was perfectly plausible in an era when the team never used to meet until the Friday afternoon before a match. It was not unknown for total strangers to be introduced to one another the day before they played for the same team.

Even so, the railway compartment exchange was exceptional, but utterly in keeping with Aarvold's life. After 16 internationals for England and four for the Lions, he retired in 1933 at the age of 26, the year after he had been called to the bar by Inner Temple. 'I think 27 is about the right age to stop playing strenuous games,' he said years later. 'If you go on any longer, you go downhill.'

The most rewarding of all Aarvold's rugby matches was not for the Lions or England but for Headingley, whom he had joined from West Hartlepool. What appeared to be a routine home match towards the end of 1928 turned out to be nothing of the sort because he met Noeline Hill. She was a redoubtable Yorkshire lady from Denton Park who excelled at tennis, squash, golf and fencing. They were married in London six years later at St George's, in Hanover Square, by the Bishop of Worcester.

Seventy years later, Lady Aarvold was recalling some of her golden memories, from the family's home in the lovely rolling Surrey countryside around Dorking, not least the picnic ritual of the west car park at Twickenham. Despite her husband's flourishing legal career, the ever-darkening cloud of Nazism loomed over the early years of a marriage which survived the Second World War and spanned more than half a century.

Aarvold, an officer in the Royal Artillery, had a distinguished war record and was awarded an OBE in 1945. Two of his teammates with Blackheath, England and the Lions paid the supreme sacrifice. His great friend, the goal-kicking back-row forward Brian Black, a South African Rhodes Scholar, lost his life on active service as a Pilot Officer in the RAF in July 1940. A few months later that same year Henry Rew, the outstanding front-row Lion in all four Tests in New Zealand ten years earlier and a career soldier as an officer in the Royal Tank Corps, was killed in Libya.

Returning to civvy street and resuming where he had been so rudely interrupted six years earlier, the former Durham School, Emmanuel College, Cambridge University, West Hartlepool, Headingley, Blackheath, Barbarians, Durham, England and Lions three-quarter established a thriving legal practice in London. In 1948, he became deputy chairman of Surrey Quarter Sessions, which he combined with duties as Recorder of Pontefract for three years until 1954, when he was appointed a judge of the Mayor's and City of London Court.

His career at the Old Bailey began when he became Common Sergeant of the City of London in 1959. As Recorder of London, he was the senior, permanent judge at the Old Bailey from 1964 to 1975, during which time the Central Criminal Court expanded from four courts to twenty-nine. He presided over every kind of criminal case, including no shortage of causes célèbres: for example, the trials of the Kray twins and the notorious insurance swindler Emil Savundra.

As Aarvold's stature rose ever higher, he chaired a Home Office committee after the trial of the poisoner Graham Young, who had been found guilty of a double murder committed while on conditional discharge from Broadmoor Hospital: the Aarvold Report subsequently recommended restrictions on the parole of mental patients. But it would be easy in highlighting a few of his many achievements to lose sight of Aarvold the human being.

He had earned a worthy reputation as London's most colourful and popular judge of his time. 'Humility becomes a judge even more than it does anyone else,' he said. 'A vain man is usually a bad judge.' *The Times* recognised this side of his character in his obituary:

> He had a natural capacity for dispensing justice with unfailing courtesy and humanity and with a complete lack of the irritability and impatience which sometimes afflict incumbents of the bench. He had a deep appreciation of the problems of the inadequate and the disadvantaged.
>
> Indeed on his last day in office, he celebrated what he called his 'feeling of enlarged freedom' by releasing on bail a young man on a violence charge because the accused's son was ill, and Aarvold felt he ought to be able to be with him. This was utterly characteristic of Aarvold's unaffected compassion.

Despite the heavy demands of his professional life in ensuring that justice was not only done but seen to be done, he found the time and energy to work for Toynbee Hall, the charity set up to combat poverty in the East End of London. Its location, in the Tower Hamlets area of London, backed on to Gunthorpe Street, where Jack the Ripper killed the first of his victims in 1888, and the charity became the life's work of the disgraced politician John Profumo, forced to resign from Harold Macmillan's Conservative government as a result of the Christine Keeler scandal in 1963.

There were more facets to the multi-dimensional judge of Viking stock. He gave another sport the benefit of his dignity and wisdom throughout 19 years as president of the Lawn Tennis Association (LTA). His tenure spanned a period which saw the historic decision to abolish the sport's distinction between amateur and professional, with effect from 1968.

In December the previous year, immediately after the LTA had taken their decision, Sir Carl wrote a letter to Dr Giorgio de Stefani, his presidential counterpart at the International Lawn Tennis Federation. He wrote:

> We are convinced that the action we are taking will prove of immense good for the game and will abolish the dishonesty and hypocrisy at present so rife.
>
>   We think that to authorise a player to make as much money as he can from playing the game and yet try to distinguish him from another category of professional would be the quintessence of hypocrisy. Far better call them all 'players' and legislate accordingly, both nationally and internationally.

Throughout his long life, Sir Carl never allowed his abiding sense of fair play to be compromised, a point he made during his outgoing speech as president of the LTA in December 1981. 'It is easy enough to blame someone else but a game is a game and temper has no part in it,' he said in pleading for the sport not to be ruined by bad behaviour from players or spectators.

Virginia Wade's triumph in winning the Wimbledon singles title in the midst of the Queen's Silver Jubilee celebrations, four years earlier, had been another landmark of his presidency. Presenting her with a 49-piece Waterford Crystal set, Sir Carl said, 'Her success was no fluke. For 12 months she had been determined that 1977 was to be her year. She may have put a shekel or two in her handbag as she did so, but to win at Wimbledon in this very special year was her declared intent. She taught us that skill by itself is not enough. It requires determination and courage, plus the inspiration of purpose, to yield its reward.'

Knighted in 1968, he served as a steward on the British Boxing Board of Control and was chairman of the RAC for three years, from 1978. His sense of humour remained intact throughout, as reflected in a mock complaint at the behaviour of the guests when he spoke at the Saracens' centenary dinner in 1976. It was, he mused, 'a sign of England's decadence that the president of the Rugby Football Union could stand up and address you and not have a single bread roll directed at him. It would never have happened in my day . . .'

A seven-handicap golfer, he rarely missed an international at Twickenham and the traditional west car park picnic. No occasion there gave him greater pride than the England v. Scotland schoolboy match in January 1964 when 17-year-old James, the middle of his three sons, maintained the family tradition of representing his country, not in the centre but in the back row. 'I'm afraid Scotland won by miles, but Dad enjoyed it,' said James, who went on to play for Richmond in the same pack as England lock Chris Ralston, and the Springbok number 8 Tommy Bedford. 'Dad's rugby philosophy never changed. It was a game and, when all was said and done, that's all it was.'

Two of his grandsons played at club level. Alexander Aarvold appeared at centre for Heriot's, Scottish students and, on more than one occasion, in the same Edinburgh University team as his cousin, Robbie. There was never any question that either would allow the pursuit of a professional contract to interfere with their academic qualifications.

Their grandfather died at the age of 83 on 17 March 1991, the day after England beat France to win the Grand Slam despite conceding a try that would probably have given Sir Carl more pleasure than the result itself. It contained everything he loved about the game, from the moment Pierre Berbizier caught Simon Hodgkinson's failed penalty attempt and launched the counter-attack from the French in-goal area, to Didier Camberabero's exquisite cross-kick which sent Philippe Saint-André plunging over under the English posts.

An oval-shaped marble plaque in the parish church of Mitcheldene, barely a mile from the family home in West Humble, serves as a permanent memorial to the stylish Englishman whose epitaph comes from the pen of one of the literary giants of his time:

> Remembered with love and affection:
> Sir Carl Aarvold, 1907–1991
> Recorder of London and sportsman.
> A staunch supporter and lifelong friend of this community.
> 'There's nothing worth the wear of winning but laughter
> and the love of friends.' H. Belloc.

Ole Aarvold could never have dreamt, when he set sail from Tønsberg at the start of the last century, of the impact his voyage would have on so many facets of English life over so many decades.

2

A FLASH OF LIGHTNING

HECKMONDWIKE HAS HAD MORE THAN ITS SHARE OF CLAIMS TO FAME OVER THE YEARS.
Showbiz, chemistry, literature, sport and music all have connections
of sorts with the little textile town in West Yorkshire. Bing Crosby,
for instance, is said to have 'served' at a private mass in the Holy
Spirit Church. More recently, another American singer of a very
different genre, Madonna, gave the local economy a bit of oomph
with the order of a carpet – all 160 square feet of it – for daughter
Lourdes' play-room. When word got out, *The Sun* marked the
occasion with a characteristically saucy observation: 'Madonna goes
to Heckmondwike carpets when she wants her underfelt!'

The town has other uplifting links to famous people. Joseph
Priestley, the eighteenth-century chemist who specialised in gases
and shared with the Swede Carl Scheele the discovery of oxygen,
was born there as was Sammy King. He wrote the song 'Penny
Arcade' which became a smash-hit for Roy Orbison, who was not
born in Heckmondwike.

The Brontë sisters also lived in the locality. Roger Hargreaves,
another storyteller and the author of the *Mister Men* books, grew up
in the town as did two Lions who shared the same initials, as well as
the same birthplace and some stirring deeds in South Africa during
the second half of the twentieth century: John Bentley and the late
Jeff Butterfield, the latter born on 9 August 1929.

Both went to school in neighbouring Cleckheaton, another,

larger, textile town that once found itself the butt of a joke cracked by an inimitable comedian from the other side of the Pennines. Les Dawson, the self-styled 'Battling Rembrandt', a soubriquet inspired by the amount of time he spent on the canvas during a largely horizontal career as an amateur boxer, would poke a little fun at Cleckheaton, suggesting that it was some distance from the centre of the universe. Another of the much-loved, greatly missed comedian's jokes conferred a back-handed compliment on the place. Describing the 'Cleckheaton Carnival', a figment of his fertile imagination, Dawson pulled a suitably melancholic face and said it was 'the day when they turned on both street lights'.

One plausible explanation could have been that Heckmondwike's last captain of England was otherwise engaged illuminating a larger stage elsewhere. 'Butterfield in those Twickenham winters was like a lightning flash across a sombre sky,' A. A. Thomson told his readers in *The Times*, and nobody could ever have written a more vivid appreciation of his skills.

Jeffrey Butterfield was still in short trousers in the late '30s when his father took him, as a special treat, to watch Bradford Northern at Odsal. The nine-year-old boy saw something that day that he would never forget, and he had enough nous at such a tender age to appreciate what made Willie Davies a special player.

A couple of years earlier, the Welsh teenager Davies had gone straight from school to play the proverbial blinder for his native Swansea in their celebrated victory over the 1935 All Blacks: the first by a British club. Davies made such an impression that he became Butterfield's inspiration, and the astute Yorkshire boy would learn the lesson so well that, years later, he would make it count in the shape of a rare English Grand Slam.

'I modelled my running on Willie Davies,' Butterfield said. 'He always ran holding the ball in both hands so that the opposition could never be sure what he was going to do with it. As a boy, I watched League all the time because that's where the stars were, and Willie was one of my big heroes.'

The others, for the record, were another England captain in the making, Len Hutton – later Sir Leonard – and Johnny Weissmuller, the American Olympic gold medal winning swimmer who transformed himself into Tarzan. 'I tried to be as fast as him in my little pool in Cleckheaton,' said Butterfield, 'and I could go fairly quickly.'

Quickly enough to be a schoolboy champion, but, when push

came to shove, he was moved more by Davies than by any desire to swing from tree to tree with a girl called Jane or play a straight bat for the White Rose county, as he always imagined he did at home where his father had 'erected' stumps in chalk on the wall of the backyard.

Davies had made a winning debut in the centre for Wales against Ireland at Cardiff in 1936 at the age of 19, before switching to stand-off against England at Twickenham the following season when he partnered his cousin Haydn Tanner, who had then just turned 20. By August 1939, Davies had turned professional, and while he went north, so Butterfield was destined to go south with the blessing of his headmaster: 'I went into the sixth form for a higher school certificate and the inevitable interview with the headmaster, Arthur W. King. He was the gentleman who walked round the school carrying a cane so we knew what discipline was all about. You got it instantly if you did anything wrong.

'He said, "What would you like to do?" The only colour magazine at the time was a Sunday paper called *Picture Post* and on the front they had a guy throwing a discus at Loughborough College.

'I said, "I'd like to go to Loughborough."

'He said, "Apply." I did and got in at the age of sixteen.'

Loughborough provided a stimulating education, not least in opening his eyes to influences beyond the English shires. 'That was where I discovered who the Welsh were,' he said. 'The war had just ended and a lot of ex-servicemen at Loughborough [who were] doing what I was doing – physical education – were Welsh. They played wonderful rugby, and I learnt how to play rugby from them. We could beat any first-class club at the time on sheer fitness. What a pity we couldn't have played Oxford or Cambridge Universities because we would have beaten them, too.'

His emergence as the pre-eminent centre of his generation owed much to those impressionable early days at Odsal and his almost innate mastery of the art of giving and taking a pass: 'My creed was to catch it in one stride and pass it in the next one.' Never did Butterfield use such skills to more devastating effect than during the opening minutes of the opening Lions Test against South Africa in 1955; the first game in an epic series over four matches that resulted in the only squared rubber of any such post-war tour. A Welshman started the move from a set-piece lineout, and an Irishman finished it off, but it was Butterfield who made it possible, stitching the whole thing together when a lesser player would have been unable to prevent it coming apart at the seams. He made light of a poor pass, produced a classical outside break and drew the full-back in textbook fashion to give Cecil Pedlow, the Irish wing, a clear run to the corner.

Cliff Morgan, the mercurial Welsh stand-off that afternoon, before what was then a world-record crowd of approximately 96,000 at Ellis Park, remembers it well: 'When we scored the first try, not one Springbok touched the ball. There was a throw-in to our lineout where Rhys Williams of Llanelli caught the ball, turned in the air and dropped it down to [Dickie] Jeeps. From Jeeps to me and I made a half-gap. Phil Davies took my pass and running, as he always did, with a tremendous sense of power in his enormous shoulders and hips, swept through the gap and gave the ball to Butterfield. Now Phil wasn't the world's best passer of the ball, and it went somewhere behind Jeff's right ear. But Jeff put his arm back and, without checking his stride, took the ball, brought it in front of him, leaned in, drew the full-back and finally gave Pedlow the perfect pass which took him across the line. It was all magical – a flawless, text-book movement.'

As a centre-three-quarter par excellence, during an era when the game would all too often submerge itself in a war of attrition between the forwards, Butterfield always had a clear vision of how rugby should be played once the ball was put in the hands of the craftsmen behind the scrum. Because he had always relied on brainpower to create a shaft of space during his career, it was understandable that he condemned the crushing emphasis on brawn that gave birth to the crash-ball of the Seventies.

'I don't like blood-and-thunder rugby,' he said when I spoke to him on an idyllic summer's day at his home in rural Buckinghamshire less than two years before his sudden death in April 2004. 'I call it pugilistic rugby. Watching the professional game leaves me very unhappy. I have not seen one skill which has been improved by professionalism. Instead of finding space, they all keep running into each other. Fitter, faster and stronger they may be, but there's no great passing skill. They throw the ball anywhere, and they run across the field from touch to touch. There's only one way to run and that's up the middle. I've been to Northampton on a few occasions, but I have left once or twice before half-time.'

Having warmed himself up, Butterfield duly went into overdrive in his tirade: 'I call it "brutal rugby", and I don't get any pleasure from watching it. They just crab sideways after attending week-long seminars on how to catch and how to pass. If a coach had ever told me to run straight into my opposite number, I'd have put him in his ruddy place. I never deliberately ran into anyone in my life. No wonder the injury factor these days is so enormous.

'Mind you, there are players I admire. Keith Wood [then Ireland's captain] was incredible. To think in my day of a front-row forward passing the ball, all by himself . . . ! It was incomprehensible.

'My sole endeavour was to pass the ball and put someone away to score, but if they didn't tackle me I kept running. I could run fairly fast, and I could run forever. Sometimes these days they run so fast, they don't know where they are going. They need to be calmed down occasionally.

'Kicking was never my game. Passing was the one thing I was crazy about, but I would have found it awfully difficult to play in the professional game because I wouldn't have wanted to be involved in a roughhouse. I never went to rugby league because it was equally brutal.'

Making that particular decision cost him a small fortune. Bradford Northern came knocking, amongst others, once Butterfield had established himself at Northampton. He had gone to Northampton after the headmaster at Wellingborough Grammar School had recommended his young PE teacher to the club's former England back-row forward Don White. Bradford offered a £3,000 signing-on fee that would have bought him a nice detached house, except that Butterfield, like his contemporary Morgan, could not be diverted from the union catechism that rugby was meant to be played for fun, not for money.

No matter how much he may have welcomed the cash as a newly qualified schoolteacher, the money men were given short shrift. 'These people came knocking on our front door, and I shall always remember them because they were wearing dinner jackets. My mother opened the door and thought they were in fancy dress. They introduced themselves and said, "Can we speak to your son about signing for us as a professional?" My mother nearly fetched her rolling pin and sent them packing off down the road. And that was that.'

Butterfield was too good for the money men to give up that easily, but he never succumbed to the age-old principle that every man has his price. The same could not be said of his Welsh contemporary Lewis Jones, a teenage Lion in New Zealand in 1950, who went to

Leeds two years later for £6,000. Back then, it would have bought him a house on a grand scale with enough left over to throw in a car for good measure: some compensation for offending the Establishment.

Their contempt for the northern code would descend, every so often, into paranoia. On one infamous occasion, George Parsons, a Welsh international, was ejected from the train taking the team to Paris merely on suspicion of having talked to a league club. For a union player to cash in his chips back then may have been considered very bad form but how the tin-pot dictators of the Welsh Rugby Union were allowed to get away with their disgraceful treatment of the hapless Parsons beggars belief. To their eternal shame, it stands on its own as the supreme example of union bigotry.

Two years later, Jones was in the midst of doing his national service with the Royal Navy at Devonport, when his commanding officer Captain R. W. Marshall left him in absolutely no doubt as to what he thought about rugby league. 'Look here, Jones,' he told the bemused sailor, following an early attempt by an adventurous northern club to offer him something rewarding once he had done his bit for the Senior Service. 'I've had a couple of fellows here looking for you. They said they were from a rugby league club, so I had them escorted out and turfed overboard! For your own good, my boy . . .'

Within months of Jones signing for Leeds in November 1952, Butterfield marked his first cap in winning style against France at Twickenham, before launching what would become a formidable centre partnership with Phil Davies of Harlequins in the next match against Scotland. The cavalier Yorkshireman stayed for the next twenty-seven England matches, a permanent fixture for seven years. He retired as his country's captain and their most-capped back with four Five Nations titles and one Grand Slam to his name.

That he managed to keep the run going required no shortage of courage: he had to survive the battering the Australians gave him at Twickenham in February 1958 and still line up against Ireland the following week as though nothing had happened. Taking everything the Wallabies dished out and winning with 14 men made it, according to Butterfield, 'the match of our lives'.

He went on to explain, 'Jim Lenehan [Australia's centre] knocked me out four times with the type of tackling they do now. I am not sure I had the ball. All I knew was that on four occasions I saw stars, and I can assure you I was not looking at my colleagues in the England team because I wasn't able to!

'After the fourth time, they put me on a stretcher, and I was being carried to the dressing-room when I jumped off and went back on. I'd lost all feeling down my left-hand side, but it suddenly came back. Remember, there were no substitutes in those days.'

The fact that one international clashed with his honeymoon made his impressive run in the team all the more improbable. Butterfield and the future Mrs Butterfield, Barbara Kirton, had taken studious note of the Five Nations fixture list for 1956 and arranged their marriage more than a fortnight after the scheduled finish of the championship, in mid-March. However, fate intervened and bad weather in Paris forced a rare postponement of England's visit to the old Stade Colombes. The rearranged date, in mid-April, fell at the end of the Butterfields' first week of wedded bliss, spent on the ski slopes of a resort in the Austrian Alps. It could never happen now, but, in the finest amateur tradition, the groom negotiated the tricky logistics involved in celebrating his new partnership while still turning up in time to keep the old one going on the rugby field.

Squad training was as unheard of in those days as moon probes, mobile phones and jumbo jets. When 14 members of the England team set forth for Paris on the Friday, nobody was too bothered that the 15th had driven himself and his new bride some way across Europe, after a week on the piste. The Butterfields were already in situ on the Thursday night, when the advanced guard of the Rugby Football Union entered the French capital.

The England centre and his wife were inspecting the hors d'oeuvres trolley in the restaurant of the team's hotel when Lieutenant Colonel Douglas Prentice, secretary of the RFU, bowled over, bowler in hand, with a greeting that sounded so pure Bertie Wooster it could have come straight out of a P. G. Wodehouse novel. 'Ah, it's you, Butterfield,' the Colonel said. 'Had a good honeymoon? Jolly glad to see you and your charming wife have made it. Carry on, Butterfield. Enjoy your supper.' Whereupon he bade him adieu with a paternal pat on the back.

A fortnight or so earlier, the two had corresponded on the forthcoming clash of fixtures. 'I wrote to him saying, "Dear Colonel, I wish to advise you that the rearranged match against France coincides with my wedding and that I shall be on honeymoon." I had a letter back from him saying, "Dear Butterfield, see you in Paris."'

To get there, the newly-weds had driven for the best part of two days. Almost half a century later, Barbara still chuckles at their adventure: 'We lived on Camembert, bread and a little red wine, and by the time we reached Paris, after a week's skiing, we had virtually run out of money. Wives in those days were not allowed to book into the team hotel, so we found a cheap place on the Left Bank, before going out to dinner.

'The team were not due until the following day, so you can imagine the reaction when Colonel Prentice walked into the dining room. Jeff was horrified. That was the first year the England team had flown to Paris instead of taking the ferry, so we thought that the secretary would be flying in with the team. When Jeff said so, the colonel replied, "I never fly, Butterfield. I don't trust those aeroplanes."'

While there was a lot to be said for keeping one's feet on terra firma, Butterfield had reason to wonder why he had been grounded for quite so long on the Test runway, in the early part of his career. The stylish Yorkshireman was another victim of the irritating English reluctance to pick young players, and, while he was younger than most at 23, they were scarcely taking a risk on a player widely acknowledged as the most creative centre of his time, when they eventually selected him. The universities of Oxford and Cambridge provided a privileged production line straight into the England team during the '50s, and he would surely have been capped much sooner had he ever been granted the platform of the Varsity match.

'There was no other game then like Oxford v. Cambridge. It was as if the whole rugby world paid attention to it. We had our local derbies like Northampton v. Leicester and Northampton v. Coventry, but there wasn't a club match in England like the Varsity match. If I'd had the chance to play in it, I think I would probably have been an England player at 19. I should have played for England then, but I wasn't in the right place and didn't play for England for another five years. That was the strength of the old school tie.'

An almost suspicious selection policy towards precocious talent existed during his formative years: a policy that decreed that even the most gifted had to do time before they were considered ready, unless, as Butterfield put it, 'you were at Oxford or Cambridge'.

'There was one thing, in particular, which I never approved of. There were three England trials per season with the Oxford and Cambridge players excused the first. I could not see any reason why that should have been. But they ruled the game, didn't they? The sport had that old-boy network running right through it over the years. It's gone now, thankfully.'

Once he had arrived on the grand stage, there was no stopping him, least of all during the tour that did more than any other to establish the magnetic appeal of the Lions: the famous squared series against the Springboks in 1955.

It confirmed Butterfield as a master craftsman: his incisive running and the often perfect timing of his pass made him the most dangerous component of a back division featuring the mercurial Cliff Morgan, the fearless, uncapped scrum-half Dickie Jeeps and the teenage phenomenon Tony O'Reilly on the wing. Butterfield had many gifts, but an ability to swivel his hips, through what must have seemed like 360 degrees, to bamboozle opponents was arguably the greatest gift of all. He was also able to split defences by the sheer speed with which he took and gave a pass.

He could finish, too, scoring a try in each of the first three Tests: something which no other Lion had done before or since. Comparisons between the greats of different eras are as inevitable as they are invidious, but Butterfield is universally accepted as the most complete Lions centre: so good that his admirers talk of him in the same breath as Mike Gibson, the Belfast solicitor who proved his greatness over a period of 15 years with the Lions.

On top of all his attributes on the field, 'Buttercup' – as the inventive Morgan dubbed him – acted as the first trainer in Lions' history, using his expertise in physical education on a daily basis. However primitive by modern standards, it represented a real break-through at a time when coaching was a dirty word, and any attempt to put in extra practice was frowned upon as a poor show. In the misguided Establishment view, it was not quite playing the game.

The Lions of 1955 under the astute management of Jack Siggins, a perceptive Ulsterman from Belfast who had captained Ireland during the '30s, knew they had to close the fitness gap on South Africa, then the best team in the world. 'Jeff was given the responsibility for getting us fit, and we didn't want to let him down,' Morgan said. 'We got fairly fit, all right, but, as with most international teams of that time, we didn't go in for any strategic planning for the games ahead. What a difference it might have made if we'd had a coach to direct us and teach us moves and techniques. If we needed a massage or medical treatment in South Africa, we had to go down to the local hospital. The whole thing was run like a casual trip for amateurs abroad.'

That underlined the scale of the Lions' achievement in drawing the series 2–2. The way they won games captivated South Africa and shattered box-office records wherever they went. A young Nelson Mandela was said to be among the crowd of almost 100,000 crammed into Ellis Park for the first Test, which the Lions won 23–22. Forty years later, shortly before he died, Dr Danie Craven, the godfather of Springbok rugby, described it as the 'greatest' international match he had seen.

Clem Thomas, a young Welshman who forced his way into the back row for the last two Tests and who would become one of the leading authorities on the game, was in no doubt that the 'immaculate' Butterfield ought to have captained the Lions on that trip. The honour had gone instead to the Irish second-row forward Robin Thompson, and when the Lions came to picking their captain for the next trip, to Australia and New Zealand in 1959, Butterfield had just completed his one season in charge of England, following Eric Evans's retirement.

A rather desperate set of results for England that season called for some decisive action. Before the last match, at home to Scotland, the chairman of selectors Carston Catcheside, a prolific scoring wing in Lord Wakefield's Grand Slam team of the mid-'20s, approached Butterfield. 'Right, Jeff, the game's getting to a bit of a serious stage,' he told the skipper. 'We are going to have a meeting before the match tomorrow at midday. We just want to talk to the team before you go onto the field.'

Intrigued, Butterfield wondered and waited for high noon to arrive. 'I'd had my usual pre-match meal – raw eggs and sherry – and Ron Jacobs had just finished his customary big steak. Carston got us all sat down and said, "Gentlemen, this is one of the most disappointing seasons England have had. We have had three matches now, and we have not scored one single try. Right, gentlemen. We have got to improve and this is what I've got to say to you fifteen boys going out now to play for England: if you don't pass the ball to the wings, you might as well use my backside for shooting pigeons. I have nothing more to say."'

The players barely had time to digest the ramifications of this revolutionary idea than they were given another odd piece of advice from another selector. According to Butterfield, this is what happened next. 'Brigadier Haslett, one of the selectors, got up and said, "Carston, can I have a word?"

'"Yes, of course. Fire away."

'"I'd like to say to all of you: don't go to the toilet and have a crap before the game. If you do you give out heat, and heat and energy are the same. Good luck to you all."'

Whether anyone heeded the advice is not known but, surprise, surprise, it made not a blind bit of difference. Armed with what Butterfield called 'the first coaching hint any England selectors had ever given to the team', England again failed to score a try in a 3–3 draw. No one could recall whether, as a consequence, the chairman bared his backside for a pigeon-shoot.

Another new skipper had emerged that season to compete with Butterfield for the captaincy of the Lions later that year: Ronnie Dawson of Ireland. Both were summoned to be interviewed by the organisers, the Four Home Unions' Tours Committee, at the East India Club. It was the Lions' traditional watering hole in central London where news of the Duke of Wellington's victory over Napoleon at Waterloo was delivered from a balcony overlooking St James Square.

'They asked me what I thought about playing and coaching and what my aims were for the tour,' Butterfield said. 'I said we'd have to play better rugby football than we'd ever played before. Then they made their decision. I said "well done" to Ronnie Dawson and that was it. I wasn't angry. I just accepted it. There might have been a little bit of bias – might have been – but I wouldn't have said it was a crucial factor. The main point was that we didn't play competitive rugby at that time. South Africa and New Zealand have always played competitive rugby. Ours, by comparison, was friendly. The only competitive stuff we had in our day was the county championship.'

In that respect, Butterfield was way ahead of his time, and the 1959 trip to New Zealand with the Lions, when recurring injury eliminated him from all four Tests, underlined his point. It was to his huge credit that, in adhering strictly to the amateur ethos, he brought a professional attitude to the game: one that had nothing to do with money but everything to do with pride of performance and a desire to improve.

He could have been England's first coach – in a strictly honorary capacity, of course – and would have been in more enlightened times, but the ingrained Establishment view of coaching appearing to be too much like professionalism undermined unofficial approaches about his taking charge of the national team.

Nobody was more acutely aware of the general hostility towards the new breed than the kindred spirit Ray Williams, a lifelong friend of Butterfield's from Loughborough and his Northampton teammate. In 1967, Williams would become rugby's prototype professional as the full-time coaching organiser for the Welsh Rugby Union. The RFU attitude to the notion of a coach – even an amateur one – helping an amateur team was summed up perfectly during the winter of 1958–59 by the then president, Wing Commander James (Jimmy) Lawson, CBE. Williams said, 'I remember the president saying, "Ray, can we find another word other than coach?"

'I replied, my voice a mixture of amusement and incredulity, "Well, I don't really know whether there is one."

'Jeff then came up with an alternative description. He said, "If we can't call the coach the coach, then we could call him the Team Practice Organiser."'

Some years later, the Scottish Rugby Union did something very similar. Rather than concede the terrifying truth that Bill Dickinson was coaching the team, even though it was purely for the love of the game, they concocted another euphemism. Dickinson was to be known as 'the adviser to the captain'.

'The whole thing was ludicrous, wasn't it?' Williams said. 'They didn't think coaching was appropriate at club level. It was inbred in the amateur concept that you must not try too hard to be too good. Their popular concept of rugby union in general was of a sport for recreational purposes. I was totally opposed to that. It was a question of how good you wanted to be. Butterfield wanted to be very good. We had gone past the stage where you played rugby to get fit. Now you had to get fit to play rugby, and that's when people said, "We can't do it because the game will go professional." I said the game would not go professional in the foreseeable future, and I was proved right because it didn't happen for more than another 30 years.'

Along with another contemporary from their student days, ex-Scotland hooker Bob MacEwan, Butterfield and Williams persisted. 'Back then, we were largely wasting our time so we decided to organise two conferences at Lilleshall, in 1964,' Williams said. 'As a result, the RFU set up a coaching advisory committee chaired by the former England player, Ian Beer. We produced the "Guide to Coaching", in 1966, and the WRU bought one hundred copies.'

Williams recalls that the RFU gave the impression of being less than enthusiastic: 'Sir Augustus Walker, the president at the time, told us, "Well, I have to congratulate you chaps on bringing out these coaching books. Very good. But there is only thing we should concentrate on in rugby football. And that is passing the ball to the wings."'

Butterfield, frustrated at the futility of picking a team to turn up the day before an international without anyone qualified to coach it, issued a prophetic plea in that same year. His words sound like a statement of the obvious by modern standards but they would have been considered revolutionary by the reactionaries who claimed to be the guardians of the amateur game: 'I wanted a team of athletes, not guys who would push in the scrum and toddle round the field. The forwards we had were mighty men, but I wanted forwards to be in the game other than for the set-pieces. Jean Prat [captain of France] was not a very big chap but once at Twickenham [February 1955] he took a ball off the top of the lineout and dropped a goal. And then he did it again. You wouldn't see a forward do that, even today.'

In 1968 Butterfield was approached about becoming England's first honorary coach: 'Albert Agar was chairman of selectors. He walked me round Richmond on the morning before an international and he said, "What about you coaching England next season?"

'I said, "I'd love to but I have to work. Being coach is a full-time job. I don't see it as someone turning up for the day for a chat."

'One of my best friends, Don White – great player, dirty so-and-so – said, "I'll do it." He turned up on the Friday afternoon, but that was hardly even scratching the surface. The possibilities of a full-time coach were a long way off then, and we were just as far away from the thought of paying someone to do it.'

Butterfield's contribution on back play to the loose-leafed coaching manual, produced in consultation with Williams, MacEwan, Beer, Mark Sugden (Ireland's pre-war scrum-half) and Hywel Griffiths, another Welshman and former Cambridge University wing, proved an inspiration to the Lions for their two most successful tours: New Zealand in 1971 and South Africa three years later. Even after that, the coach was still being given a hard time.

The RFU, for example, complained about Williams on the basis that he was a professional and as such could not work with the Wales team. 'There was a picture of me and the Pontypool front row on the back page of the *Western Mail*, in 1976,' he said. 'The RFU saw it and made a complaint. When a very senior member of the WRU told me about it, I said, "Tell them to mind their own bloody business. I do not coach the Welsh team.'"

Butterfield never did get to coach England, but, despite playing the last of his 227 matches for Northampton in 1963, he spent virtually the rest of his life immersed in the game. He was never more in his element than at The Rugby Club in central London, which he and Barbara ran for 25 years, providing a buckshee public relations service for the English game, while still finding the energy to champion various sports causes.

He founded Freedom in Sport with the objective of saving sportsmen and women from 'being hammered by politicians'. At the launch in 1981, with South Africa ostracised by the global community in condemnation of their race laws, Butterfield said, 'We would all like to see the disintegration of apartheid. But sport is one area which really is multiracial, yet the only people to get blacklisted are sportsmen. It doesn't make sense. We will work hard to change people's minds.'

Work hard he did. A letter to *The Times* in April 1988 captured the vigour of his campaign:

> Sir,
> Surely the time has now come to pose the one vital question concerning the future well-being of international sport which no one has yet dared to put before a gullible sporting and general public. We, Freedom in Sport, challenge publicly Sam Ramsamy, Sony Ramphal and all other anti-sports apartheid activists to justify the exclusion of black South African sports persons from international sport.

While his drive created the first European Golden Oldies Rugby festival staged at Denbosch in Holland in 1992, he found himself increasingly disenchanted by professionalism and the haphazard way it was introduced overnight, in August 1995: 'The day before it happened, I was in Johannesburg, and the people I met were all taking about anarchy in this great game of ours. I think it had to come but the RFU, for one, ought to have paved the way. Instead everything was done in a panic.'

In March 2004, the holy trinity largely responsible for changing the sport's sniffy attitude to coaches and coaching held what would be their last reunion. Butterfield and Williams and their wives met in Swansea, along with the widower MacEwan, to reminisce about old times and bemoan the state of rugby union as they saw it.

'We chatted about how the game had deteriorated and how much better it was in our day,' Williams said. 'I was so glad that we had those two days together, which we all enjoyed greatly.'

Just a few weeks later, on a bright spring morning, Butterfield was sweeping up in the garden of his home while his wife tidied up the lawn. As usual, the double heart bypass operation, which her husband had undergone seven years before, was uppermost in her mind: 'I said, "For goodness sake, don't overdo it," which is what I said every day. He said, "All right." I did a bit more strimming, and when I turned round he was flat out.' He was mourned as much in certain parts of Wales as he was in England and thereby hangs a tale.

Butterfield, strictly speaking, was never capped as a player. The RFU gave their players the choice between a cap or a blazer badge. Having opted for the latter, another 20 years elapsed before Butterfield wrote to Twickenham asking for a cap: 'I said, "I never got one as a player, so could I possibly have one now?"

'They said, "Yes. It will cost you £9." So I paid them the nine quid and gave it to some Welsh friends who wanted to put it on show in their clubhouse down Pontypool way. I was very close to some of the Welsh players. Ray Prosser [a 1959 Lion who coached the fearsome, all-conquering "Pooler" team of the early Eighties] was a great friend.'

Such generosity was typical of a great rugby man. Had he been Welsh, they would have given him a state funeral.

3

NIJINKSY

AS BRITAIN'S WAR CABINET CALCULATED THE COST OF THE LUFTWAFFE BOMBARDMENT during the early weeks of 1941, Prime Minister Winston Churchill sent a memo to the Minister of Supply on the steep reduction in rifle manufacture over the previous five months.

'I understand that this fall is due to raids on Small Heath, Birmingham, which completely stopped production,' he wrote on 23 January. 'Pray inform me what progress has been made towards resuming production.'

Albert Jackson, a footballer and cricketer of note, while pursuing a career as a metallurgist, played for Small Heath in the days before the club transformed itself into Birmingham City. His two sons were born in Small Heath, and by the time Churchill tackled the rifle issue, they had been moved to the relative safety of the countryside, joining thousands of other evacuees in taking refuge from the fearful blitz of the West Midlands, in their case on a farm in the Staffordshire village of Moreton.

In moving to the country, the younger boy had been forced to take the sort of evasive action that would later in life become his trademark. One day Peter Jackson, born on 22 September 1930, would rescue his country on the rugby field against Australia with a try of such daring and improbability that it will forever be remembered as one of the greatest – if not the greatest – ever seen at Twickenham.

Few can ever have got there against more crushing odds. Ironically, the one time that the boy did end up in hospital, the emergency had nothing to do with the deadly nocturnal raids from the Nazi war planes. At the age of ten, Jackson had become ill with nephritis, a serious kidney disease similar to that suffered by the All Black Jonah Lomu. 'The doctors told me I would not be able to play any sport,' he said, during one of his last interviews. 'That was really worrying because sport was what I was good at. They told me that I had to do nothing but rest for six months. I couldn't swim, I couldn't play rugby or cricket or tennis and I couldn't do any athletics. I couldn't do anything. The thought of never being able to do that [play sport] again was pretty dreadful, but I had to accept it because the important thing was to get better. Mother was a very strong character and her reaction was, "Look, these are the sort of things you have to put up with in life. You have to learn to adapt."'

Discharged from hospital later that year, he adapted, initially at any rate, by trying something completely different during that long summer of 1941: 'I took up the clarinet. [I] Didn't do very well, but it was something to do because I wasn't allowed outdoors for six whole months.'

By the age of 11, his restoring health encouraged him to think that the doctors had been unduly rash in their no-sport prognosis and that he would soon be moving to the beat of a different drum. 'After six months, I kept saying, "I must do something. I'm raring to go." I persuaded one of the doctors to let me go for a run. He agreed but only on condition that I saw him every ten days for a urine sample. They were afraid that the nephritis would flare up again. Luckily it didn't, and I threw myself back into sport as though I was trying to make up for lost time.'

The war had ended when another sledgehammer blow landed: this time in the form of a fractured skull. It sounds ludicrous today to think that someone of his calibre was still playing old boys' rugby at the age of 22 for Old Edwardians and even more ludicrous that the fracture was not diagnosed on the spot.

'I tackled a man in the wrong way, and my head took the impact,' Jackson explained. 'It wasn't until two or three days later that it caught up with me. I was working for a packaging company at the time, and someone came in with a load of cases. I picked up one case, and when I tried to carry it I fell over. I got up with one hell of a headache.

'The boss took me home, and the next morning I was all over the place. I went to see the doctor, and he saw that my left eye was a bit funny. He sent me off for an X-ray and that was how they found that I'd fractured my skull. So, for the second time, I was told to forget about rugby.' For the second time, he proved them wrong: after a year's absence, he was back on the wing for his old school team.

With all due respect to Old Edwardians, it said something about English rugby's chaotic structure and, more alarmingly, its inability to recognise a rare talent that someone like Jackson was almost 24 before he gravitated to the first-class stage with Coventry. Club loyalty was a big thing back in the '50s – even in soccer – and Jackson's to Old Edwardians never wavered. As if to illustrate the point, he once said, 'I still think of myself as an Old Ed.'

He represented Old Edwardians for Midland Counties against Bob Stuart's All Blacks at Villa Park in December 1953, and the experience changed his career. For the first time, he began to think about how far he could go in the game and realised that in order to get there he needed to test himself in a more demanding environment.

Coventry, then the provincial powerhouse driving the alternative English game as compared to the traditional, privileged one run by Oxford and Cambridge, duly provided it. Having overcome so many obstacles, Jackson then discovered, to his chagrin, that the English selectors presented what seemed to be an even more awkward stumbling-block to his international ambitions than the *Luftwaffe*, his kidney disorder and a fractured skull put together. Anyone with half an eye for the game could see that he was different in a way that opened up all manner of possibilities. Luckily for their opponents, the national selectors discarded him as being a bad risk, a conclusion that Jackson reinforced during a final trial in 1954 by attempting to run the ball out from behind his own posts.

They simply didn't know what to make of him. 'The selectors were looking for straight-forward runners on the wings,' he said. 'They were looking for speed, and speed was not my forte. I was so unorthodox that I was just as likely to go inside as outside, and they didn't think I was that fast. It didn't worry me.'

Even when they finally got round to picking him, against Wales at Twickenham in January 1956, the newcomer was given a disgraceful vote of no-confidence along with his cap. No debutant, regardless of colour or creed, can have been subjected to a more demoralising condemnation of his selection from one of those whom he, not unnaturally, assumed had been responsible for picking him. On the eve of representing his country for the first time, Jackson might reasonably have expected an encouraging slap on the back. What he got, as the result of a chance meeting in the team hotel, was more akin to a figurative kick in the teeth: 'This is the gospel truth. Sometime during the Friday evening I went into the toilet and found this big fellow standing there. I soon realised he was as pie-eyed as a newt. When he saw me, he said, "And who the hell are you?"

'"Peter Jackson."

'And he said, "Ah, the right wing. You should never have been selected."

'I said something like, "Sorry, but I have," and walked out. How's that for a story? I later learnt that he was the chairman of selectors. He liked wingers to be big and strong. He'd been one himself, and his forte, apparently, was to hurdle his opposite number.'

Eric Evans, the new captain, had enough on his plate, leading a team that included nine other new caps, without the tenth being made to feel unworthy of such an honour. Evans, a player so far ahead of his time that he trained at Old Trafford with the revered 'Busby Babes', many of whom were to lose their lives in the Munich air disaster two years later, deserves a permanent place amongst the most inspiring of English leaders. Told of the chairman's objection to Jackson's choice, Evans dismissed the matter with the reassuring deduction that, 'He was obviously out-voted.'

The new boy's frame of mind was hardly eased by what he overheard out on the street the next morning, as a group of England supporters from Yorkshire discussed the switch of wings caused by Ted Woodward's late withdrawal through injury. To offset the loss, Jackson switched wings to replace the burly Wasp on the right with Peter Thompson of Headingley, another new cap, drafted in on the left. The fans were of the opinion, as Peter remembered it, that their man was 'a better player than that Jackson'.

At Twickenham that day, as well as a brand-new pair of wingers, England had a new pair of locks and a new fly-half who became, however fleetingly, the last of the dual internationals. The two locks, Richard Marques and John Currie, lasted a lot longer than Mike (M. J. K.) Smith, a one-cap wonder who reappeared in a very different guise two years later, opening the batting for England against New Zealand before succeeding Ted Dexter as captain in India during the winter of 1963–64.

Smith's rugby career might well have lasted a little longer had Jackson not been disallowed a debut try under the posts, which would have given the new England team every chance of a satisfying draw with Wales, instead of losing 8–3. 'I was penalised for not playing the ball with the foot after a tackle as the law required in those days. The way I saw it, I was not tackled. I tripped over someone's hand but was not held.'

His first international try came in the next match against Ireland, and he scored three more the following season: 50 per cent of the total for that Five Nations Championship, which provided a major contribution to the first English Grand Slam since the '20s. In retrospect, these tries could be seen as dazzling preparation for his greatest moment, against Australia at Twickenham on 1 February 1958.

Against seemingly impossible odds, the match-winning try in the dying seconds encapsulated Jackson's sheer brilliance as a runner, his mastery of the feint and almost bewitching balance. It was all achieved despite a physique that one critic described as 'wraithlike'. Weighing in at barely 12 st., he never had any option but to put mind above muscle.

Even now, almost half a century later, the try is still right up there alongside Prince Obolensky's against the All Blacks in 1936 as the finest scored by an Englishman, or a Russian prince for that matter, at Headquarters. The old black-and-white video clips record both for posterity, but what the film can never show in Jackson's case was the sense of anger which drove him through on his magical dance to the corner. England, not content to settle for a draw, despite having been reduced to 14 men for most of the match, were enraged at the Aussie thuggery, which was responsible for fly-half Phil Horrocks-Taylor being knocked unconscious and other instances of gratuitous violence.

'There was a certain amount of fury at some of the things which one or two of the Aussies had done,' Jackson said. 'It was shameful. Some of the late tackles were so late, it was unbelievable that they were allowed to get away with it. The crowd were yelling like fury, and I was raging when I got the ball.'

By then, the crippling loss of Horrocks-Taylor meant that Jeff Butterfield had to stand in at stand-off whenever the Wallabies were not laying him out with late tackles. Coventry flanker Peter Robbins had been withdrawn from the pack to plug the vacancy left by Butterfield at centre and Evans responded to the emergency magnificently, galvanising his depleted pack for one last heroic effort.

A lineout in the Australian 25-yard area gave them the platform for Jackson to weave his magic and ghost through a wall of Wallabies, handing off the first challenger before leaving at least three more on their backsides en route to the corner. It was hard enough to imagine let alone execute, against a defence that had given away nothing but a solitary try to the new England centre Malcolm Phillips.

Jackson had found room hard to find on the right wing against his marker Rod Phelps. In achieving that stupendous finale and ensuring that English brain trumped Australian brawn, the Old Edwardian had outwitted the Wallabies by thinking his way through them, as opposed to closing his eyes and hoping for the best.

'Phelps followed me all day, giving me very little room but when that last move began, we had a lot of space on my side. Having fended off Phelps, I could see the full-back [Terry Curley], and I sensed that he was anticipating me going inside him. So, with a couple of sidesteps, I went the other way. Phelps had done extremely well to run back and get to me at the right-hand corner of the old South Stand.'

Typically, and with no false sense of modesty, Jackson always made a point of referring to it as a team try, despite the solo aspect of his role. 'OK, I scored the try, but, basically, it was the result of a fantastic effort put in by those seven forwards. It was scored because of the huge impetus the skipper [Evans] gave in making us believe that we were going to win despite being a man short. Without a shadow of a doubt, Evans was the best captain I ever played under.'

Soon it would be the All Blacks' turn to cope with a will-o'-the-wisp whose almost balletic poise in the tightest of corners would earn him the ultimate nickname of Nijinsky, after the supreme Russian dancer – not the classic racehorse, which would not be heard of for another ten years. Jackson left with the Lions for New Zealand in May 1959, and by the time he headed for home, a few months later, New Zealand had acclaimed him as the world's number one winger: some title considering that his fellow Test wing Tony O'Reilly was then at the zenith of his career.

The pair cut a swathe across the length and breadth of New Zealand the like of which had never been seen before and will certainly, in these days of abbreviated tours, never be seen again.

Between them they scored 33 tries in an aggregate of 31 appearances. While O'Reilly averaged a try a match – 17 from 17 – Jackson went fractionally better with 16 from 14.

It was O'Reilly who gave him the nickname. 'He used to say to me, "You're like that fellow Nijinsky, you are,"' Jackson recalled. '"You never know where you're going but you always seem to get there." O'Reilly was a great one for nicknames. He also called me "Nikolai the Russian spy".'

And to think he almost declined the invitation that dropped through the letter box of his Castle Bromwich home one day in late March of 1959. It was from the Hon. Secretary of the Four Home Unions' Tours Committee, and it contained some exciting news, even if it was couched in the cold formality of 'Dear Jackson', a tone that sounds terribly condescending today but which was pretty much par for the course back in the austere '50s.

For a family man aged 28, it posed a problem which became acute once his employers Remploy Ltd expressed initial disquiet about granting him paid leave for the five months of the tour. 'I had a wife [Jean] and two little boys [Martin and Philip] to support and a mortgage to pay. Someone suggested I could use my savings. What savings? I didn't have any. I explained to Jean what it was going to cost. Her reaction was to say, "I don't want you to go in one sense, but it would be a terrible shame to miss such a wonderful opportunity." Luckily, her parents and my parents came to the rescue by offering to look after everything on the financial side so I could go.'

His acceptance drew a congratulatory note from the Hon. Team Manager Alf W. Wilson, a 50-year-old quarry company director from Dunfermline who had played three times for Scotland in the 1931 Five Nations: twice in the centre and once at full-back during the course of captaining his local club for eight years. With his deep-rooted, true-blue amateur principles, he upset the Australians during the opening leg of the tour, provoking accusations that he had banned Bev Risman, the 21-year-old English fly-half, from attending a rugby league function in honour of his celebrated father Gus, Wales's gift to the 13-a-side code.

At least one Kiwi journalist considered that the autocratic Wilson had the capacity to be 'a very frightening little man', not to mention a very brave one as reflected in the DSO won during the Second World War when he commanded a heavy anti-aircraft regiment during the Allied landings in Italy. There was nothing of a fearful nature in the letter he sent to the Coventry wing, dated 27 March 1959:

> Dear Jackson,
> Many congratulations on coming with us on tour. I would like to wish you the best of good luck and hope you have a very happy tour. It will be a most strenuous tour and I hope therefore you are able to lay off rugger as soon after the 4th April as is possible.
>   Yrs,
>   Alf W. Wilson

When the Lions gathered at Eastbourne prior to departure, Jackson, the pale Brummie, roomed with O'Reilly, the young Irish superstar, who at just 23 was already a Lions legend. His exploits during the previous tour in South Africa four years earlier had even inspired one Hollywood director to consider casting him for the principal role in *Ben Hur*.

The Irishman, whose enterprise would soon make him, arguably, America's top businessman as head of the Heinz corporation, made such an impression on his English teammate that it was still indelible more than 40 years later. 'On the day we checked out of the hotel to go to London for departure, he left about ten of his books on the windowsill of our room,' Jackson recalled. 'I said to him, "You've forgotten these books."'

'He said, "No, I've read them." He had the ability to read a book, digest whatever he thought necessary and retain it. He had absorbed what he wanted from the books which he left behind. Tony could hold discussions on subjects about which I had very little idea. His knowledge of people and issues was phenomenal.'

Jackson justified the legendary status endowed on him by his hosts, by matching his more famous colleague stride for giant stride. Terry McLean, the most authoritative of New Zealand rugby journalists who died in 2004 in his 90s, acclaimed the deceptive Englishman as '. . . the zaniest runner of all time. He would sidestep, dodge, swerve, jump sideways, cough apologetically off the ball to a tackler and try anything at least once as a means of beating an opponent.'

During that New Zealand winter, the Lions and Jackson were made for each other. Right from the start of the tour, in the seaside town of Napier, he so entertained the crowd in the drubbing of Hawke's Bay that they could only laugh at the sheer audacity of his running. Even as hard-bitten a Kiwi critic as the perceptive McLean was moved enough to write of Jackson's 'wondrous weavings' and how 'a bright golden haze had descended on the Lions tour'. Waxing lyrical, he went on to write:

> Speed of thought with the Lions was never better expressed than by Jackson, though he had formidable competition from some of his fellows. He plucked the strangest schemes out of the air.
>
> Playing against Wairarapa-Bush Districts, he swerved and darted into midfield, plainly in an attempt to beat the full-back by a characteristic shift and sidestep. Then, out of the blue, he noticed a teammate crossing behind him. Without even a moment's consideration, Jackson (who it should be emphasised, was meanwhile travelling at almost his fastest speed) performed a fantastic manoeuvre by spinning from right to left, bringing his arms around in a sweeping movement and making as if to pass behind and to the right to the man crossing at the rear.
>
> The poor full-back, who had probably never imagined that such a feat could be performed, even by travelling gymnasts, like a sensible fellow immediately shifted ground to deal with the newcomer. Lo and behold, Jackson still had the ball, the path was now clear and onward he headed to the goal line and a try which proclaimed that the quickness of the mind will deceive anybody, if you care to exercise it.

Jackson duly marked the start of the four-Test series in Dunedin with a try as did O'Reilly. Malcolm Price, the Wales centre, doubled up with two of his own, with the Lions winning 4–0 on tries. Ludicrously, they lost the match 18–17, beaten by six Don Clarke penalties. Never can a single Test match have delivered a more damaging blow to the credibility of rugby football than the one at Carisbrook on 18 July 1959.

It created an unholy stink across the rugby world and beyond as the aficionados and the uninitiated alike pondered the same question: what kind of game is this when six penalty goals count for more than four tries? Another, more awkward question ought to have been asked of the Lions but presumably wasn't because they were pre-occupied by the pervading sense of injustice: why didn't they kick their goals?

The Lions missed seven that day at Carisbrook – four penalties and three conversions – any one of which would have put the game beyond Clarke's telescopic boot. Even the hosts found it hard to stomach, with the Dunedin crowd abusing the Dunedin referee for awarding the fateful last penalty. One Kiwi journalist even condemned the proceedings as 'a day of shame'.

What was almost as ludicrous as the result was the fact that it took the sport's law-makers on the International Rugby Board fully twelve years to introduce the four-point try and accept what had been blindingly obvious for more than a decade: that the try had to be worth more than the penalty goal, especially if the Lions were taking on the All Blacks in a game refereed by a New Zealander.

At a time when the sport was still many years away from appointing neutral referees, presumably on the basis that New Zealand was too far away to justify the expense, the Lions had a rough idea what to expect from the outset. For the first Test, the hosts chose a referee who would be at home in every sense. Rather than choosing an 'outsider' from Auckland or Wellington they opted for someone from the very province in which the match was played: Mr A. L. Fleury of Otago.

The Lions' sense of injustice was not helped by the fact that their touch judge, the Irish fly-half Mick English, did not raise his flag for one of Clarke's penalties, thereby signalling that he had missed it. Mr Fleury, apparently, had no such doubts and the penalty stood. By the end large sections of the 41,000 crowd had given vent to their embarrassment.

While his performance invited general condemnation, it ought to be pointed out in Mr Fleury's defence that he did disallow the All Blacks a try which fly-half Ron Brown was convinced he had scored. Once the Lions had fired their magnificent four-try salvo, Clarke still managed to outpoint them with his fourth, fifth and sixth penalties, unheard of in Test rugby at that time.

'Three of those penalties should never have been given, especially the last one in front of the posts,' Jackson said. 'We were far superior, but that all changed later in the series. I have never been as humiliated in all my life as I was by the sheer mastery of the All Black game during the third Test in Christchurch.'

Few Lions can have made more of an impact on their first tour. During the Australian leg of the tour, en route to New Zealand, Jackson created such an impression that one newspaper acclaimed him as having 'taken over the crown of the world's best wing from teammate Tony O'Reilly'. In New Zealand, where he achieved the distinction of scoring four tries one Saturday, against West Coast-Buller at Greymouth, and four more the next Saturday, against a combined Marlborough, Nelson, Golden Bay and Montueka XV at Blenheim, he had them rolling in the aisles as a result of some of his tricks. Fred Boshier, the experienced sports editor of the *Evening Post* in Wellington, captured the sense of fun and colour that 'Nijinsky' brought to the home crowds all over the Land of the Long White Cloud:

> If there was one player who epitomised the British style, it was Jackson. The right wing possesses as dazzling a sidestep as this country has seen for a long time, and it was something which the All Blacks simply could not cope with. Jackson often makes up his own rules and it is nothing for him to suddenly boot up on the left wing when he is supposed to be playing on the right.

As if to prove that his masterpiece against the Wallabies the previous year was no fluke – not that any proof was required – he conjured up something similar for the benefit of the New Zealanders when the Lions gained the meagre consolation of winning the final Test 9–6, thereby avoiding a black-wash. It was the rugby equivalent of Michelangelo painting the ceiling of the Sistine Chapel and then going back to give it another coat. O'Reilly's one-handed pass found Jackson thirty yards out with three opponents standing in the way. Those who saw what happened next still talk in reverent tones of how the Englishman ghosted past the three defenders. Included on the list of witnesses that day was the ubiquitous McLean, who gave chapter and verse in his book about the tour:

> Jackson weaved past [Ralph] Caulton [the All Blacks' outside centre]. He offered a simultaneous dummy and dodge to beat another man and, approaching [Roger] Urbahn [the All Blacks' scrum-half], who faced him four-square, Jackson began jiggling like a rock-'n'-roll dancer, at the same time holding the ball out in front of him with both hands.
>
> It was mesmerism. No, it was more than mesmerism. It was magic. By some incredible means, he was past Urbahn and going over the goal line as Caulton came at him again, too late to save the try but early enough to get into the

photographs of its scoring. As a try, technically speaking, it was stupendous, a tour de force.

Jackson's one misfortune, perhaps, was to have been a wing of wit and imagination at a time when the English, probably more than anyone else, frowned on anyone courageous or foolhardy enough to flout convention and actually run a risk. When, on one memorable occasion, Jackson launched the most daring of counter-attacks from his own in-goal area that led to a try at the opposite end, an England selector congratulated him on his enterprise before adding the sober post-script, 'For God's sake, don't ever take a chance like that again . . .' On another occasion, when he broke convention to go ferreting into a loose-maul and emerged with the ball he was 'roundly castigated'.

None of his success in New Zealand counted for much the following season. England dropped him for the entire 1960 Five Nations, preferring John Young instead. Jackson came back at the end of the following season and also played a regular part in the 1963 championship, finishing up with the title-clinching home win over Scotland before retiring at the age of 32.

It is easy in hindsight to argue that the selectors did him, and the international game, a disservice by delaying his introduction until 1956. 'I think I was at my best in '55,' he said. 'But then there were some brilliant wingers about at that time. I was fortunate that I played with a lot of good players for club [Coventry] and county [Warwickshire] because [essentially] they were one and the same.'

He cared deeply about the sport and its future, calling for the introduction of an expansive 15-man game long before the 1984 Wallabies played that way during their Grand Slam tour and the phrase 'Total Rugby' suddenly became fashionable.

'We have got to educate rugby players to believe that it is a passing game and not a kicking game,' he told the *Daily Mail*'s Charles Harrold, a few weeks before his last match:

> It means that every club must make forwards play more like backs, a question of getting possession in such a manner that forwards can become part of a passing machine.
>
> Players themselves still don't accept that forwards can pass the ball, though the French, in particular, have proved this point over and over again. Some years ago I almost felt like giving the game up because there was so little handling from

a wing three-quarter's point of view. I got so fed up waiting for the ball that I went looking for it. Things are better now, but only slightly so.

He then became every bit as prescient as an administrator, most notably with his beloved Coventry. He had long recommended a national league system and when it arrived, during the still supposedly amateur days of September 1987, Jackson saw trouble on the horizon. 'My worry,' he said, 'is that millionaires associated with clubs will provide jobs and money to attract leading players. The championship will lead to more publicity, so attracting power-seeking individuals with no feeling for the spirit of the game.'

How right he was and how sad that he ought to have been denied the privilege of playing for the one club which, more than any other, prides itself in upholding the spirit of the game. Peter Jackson, probably more than any other player of his generation, epitomised the essence of the Barbarians and yet, to their shame, he remains by some distance the finest player of that era never to appear for the celebrated touring team of no fixed abode.

They did invite him to join the annual Easter tour of South Wales in 1956 and it was then that his perennial blackballing by the Baa-Baas began, lasting until his retirement seven years later. 'I had been injured in one of the internationals prior to the invitation, and I was not fit to play,' he said. 'I was desperate to turn out for the Barbarians, and the specialist whom I was under worked like fury to get me fit. Unfortunately, he ruled me unfit for the match against Scotland and also for the Barbarians tour which was starting a fortnight after the international. I was bitterly disappointed. I got home and phoned the president of the Barbarians to say that I was not fit to play.

'He said, "Why don't you come on down anyway?" I explained that it was very difficult with my boss frowning heavily at the prospect of losing a Saturday morning's work. The president tried to be insistent but I said, "No. I must stay at home and get on with my work."

'I think I upset him because he told someone else that I'd never be picked again. I learnt after the tour that he had gone back to wherever they were in the bar, and said, "He's had it", or words to that effect. I suppose he thought I was a bit late letting them know.'

At that time, England still had to complete their Five Nations fixtures, with bad weather causing the outstanding match against France in Paris to be postponed until after Easter. 'I thought it was more important for me to be fit to play for England than for the Baa-Baas,' Jackson said. 'If the doctor is doing his level best and he says it would make matters worse to play, you listen to him.

'I felt disappointed at the Barbarians' reaction but philosophical about it. If that was the way people operated, there was very little I could have done to change them. They never picked me again. I felt whoever made that decision had no consideration for anyone.'

The late Dr H. L. Glyn Hughes began his association with the Barbarians as a player in 1913, became the honorary treasurer 15 years later and duly ascended to the presidency. In addition to having gained the distinction of being made the first president of Blackheath, Dr Hughes had also served on the Middlesex County Committee for 25 years: all of which made him an 'alickadoo' – or 'blazer' in modern parlance – of some stature.

'Dr Hughes ignored me on one occasion completely. I didn't know him as such but in the bar after a match, someone asked me to join a group of people. [When] I went across, we were talking and this chappie turned round and walked away. I didn't know who he was. A little later, I was told that it was Dr Hughes. I thought to myself, "So, I blew it."'

How sad and how ironic that such treatment should come from a great club, justifiably proud of what it stands for: an ethos that is perhaps best encapsulated by the opening lines of the club song:

> For it's a way we have in the Baa-Baas
> And a jolly good way, too.

As a team for pure stylists, Jackson would have been right up their street and yet they showed him precious little in the way of jolliness.

It was not as if he would ever have abused their hospitality at the bar. As a player, he never deviated from his favourite tipple: a good, strong cup of tea. All that changed after his first heart operation: a triple bypass in 1982 at the age of 51. 'Until then, I didn't drink alcohol of any kind,' he said. 'It wasn't that I was against drink. I just didn't like it. I still went into the bar because I enjoyed the company, and I was lucky enough to meet many wonderful people down the years. There is a spirit about rugby which you don't get in any other sport. You knock the hell out of one another and have a chat about it over a pint or, in my case, a cup of tea.

'There were three of us non-drinkers on that [1959] Lions tour – John Faull of Wales and Hugh McLeod of Scotland. After the heart operation, the doctor said, "Drink that. It's good for you." It was whisky. He said to Jean, "I want you to make sure he takes a tot of that at half-past eight every night. I'm serious. The one thing whisky will do is thin the blood."

'Put it this way: I certainly got used to a little whisky . . .'

In some respects, he succeeded in spite of the old, safety-first English attitude to the game which stifled many of his successors, most notably Rory Underwood during the barren years at the start of his long career in the '80s. If Jackson could make that sort of impact under that kind of handicap, the mind boggles at how much more he would have done had he been around when Clive Woodward liberated the English game from its shackles.

'Ah yes, I would like to have been playing now,' Jackson said. 'It's a far more exhilarating game. You don't have them [forwards] and us [backs]. You have a whole team working together.'

After a second heart operation – a quadruple bypass in 1995 – and having recovered from three strokes during 1997 and '98, he had been looking forward to one day watching England win the World Cup. Cruelly, a fourth stroke denied him the pleasure, and he died five months later, in the spring of 2004, without regaining consciousness.

There was standing room only at the church of St Peter and St Paul long before the hearse arrived bearing the 'Prince of Wings' on his last journey. On a glorious spring morning, beneath the bluest of skies in the little Warwickshire village of Water Orton, they came from near and far to pay their last respects to a true legend of the game.

Nobody could have brought more credit to the club, county and country which they served. The names of those teams, printed in black capital letters on his red luggage label, in New Zealand all those years ago, provided a chronology of his career and reflected the enormous pride he felt at playing for them: Old Edwardians; North Midlands; Coventry; Warwickshire; England; British Lions. They were all represented at the funeral, gathering to remember a wonderful human being. John Butler, a life-long friend, movingly described Jackson in his eulogy as, 'This lovely, lovely man.'

Once, during an England trial at Otley, as a fearless 20 year old in December 1950, he ran round behind his own posts (rather than concede a five-yard scrum), lost the ball and committed the cardinal sin of conceding a try. The selectors finally forgave him five years later. More fool them for failing to recognise pure genius when it hit them between the eyes.

4

DEVASTATING DICKIE

IN THE SUMMER OF 1955, WHEN BRITAIN'S DON COCKELL FOUGHT ROCKY MARCIANO FOR the world heavyweight title and a rock 'n' roll singer from Tupelo, Mississippi, called Elvis Presley began knocking them out all over the place, Dickie Jeeps did something that had never been done before.

The nugget of a scrum-half, from the flatlands of the Fens, played an entire Test series for the Lions in South Africa before he had played for his country. Nobody has emulated him during the last 50 years and it is hard to imagine that anyone will in the next 50. In the annals of the Lions, Jeeps ranks alongside two compatriots whose names are not to be found in the roll call of England internationals.

During the previous tour of South Africa, in 1938, Gerald 'Beef' Dancer sprang out of Bedford's team straight into the front row for all three Tests. A try-scoring prop whose touchdown at Newlands initiated the Lions' recovery from a ten-point deficit to win the final match of a lost rubber, Dancer went on that tour with another uncapped English prop: the Old Birkonian Bill Howard.

What makes them unique is that neither was ever considered good enough to play for their country. Dancer, in particular, might have thought he had done enough to justify an England place the following year, but, despite a final trial and a consistent season for Bedford, he never made it. The outbreak of the Second World War meant that by the time it was over, he was too old at the age of 34.

Jeeps, mercifully, had no such problem. The England selectors,

58

often a law unto themselves, wasted no time recognising his success as a Lion, picking him for a belated debut against Wales at Twickenham on 21 January 1956. His partner, for what would be a strictly one-off performance, was the future England cricket captain, Mike (M. J. K.) Smith.

Smith succeeded at the highest level as a cricketer despite the inconvenience of having to wear spectacles, a luxury he could not afford on the rugby field. The new half-backs had not met before they shook hands at Richmond on the Friday afternoon for the first and last training session. The introductions over, Jeeps made the most rudimentary of enquiries: 'How do you want the ball?'

'Not too far in front of me,' came the reply. 'I can't see too well . . .'

England lost 8–3. Smith, undaunted at joining the ranks of one-cap wonders, resurfaced in another Test arena two years later and went on to captain his country through a drawn Ashes series in Australia during the winter of 1965–66, by which time Jeeps had long established himself as the best scrum-half produced in the British Isles up to that point. Of course, the mid-'60s came slightly before a teenager from Gwaun-cae-Gerwyn burst out of his native valley with a name that rang around the rugby world: Gareth Edwards.

Cliff Morgan, another of Wales's most revered rugby figures, played an influential role in enabling Jeeps to bypass England and make the quantum leap from Northampton to the Lions. For the first time, the tourists chose to take an extra scrum-half with them. The uncapped Jeeps travelled as the third man behind Trevor Lloyd of Wales and the putative first-choice Johnny Williams, the Old Millhillian, whom England had chosen in the months before the Lions tour throughout a Five Nations series that produced a solitary win from the last match against Scotland.

Morgan, the prototypical post-war model to roll off the assembly line at the fabled Welsh outside-half factory, came across Jeeps during a Northampton v. Cardiff match at Franklin's Gardens in the first half of the 1955–56 season. The Saints won an extraordinary match, and their ambitious young scrum-half left an indelible mark on the Welsh opponent who would be the Lions' Test number 10. 'I had a terrific match, and, luckily, the best fly-half in the game liked me,' Jeeps said. 'That helped me a lot.'

He went on, 'Cliff wanted the ball thrown in front of him. Johnny Williams, without a doubt, had a longer pass than mine – a good, long service – but sometimes it was high up in the air, and Cliff couldn't cope with that. He scored a brilliant try in the first Test. He called for the ball, got it exactly where he wanted and I can see him now tucking his backside in: the wing-forward missed him by a whisker and Cliff was under the posts in a shot.'

England may have preferred Williams, but Morgan knew he had seen someone special in the Northampton club match which, almost half a century later, he still considered the best he had ever played in: 'It was a privilege to take part just to see Bleddyn Williams, who was our captain, sell a dummy, pull the ball back and dive over for a try, making them look stupid. And then, ten minutes later, to see Jeff Butterfield reply in kind, running around and making his own gap to score. I think the ball went into touch only nine times from start to finish.'

The ease with which the supposed novice from Northampton made the Test team and stayed there questioned the judgement of the English selectors who had clearly been of the opinion that Jeeps was not quite good enough for his country, let alone for a superior body representing an amalgam of the best of four countries. At 23, it wasn't as if he had suddenly appeared from nowhere.

Jeeps was, by any standards, an extraordinary scrum-half who flourished in the rarefied atmosphere of an extraordinary tour. The drawn series against the Springboks, during that summer of 1955, will forever retain a special niche in Lions folklore, with Jeeps long assured his place in the rugby pantheon. Morgan had known as much all along. 'He served you like a dog,' Cliff said. 'He was tough and he knew the game. I am convinced that if his fellow Northampton player, Don White, had been in the party and working closely with him in the back row of the scrum, we'd have won the Test series.'

His priceless mixture of courage, strength and technical skill would provide Morgan with the time and space to launch the Anglo-Irish three-quarter line. The English centres – the rapier-like Jeff Butterfield and the bludgeoning Phil Davies – provided the perfect mix of panache and power to unleash a pair of wings from either side of the Irish border: Cecil Pedlow and Tony O'Reilly. Both scored in the first Test, and whenever the definitive list of all-time Lions' classics is drawn up, Johannesburg on 6 August 1955 will be somewhere around the top.

Nobody had any way of finding out exactly how many squeezed into Ellis Park and its steep stands that day. Estimates varied from

95,000 to 105,000, with public demand creating a black market which pushed the price of a ticket up to a staggering level, and the Lions did not require too many entrepreneurial skills to ensure they got their cut, even if it meant running roughshod over the amateur regulations. Clem Thomas revealed how they managed it in his book *The History of the British and Irish Lions*:

> The black market got up to £100 a ticket, a fortune in those days, but the sheep farmers coming in from the Karoo would pay anything to see that match. The Lions sold their surplus tickets to the hotel barber at £50 a time and everybody made a killing.

Talk about a snip. Having done the business off the field beforehand, they proceeded to do it on the field, where it really mattered, and set the tone for the only drawn series in Lions' history. Their victory in that first Test was settled in the final analysis by Jack van der Schyff missing a conversion halfway between the near upright and the corner flag with the last kick of the match.

As the Springbok full-back took careful aim at the posts, O'Reilly could not bear to look and turned away. When a teammate inquired in the dressing-room afterwards as to whether he had lost his nerve, the Dublin teenager revealed that he had been busy invoking a superior force: 'I was in direct communication with the Vatican.'

Billy Williams, the Swansea prop, offered his own prayer, unaware of O'Reilly's hot line to Rome. Standing under the posts, the Welshman whispered to Jeeps, 'The Lord will keep this one out. You wait and see . . .'

That the Lions had to make do for almost half the match with their English flanker Reg Higgins out of action, because of a badly wrenched knee, made a remarkable victory all the more so. 'There were one hundred thousand people there, and you could hear his ligaments go off,' Jeeps said, 'just like a shotgun.'

The Springboks were not amused, least of all by their failure to nail the winning goal and avoid the embarrassment of losing to 14 men. For van der Schyff, a prodigious kicker with either foot, there would be no shot at redemption. A big-game hunter by profession, he had missed in the biggest game of his life and there would be no second chance. 'With that last conversion he was aiming in the direction of the stand where all the non-whites were accommodated,' Jeeps said. 'They were all booing, and that put him off. No doubt about it.' Poor old Jack never set foot in the Test arena again and duly returned to pursue a precarious living hunting crocodiles in what was then Rhodesia, missing the rest of an enthralling series which finished all-square after the Lions had lost the final Test 22–8.

The most astonishing aspect of that tour can be found in a simple breakdown of how the Lions scored their points. They kicked two penalty goals in the entire series: the first by Angus Cameron of Scotland in the first Test and the second by Doug Baker of England in the third. It was amazing, even acknowledging that far fewer kicks were awarded in the '50s when internationals were often decided by a single score. They scored ten tries – five for every penalty goal – but failed to convert half of them. Contrast that to the 1997 series in South Africa, which the Lions won despite scoring just three tries. That victory was instead achieved because Neil Jenkins kicked ten penalties in the series.

It was a sign of the cavalier, or perhaps careless, attitude of those responsible that the 1955 team took off without a penalty specialist. 'We had no place-kickers so they organised a competition on a training day early on in the tour,' Jeeps said. 'We all had to have a go. We started off with a kick on the 25-yard line straight in front of the posts that proved too much for our three appointed match kickers. They dropped out and the rest of us had one kick from each touchline. To finish it off, we had a shot from the ten-yard line. On the way to the first Test match, they presented me with this cup engraved with the words "Dickie Jeeps, place-kicking champion, 1955 Lions".'

It did not do him, or the Lions, much good. When it came to the real thing against Rhodesia – now Zimbabwe – in Kitwe, the newly elected penalty expert lasted for one kick. 'I lined it up from 40 yards out, and this bloody great forward stood between me and the posts. I kicked it straight through his legs and that was that!'

Jeeps had established himself as an ever-present throughout the series, a feat matched only by Morgan, Butterfield and O'Reilly. With their stylish approach on the field and their singing, winning ways off it, the '55 Lions created a mystique and aura around their name: no mean feat considering the lack of exposure in Britain and Ireland at a time when television was still in its infancy. On top of that, only two journalists, J. B. G. (Bryn) Thomas of the *Western Mail* and Vivian Jenkins of the *Sunday Times*, covered the three-month adventure from start to finish.

The triple scrum-half policy turned out to be way ahead of its time with Lloyd sitting out all but five of the 24 matches. Jeeps tried to enter a plea on the Welshman's behalf with the tour manager Jack Siggins, a 45-year-old insurance manager from Belfast who did not take kindly to players advising him on selection.

'I went up to the manager towards the end of the tour and said, "It's time you picked Trevor Lloyd," because at that stage he'd only played four matches,' Jeeps recalled. 'The manager gave me short shrift and said, "I pick the team, not you." Mind you, the management of the Lions, in my experience, was usually terrible.

'In South Africa we took Danny Davies, a Welshman from Cardiff. He was supposed to be the assistant manager-coach. Nice man but, at the end of the day, we had to do our own training and our own thinking. The Lions back then picked their management as a way of rewarding people for their long service in the game, not because they were necessarily the best people for the job. That didn't appeal to my competitive nature. I played everything to win – still do – whether it's half-a-crown [12½ pence in new coinage] for a game of golf or darts.'

Competitive barely does him justice. From an early age Jeeps displayed an aptitude to succeed in a wide range of sports, founded more on an indomitable will to win than pure ability. Whatever he lacked in natural talent he more than made up for in a powerful refusal to be beaten: a feisty doggedness that was to be one of the hallmarks of his rugby career.

Born in the Cambridgeshire village of Willingham on the edge of the Fens, Jeeps excelled as a speed skater. Whenever the river Ouse burst its banks and the temperature plummeted, as it did on an unprecedented scale during the polar winter of 1947, the frozen low-lying fields provided the course for the Fenmen's Sprint Championship over a distance of more than a mile. He finished third one year, not bad considering that he used skating purely as 'a way of keeping fit' on the rare occasions when his preferred Saturday pastime had been frozen off.

At Bedford Modern School, the teenage Jeeps won colours in four sports: rugby, cricket, rugby fives and cross-country running. 'I wasn't the best player, but I had the most determination,' he said. 'Others were better technicians. I was never that quick when I ran for the school, but I did it on guts more than anything else. I came second one year in the Bedfordshire cross-country championships over four miles which was a real surprise. It was half-term and my old man had come to fetch me. At the start of the race, I thought, "I'd better get on with this and get home . . ."'

His will to win made him perfect for rugby, despite the temptation to change tack brought about by a stack of runs for the school cricket XI for whom, in one bountiful season, he returned an average of fractionally more than 100. His contemporaries included his fellow opening batsman Bob Gale, who went on to score runs by the thousand for Middlesex, and Geoff Millman, the wicket-keeper whose career took him into the England Test team via Nottinghamshire. Jeeps contented himself with a few seasons for Cambridgeshire in the less demanding environment of Minor Counties Cricket, ensuring that it would never interfere with his rugby. It satisfied his competitive desire during those summers when the Lions did not require his services.

His success in South Africa in 1955 made him an automatic selection for the two subsequent Lions tours, to New Zealand in 1959 and back to South Africa three years later. Before retiring, he had played in 13 Tests out of a possible 14, a total exceeded only by Willie John McBride.

Nobody will ever get close to Jeeps's total, let alone McBride's. Now that tours take place once every four years with Test series down to the best of three matches, a player would have to stay at the highest level for a minimum of twelve years, long enough to make four tours and play in every Test. Even then, he would still finish one short of Jeeps, which makes his achievement untouchable.

Gareth Edwards may have been voted the player of the 20th century, but even he fell some way short of matching his English predecessor. For those three tours, Francis Jeeps effectively financed his son's Lions trips by forking out for hired hands to do the work his only child should have been doing on the family fruit farm spread out over almost 300 acres around Willingham.

In other parts of the country, they scrimped and saved, and any club lucky enough to boast a Lion in its midst would push the boat out to ensure that he could make ends meet. That was what Swansea did in honour of their two 1955 Lions, Billy Williams and Clem Thomas. They presented them each with a suitcase and £50, a small fortune back then. A gift, especially one involving such a vast sum, had to be made strictly on the q.t. because it broke the amateur regulations.

Fifty quid in a suitcase at least made a change from fifty quid in a brown envelope and with the Welsh lads taking care not to flash too many of those big old white £5 notes all at once, nobody was any the wiser, and their amateur status was never compromised. Each player was also entitled to a weekly tour allowance of £2.50, which he was supposed to account for, penny by penny, while the South African Rugby Football Union raked in a fortune from an aggregate attendance of approximately 650,000.

That figure was raised to 798,000 in New Zealand four years later, in a series that was lost before the Lions averted a black-wash by winning the final Test: the only one that Jeeps missed. In the face of adversity, he made such an impact that not a year of his life has gone by since without New Zealanders making the long pilgrimage to his home in Suffolk. The eulogy penned by Terry McLean – until his death in 2004 the most authoritative journalist on all matters All Black – helps explain the Englishman's enduring appeal on the other side of the world:

> It was a common occurrence for him to wind himself up to a reckless courage and in this mood he became a combination of Horatius, Wild Bill Hickock and the boy who stood on the burning deck whence all around had fled. He had the torso and arms of a heavyweight and with his courage he would take on anything. He had a furious temper, too.
>
> He hated to be beaten and everything he could raise went into every game. I admired Jeeps greatly as both an outstanding scrum-half and a fine team player and it was astonishing to discover that some of his teammates did not entertain a similar regard either for his football or his personality.

Jeeps demanded a lot of himself and expected the same from others in return. As he himself put it, 'Sadly, there were some players who were not up to being on a Lions tour. That didn't necessarily mean I wasn't friends with them.'

Time has not dimmed his frustration at what he saw as some basic flaws in selection, and, in Jeeps's view, the Lions handicapped themselves by not picking their strongest XV. 'We had the wrong captain, and I say that quite outspokenly,' Jeeps said. 'Ronnie Dawson, the Irish hooker, was captain. The other hooker, Bryn Meredith, was a better player but he was always the number two hooker. He'd played really well in South Africa. [He was] very quick at the front of the lineout, and he knew how to obstruct them as well. [However,] there was no way he could get Dawson out of the side. Meredith probably should have been captain.'

Jeeps has never forgotten how the Lions threw away the second Test in Wellington nor, one suspects, forgiven those responsible for an 8–6 victory dissolving into an 11–8 defeat. 'We're ahead with a minute to go and we get a penalty. Terry Davies says, "Right, I'll have a kick at goal." Ronnie Dawson says, "OK." If we'd kicked it into touch, it was the end of the game. Don Clarke caught the missed penalty, and they scored a try at the other end of the field to win the match. Sorry, we just played with no brains.'

The late Vivian Jenkins, the *Sunday Times* correspondent, saw it differently, reporting that Davies, the Wales full-back from Llanelli, '. . . shaped as though he was going to take a kick at goal, but Dawson came up and told him to kick for touch. Davies' kick failed to find touch . . .'

At that time, television had not yet reached New Zealand – never mind videotape – and so the players had to wait until the following week to see highlights of the match on a cinema newsreel. 'I stood outside the posts for one of the Clarke penalties and the ball missed but it was edited out of the film,' Jeeps said. 'We actually scored a very good try which the referee disallowed from 50 yards away. That was hard to take.'

Jeeps felt the tour management left a lot to be desired. 'They needed to be a lot closer to the game. I had the impression that they were out of touch. The manager, Alf Wilson, did play for Scotland, but that was way before the war.

'In my time, the honorary manager and the honorary assistant manager were chosen on a Buggins' turn basis. It wasn't the man who was best qualified or best equipped to be the manager. It was done because it was the turn of a particular country to provide the manager and, nearly always, they were not English. Sorry, but that's the way it was.'

At 12 st. and 5 ft 7 in., Jeeps was never the heaviest nor the tallest of scrum-halves but he was among the strongest, a quality that came from the farming of the country of his native Cambridgeshire. 'We used to plant an orchard every year and our land was heavy land,' he said. 'I held the side of the apple tree, two other fellows chucked the soil into the hole and I stamped it in. Every tree took five minutes to plant, and we would plant 2,000. All told that took around 160 hours and you can imagine what it did for your leg muscles. I went into one game, for Major Stanley's XV against Oxford University, totally knackered.'

Brian Finlay was one All Black who could always vouch for the effect of all those apple trees. The Manawatu flanker won his first cap in the first Test at the age of 31, but the consequences of tackling Jeeps ensured he would not get another one. That Finlay, for all his hobbling, still finished on the winning side was the biggest single regret Jeeps had as a Lion, and all the more so because a number of leading All Black players had dropped out during the week before the match.

The All Blacks admired Jeeps to the point that they would have loved to have claimed him as one of their own. In his report on the tour as a whole, Fred Boshier, sports editor of the *Wellington Evening Post*, emphasised the impression the Englishman had made. 'Before the team was chosen, Jeeps was alleged to have come almost to the end of his tether,' Boshier said. 'What must he have been like at his best? Tough enough to take on the biggest forward, a fine passer, a dangerous runner, a splendid kicker with either foot and saturated in Rugby know-how, Jeeps will always be remembered here as a true champion.'

England elevated him to the captaincy the following season (1959–60) only to be denied a Grand Slam because Mike Weston's try failed to outpoint Michel Vannier's penalty in a 3–3 draw at Stade Colombes in Paris. Jeeps had done the Slam three years earlier under Eric Evans, the Sale hooker. Jeeps remembered him as 'a great captain who had little knock-knees, but he got us through because he was such a great enthusiast'.

Others, some in prominent positions at the Rugby Football Union, often showed their enthusiasm for different aspects of an international weekend. For example, the chairman of selectors rather let the side down at the after-match banquet in Paris one year by letting down his trousers. 'He got stripped to his underpants, and the lady who was playing the violin fled from the room,' Jeeps said. 'The same chap had given us our first and only team meeting at eleven o'clock that morning. All he'd say was, "Right, lads. Get the ball out to the wings. Let's play a bit." Then this waiter came in carrying a telegram on a tray which had all been arranged in advance so the chairman could make a quick exit. He stopped, read the telegram and said, "Sorry, got to go. Cheerio, lads. Good luck." Being a nosey bugger, I picked the telegram up, and do you know what it said? "Bollocks". I'll never forget that as long as I live.'

Like Evans before him, Jeeps rapidly discovered that not everyone in the RFU would thank him for being so willing to bust a gut for

England's glory. Teams were forbidden under the amateur regulations to train any earlier than 48 hours before the game, and, while others were not averse to turning a blind eye, England followed the law to the letter: it was a case of woe betide anyone who tried too hard. Jeeps discovered this for himself in laughable circumstances that exposed the blimpish attitude at Twickenham: 'Before England played The Rest in a final trial, I wrote to the other 14 players. Basically, I said, "If you blokes want to play for England, make sure you win this trial. So, why don't we all get together at Richmond for a practice?" The RFU heard about it, and boy did I get a rollicking from Colonel Prentice, the secretary. He also sent me a letter saying this sort of thing was against the spirit of the game and all that. I tore it up. I couldn't understand his attitude. All I was doing was making a fair point. We went ahead with our preparations as planned.'

Jeeps had only one word for England training sessions: 'desperate'. His debut as England captain, against Wales at Twickenham on 16 January 1960, coincided with the selection of the Cornishman Richard Sharp at fly-half as a late replacement for Bev Risman. Rather than wait until the end of the week to go through the usual pre-match shambles, Jeeps used his initiative to get round the regulations and avoid another rebuke from 'The Colonel'.

Sharp, chosen as a travelling reserve, had journeyed across the breadth of the country from Cornwall to stay with Jeeps at his fruit farm in Cambridgeshire. 'He stayed with me all week and we went down to the local soccer club with a rugby ball. All the kids wanted to join in. That was the first time I had ever passed a ball to a fly-half before an international. I drove him down to Twickenham in my wife's little car on the Thursday night, and we very nearly didn't get there.

'We were doing about 75 [mph] near Stevenage when a stone hit the windscreen. It completely shattered so that we couldn't see a thing. Quick as a flash, I knocked a hole in it with my hand. Richard said, "Cor, that was quick thinking." It was the coldest journey either of us ever made. The following day Bev dropped out through injury and Richard had a terrific match in a win for England.'

Jeeps led England for three seasons through thirteen consecutive internationals, an inordinately large number in a period when no country played more than five matches a year. He never possessed any real pace, a deficiency which Mr Jeeps senior, winner of the

Military Cross during the Great War and centre forward for Willingham FC, exposed when he challenged his son to a race through their orchard, in the week before Dickie won his first England cap.

'He was a pretty fit old bloke, my dad,' Dickie said, laughing. 'He used to box and play football, and he was a gutsy bugger, too. He said to me, "How about I race you now?" This was about two days before I played for England. We were up in the orchards, and he must have been near 60 at the time, but he beat me.'

For his last Lions mission, to South Africa in 1962, Jeeps had been widely touted as captain. Despite his undisputed status as the world's leading scrum-half (Gareth Edwards was only 14 at the time) and his successful leadership of England, the appointment went to a Scot instead: the late Arthur Smith. Jeeps shrugged it off as '. . . one of those things. It didn't worry me at all.'

What did worry him was the Lions' lack of a competitive edge: 'We didn't have a good enough side.' Again, selection issues stretched Jeeps's incredulity, not least when Mike Campbell-Lamerton, the Scottish lock, was chosen at number 8. 'He has never played there in his life, and I am trying to demonstrate to him what his defensive roles are. This is, like, the day before the game. Don't ask me why it happened. It was the management's decision.

'South Africa and New Zealand are tough places to go and win Test series. They are a darn sight tougher if you don't have the right side. On both those tours we probably had four players who were not the right ones to be there. Players of better ability were left at home, even if some of them hadn't played international rugby at the time.'

The Lions drew the first Test, lost the next three and finished up under Jeeps's command, when Smith missed the final match in Bloemfontein. That tour to South Africa in 1962, like the two which preceded it, cost his father a small fortune as he again had to hire an extra hand on the farm while his son was away serving Queen and country. 'When I came back home, I worked even harder, but I would have given up everything to go on a Lions tour. I picked up the *Daily Mail* one morning and read that the players were objecting to £20,000 for this last tour. I'd have been very happy to play what, four or five matches for twenty grand. I'd have gone for nothing.'

Having voiced concerns about the size of the squad before the Lions left Heathrow in May 2005, nobody could accuse Jeeps of being wise after the event. 'I said before the tour began that they took too many players. As a result, they were not able to get a cohesive unit together in time for the Tests. I think the series has done the Lions a lot of harm.

'If the going for the first Test had been dry instead of wet, the All Blacks would have scored 50 points. They were far too good for us, and we have to learn from them. Almost every one of their forwards seemed to have developed greater leg muscle power.

'They had backs who could run, tackle and get the ball to the wings, which we in England don't do any more. Charlie Hodgson was the pick of the four fly-halves; the only one who showed any initiative. I picked my team for the first Test from what I had seen of the tour at that point. I got six right, ten right for the second Test and eleven for the third.'

Jeeps, who shares the same November birthday as Joe DiMaggio, Andrew Carnegie and JFK junior, retired from the big stage at the end of his last Lions tour to rejoin Cambridge City, his junior club, where he spent several seasons before reappearing on the England scene as a selector. It did not take him long to realise that the RFU's lines of communication left something to be desired: 'I'll give you an example. On a Friday night, I'm talking at a dinner somewhere which meant catching the one o'clock train out of Cambridge on Saturday morning to get to London so I could be at Redruth to see Gloucester play Cornwall. I'd gone to watch Bill Redwood, the Bristol scrum-half. When I got there I was told that he wasn't playing, that he'd dropped out the day before. Nobody thought of telling me. A lot of those selection meetings were arranged around a nice Sunday lunch.'

As luck – or lack of it – would have it, his first season as an England selector, in 1966–67, coincided with the advent of a 19-year-old student from a teacher-training college who had been close to pursuing a career as a professional footballer. Gareth Edwards played in the youth team for Swansea Town, as they were then, alongside an Italian boy called Giorgio Chinaglia, who would win fame and fortune as an international striker.

Edwards had been released from his Swansea contract to concentrate on rugby, a decision which condemned England to almost perennial defeat at the hands of Wales for 11 years until his retirement in 1978. 'I thought to myself, "The sooner that so-and-so goes to rugby league, the better it will be for England." I said after his first match against us, "Here's my half-crown. We'll start a fund for you to go . . ."'

Like Jeeps, Edwards went on three Lions tours and, while he fell some way short of matching his English predecessor's record of 13 Tests, one great scrum-half readily acknowledged the phenomenal Welshman as an even better one: 'He was so complete that he didn't have a single weakness. He was much quicker than me for a start. Playing with so many good players in a terrific Welsh side was a big help.'

Edwards was still reigning supreme when Jeeps became the youngest president in the history of the Rugby Football Union at 44. He made it clear from the outset that he would do it his way, which, no doubt, caused some consternation for the secretary: the late Air Commodore Bob Weighill.

'After my first meeting as president, Bob says to me, "We've got to do a press conference so I'll write down the things you need to say." I says, "Hang on, Bob. I don't need anything to be written down. I'll just take the questions as they come and answer them accordingly."'

With typical Jeeps zeal, he turned the presidency into a crusade, seizing English rugby by the scruff of the neck and shaking it out of its lethargy. His presidency began at a time when the game across the shires had sunk to a low ebb. It was an issue that he tackled with fiery conviction, by carrying out his own investigation into the depressed state of the sport. For most of the '70s when Wales and France monopolised the Five Nations Championship, England simply did not count.

'I have made it my business to go round the clubs to see for myself, and I don't like what I've found,' he said during an interview in August 1979. 'Far too many clubs are playing what I call rubbish rugby, the ten-man stuff which means they aren't producing backs. I won't be too popular for saying so but somebody has to say it otherwise we'll just go muddling on into another decade.

'We can't produce better rugby until skill and flair become a greater part of the training diet. The way things are with England's centres, even I could play against them. All I'd have to do would be to stand in their way, and they'd run into me. There is often no comparison when *Rugby Special* shows club matches from England and Wales. Almost without exception, it is only in the Welsh game that you see flair and skill behind the scrum. The standard of some English club games is awful.

'Our rugby is badly in need of some sort of discipline. Club coaching has become a joke. Budge Rogers went to a leading club on their main training night, in his capacity as an England selector, and eight players turned up. Eight out of forty-five. I went to another major club one Tuesday night to watch them train. Half the players arrived at 6.30, the other half at 7.30.'

Jeeps changed attitudes sufficiently for England to win a Grand Slam in 1980, the only one during a 34-year period from the late '50s. Nor did he restrict his energy to rugby. Appointed chairman of the Sports Council in June 1978 by the late Denis Howell, the former Sports Minister, he held the part-time post until his resignation seven years later.

It was long enough for one particularly memorable spat with the Duke of Edinburgh, triggered by Prince Philip's criticism of the administration of the Sports Council in his then capacity as president of the Central Council of Physical Recreation. The Duke claimed that the Sports Council was staffed by people with little knowledge of sport.

Typically, Jeeps did not take it lying down. 'For the Prince to say that the Sports Council is employing hundreds of people with little, if any, knowledge of sport is an insult to a professional body of staff,' he said in a statement. 'Most of them are highly qualified and have served a hard apprenticeship.'

More recently, he marvelled at England's Rugby World Cup success. Sadly, not every gold medallist seemed to be aware of being in his company at certain social functions held after the event. If they did know who he was, it made the lack of even the most perfunctory acknowledgement inexcusable: 'I don't go to the big dinners any more, after the internationals, but I went to one or two of the post-match receptions, and the players don't recognise you at all. It's hard to get them to talk to you. You try to. So as far as I'm concerned, I don't poke my nose in . . .'

Back in those chaotic times when England tended to be the best of losers, it was a very good job he did.

5

HOOKED ON A WELSH GENIUS

IN THE LONG, TROUBLED HISTORY OF ANGLO-IRISH CONFLICT, FEW ENGLISHMEN HOLD A more affectionate place in the annals of Celtic sport than a gnarled old farmer from the shores of the Severn. John Pullin belonged to the old school: a tough-as-old-boots front-row forward who never used two words where one would do, let alone waste any time composing a bon mot as a means of embroidering his captain's speech. On Saturday, 10 February 1973, he brought the house down at Lansdowne Road in the afternoon by turning up for the kick-off and again at the Shelbourne Hotel that evening with a spontaneous line in self-deprecation.

Wales and Scotland had refused to fulfil their fixtures in Dublin the previous year because of the Troubles: two decisions that cost Ireland the prospect of a rare Grand Slam. A victory over England at Twickenham had followed an even rarer one over France in Paris the day before Bloody Sunday. The political situation, a euphemistic phrase for the bombing and the killing, had not improved in the ensuing 12 months before it was England's turn to go to Dublin.

For obvious reasons, they had more cause to pull out than Wales or Scotland, which left Irish rugby bracing itself for another grievous blow and the Five Nations for another fractured tournament. However, England's stout-hearted rugby men refused to be put off, even if a five-try beating by Wales in the previous match at Cardiff Arms Park hardly put them in the best frame of mind to avoid another.

They made changes at full-back (Tony Jorden for Sam Doble, who made himself unavailable), scrum-half (Steve Smith for Jan Webster), second row (Roger Uttley for Peter Larter), wing-forward (Peter Dixon for John Watkins) and off they went, bolstered by the Rugby Football Union taking out £500,000 worth of insurance. England had always been guaranteed an hospitable welcome, at least for the moments before kick-off, but nobody could have imagined the thunderous scale of the appreciation that would greet them.

Lansdowne Road had never accorded anyone an ovation that lasted quite so long. The sound reverberated around the old place for fully five minutes; not even the acclamation they gave to Jack Charlton, years later, for his exploits with the Republic of Ireland soccer team could trump the reception the rugby crowd gave Pullin's team that day.

Uttley, the new cap in the back row, could still hear it 30 years later. 'I remember seeing *gardaí* with guns at the airport, and they were also stationed in the lobby and corridors of the hotel,' he said. 'As a young bloke, I was just pleased to be playing for my country. The standing ovation when we ran out made the hairs on your neck stand on end. It proved we had made the right decision.'

It all went downhill once Tom Grace scored the opening try, and Ireland's control left England fortunate to get off comparatively lightly at 18–9. Being a wily old campaigner, Pullin knew that his team wasn't up to the job, and, when the time came for him to stand up at the after-match banquet, he said so, without ever realising that his words would invite another standing ovation. 'We may not be much good,' he said, 'but at least we turn up.'

Willie John McBride, the pipe-smoking Ulster bank manager who would lead the Lions on their invincible tour of South Africa the following year, remembers the reaction as though it had happened yesterday. 'The entire company – every man in the place – stood up and roared his approval at that remark,' he said. 'I can tell you, strong men had tears in their eyes over it. I was just one of those who felt thoroughly moved by the whole experience. But that was what rugby football could do.'

Some ten days earlier, McBride had used his hitherto unknown skills as a diplomat to dissuade David Duckham, his good friend and fellow Lion, from giving the match a miss. Fearful that his withdrawal would cause a domino effect, McBride has since claimed that had he not convinced the Coventry wing of his safety the match would never have been played.

Pullin disagrees, adamant that it would have been played irrespective of how many players refused to go. He had been left in no doubt that the Rugby Football Union would find an English 15 from somewhere, even if it meant picking their tenth best team, not that the captain had any intention of vacating the bridge. The uncertainty prompted two of Twickenham's most experienced and respected selectors, Sandy Sanders and Alec Lewis, to pay Pullin a visit. He recalled, 'They came down to the farmhouse after the Welsh match, and we had lunch and a chat. I decided I'd go to Dublin and they said, "Do you think the others will come?" I said, "I don't know. It's up to them, really."

'I got the impression they [England] were going anyway, whether I went or not. That was the long and the short of it. At the back of your mind, you thought, "Well, I know if I don't go, they will find a hooker to play for England eventually, even if he would be the 25th choice." They preferred that I went as captain, and I saw no reason why I shouldn't. I didn't feel in any danger as a sportsman. I knew the Troubles were fairly widespread, but the Irish always pick their rugby team from both sides of the border. I wanted to play. Deep down, I never thought we were a target as a sporting team. For that reason, I think Wales and Scotland should have gone.'

Once he saw the extent of the security, at Dublin airport and around the team's central hotel overlooking St Stephen's Green, the phlegmatic skipper began to wonder whether they had made the correct decision to travel to Ireland: 'In the hotel, there was a policeman outside every door and two or three at the bottom of the staircase. They were all over the place. You couldn't move for them. The more you saw of the security, the more you thought, "Perhaps there is something going on." I suppose the only time you thought about it was when they played the national anthem and you were stood round dead still for a long time. You thought to yourself, "Not a good idea, this." There were never any threats, at least not that we knew, although I think it did affect a few players, like a couple of the three-quarters. The ovation was terrific. I was waiting for the match to get started, to be honest, because you just wanted to get on with it at that stage. Losing was never part of the script.'

The heady mixture of acclamation and apprehension washing all around them made it almost impossible to get their emotions back on an even keel, for what would have been a tough enough task against a rampant Irish team packed with ten Lions, past, present and future. The apologists could always seize the circumstances and use them to excuse an English failure but not the extent of that failure in finishing second by some distance, despite the 18–9 score suggesting otherwise.

Returning to his heavily guarded hotel room, Pullin had some different thinking to do. There was the ritual dinner to attend and a speech to make. 'I thought about it while I was getting ready,' he said. 'You've got to think of something to say so you scribble down a few things. When I said that bit about turning up, the reaction surprised me. It was overwhelming, and I'm not an emotional type of bloke: certainly not openly. I didn't think it was that good a quote. It just seemed the obvious thing to say, didn't it?'

England, having behaved like perfect guests on and off the field, were cheered to the rafters for the second time that day. The only difference was that this time they were sitting down in their monkey-suits instead of standing up in their kit.

Pullin was already a double Lion, in McBride's expert view '. . . a great player, an outstanding rugby man'. On his way to the top, the West Country hooker needed every ounce of his durability to suffer the slings and arrows that came with playing in the primeval-like arena of the front row: most of those slings and arrows delivered by outrageous opponents as opposed to outrageous fortune. He learnt quickly that when one door closed, another was just as liable to open and smash him in the face.

England's selectors often discarded players as quickly as they picked them, and Pullin, dropped after a losing debut to Wales at Twickenham in January 1966, was no exception. From being considered the best hooker in the country, he suddenly found himself replaced by not one rival but three. Bill Treadwell of Wasps took over for three matches, Steve Richards of Richmond for five and Bert Godwin of Coventry won eleven caps over an eight-year period, starting with a home draw against France at Twickenham in February 1959 and ending at the same venue in November 1967 with defeat by Brian Lochore's All Blacks.

Ironically, they never picked the one hooker whom Pullin then rated as England's number one: Andy Johnson of Northampton. Had the selectors known as much about the art of hooking as their Bristol specialist, Johnson would have been selected and Pullin would have been resigned to wondering whether he would go down as a one-cap wonder, instead of spending seven uninterrupted years turning himself into the most-capped hooker in Britain.

Much to his relief, he won a reprieve at the age of 26. It had taken him two years to be considered worthy of a second chance. He grabbed the opportunity and clamped it in such a vice-like grip that he became a permanent fixture throughout the next 36 internationals. Of all the challengers who came and went, only Johnson bothered Pullin as being good enough to oust him from the side, and he was persistently overlooked.

'I knew Andy was the best,' Pullin said. 'I played against him at Northampton in my first season for Bristol, and we lost fourteen against the head. Fourteen! Now that's what you call being taken to the cleaners. Andy was the only one who would ever give me any trouble in this country. We grew up together, but he had a reputation for bending the rules, which we all did. I don't know why he had that reputation, but he never got picked for England because they thought he would give away too many penalties. It was a fallacy. I also felt a bit sorry for the Welsh hooker, Jeff Young, who had the same reputation. I could get away with it but Jeff couldn't.

'Andy was the best hooker around in England, apart from myself. The only time I felt threatened was when he was a travelling reserve. I thought, "If he gets on, he'll blow my cover because they'll realise he's more than useful." I made sure he didn't get on.'

It taught Pullin a valuable lesson in self-preservation which he never forgot. Sensing that he could cope with every English hooker bar Johnson, and knowing that he had to negotiate three England trials each season, the farmer played a cunning game. He would deliberately toy with the challengers whom he considered inferior rather than rout them and force the selectors to look elsewhere. 'First trial you let them break even with you, well almost. Second trial, you take three or four strikes off them. Final trial, you stepped it up to show you were the best. But you always kept them on the scene.'

Once he had been given a second chance at the start of the 1968 Five Nations Championship, Pullin grabbed it in a manner that demanded a place amongst the 30 players picked for the Lions tour of South Africa that year. However, when there, he ran smack into another reminder that every silver lining has a cloud. It came in the unforgiving form of a fist belonging to his opposite number on his Test debut as a Lion, in the second of the four-match series against the Springboks in Port Elizabeth: a 6–6 draw that stood out amidst three defeats.

Unluckily for Pullin, his opponent was a very strong individual from the Afrikaans-speaking citadel of Pretoria. Gys Pitzer was also a heavyweight boxer and Pullin could always be relied upon to vouch for the anaesthetic effect of the South African's punching when he was not wrapping his arms around the most formidable pair of props he had ever encountered: Hof Myburgh and Hannes Marais.

Pitzer had discovered some enthusiastic sparring partners the previous year during the home series against France. The late Chris Greyvenstein, the Springbok historian, wrote of him:

> [Pitzer] not only did his job superbly well but he also proved himself to be one of the toughest men ever to pull the green-and-gold jersey over his head. Boxing ability should hardly be a qualification for a rugby player but some members of the 1967 French team often confused the two sports for it to have been an advantage in that hotly-contested series.

Greyvenstein did not appear to think that Pitzer's punches were a matter of great concern:

> There was some grumbling over the fact that Gys Pitzer had knocked out his opposite number John Pullin with a punch thrown in front of the grandstand but [Max] Baise [the South African referee] was unsighted. The Springboks insisted that Pullin had provoked Pitzer and the Lions manager [David Brooks, of Harlequins], considering the fact that he so readily complained about other matters, was remarkably unconcerned about the incident.

As if that, by some twisted logic, made the punch legitimate. Pullin saw it coming and many South Africans in the crowd saw it land but not, it seemed, the South African referee. What a surprise. 'There was a lineout and the ball had gone,' Pullin recalled. 'I was watching it [the ball] when I sort of turned into the punch just before it landed. I saw it at the last second. Too late. I was out cold for a few minutes. He'd gone by then, but he didn't do it again. Pitzer was a good player, one of the best I ever came up against. He didn't really need to do it.

'That South African side, forward-wise anyhow, was the hardest one I played against, by a long way. They were so strong: different to any team I played before or since. It was the best front row I ever came up against. You can talk about the All Blacks and their massive reputation, but, as a complete pack, the South Africans were always harder to play against.'

From a prone position in the first Test and a losing series overall, Pullin had emerged as a serious player on the global stage. The boy from Thornbury, who was not considered good enough for the 1st XV at his local grammar school ('I was a lot better than the other fellows, but I didn't get on too well with the sports master'), would soon start beating the big guns on a regular basis.

Back on his feet in a big way, he led his country to victories in rapid succession over South Africa, New Zealand and Australia: something that no British captain had done before and none would do again until Martin Johnson more than two decades later. Pullin achieved his hat-trick in less than 18 months, starting his appointment as captain with an 18–9 win over the Springboks at Ellis Park, their Colditz-style fortress in Johannesburg, on 3 June 1972.

The losers created a diplomatic incident afterwards that rather insulted their opponents and gave Pullin good reason to stress the importance of turning up in Dublin a few months later. Unlike England on that occasion, the Springboks (with one notable exception) failed to appear at the after-match reception, which gave the victors some idea of the significance of what they had achieved.

Pullin recalled, 'Their coach banned them from turning up. It was such a disgrace to lose they had to go back and have an ear-bashing rather than go to the official function. We're English. We don't do that sort of thing. Morné du Plessis did get to the reception, but I thought it a great compliment that they would stoop to such levels. I could understand it because it meant so much to them. It was classed as a national disaster and a national disgrace, especially losing to England, who'd lost four matches at home, although we were not that bad a side. But that sort of behaviour was still unforgivable.'

The All Blacks did turn up to the function in Auckland after Pullin's England had gone there the following September, although it was questionable whether the real All Black team had shown up for the match. England had never won a Test match in New Zealand until they defied the odds to the tune of 16–10 at Eden Park, when another West Country member of the front row scored the first of two second-half tries. C. B. 'Stack' Stevens, a Cornish farmer from Penzance-Newlyn, whose initials C. B. stood for Claude Brian – not that anyone outside his immediate family had the faintest clue – ensured England caused enough havoc to end the Test careers of five of Ian Kirkpatrick's team.

Back at Twickenham two months later, the 'White Tornadoes' duly took care of the Wallabies. The magnitude of England's winning sequence against the southern-hemisphere teams was not diminished by the fact that the Australians were not the force, at that time, that they would start to become in the '80s. 'Unbelievable, really,' Pullin said. 'We had quite a useful side. There was never any doubt about the Test team except for the toss-up at tight-head between [Fran] Cotton and [Mike] Burton. Otherwise the team picked itself.'

Over a period of less than thirty months, Pullin played seven times against the All Blacks' Test team for England, the Lions and the Barbarians. For someone who always thought of New Zealand as 'invincible', his record against them during that most purple of patches is unique amongst British and Irish players: won four, drawn one, lost two.

It took a phenomenal team to strip them of that invincibility, layer by layer, over a series of four matches. The 1971 Lions, who could also have been entitled 'Wales and the Rest' without contravening the Trade Descriptions Act, did exactly that, and Pullin had the distinction of being the only Englishman to play in all four Tests, along with the other ever-presents J. P. R. Williams, Gerald Davies, John Dawes, Mike Gibson, Barry John, Gareth Edwards, Iain McLauchlan, Sean Lynch, Mervyn Davies, John Taylor and McBride.

Peter Dixon and David Duckham each played in three of the Tests. That players of the calibre of Fergus Slattery, Bob Hiller and the then uncapped Derek Quinnell found themselves confined to the non-playing supporting cast underlined the strength of the squad. What they also had was a visionary coach blessed with an ability to innovate, thus challenging the traditional conservatism of the British game, and with the nerve to put his ideas into practice. Carwyn James also had the man-management expertise that made him a real people person.

Pullin had seen a lot of coaches, good, bad and indifferent, but he had not met one as good as the chain-smoking Welshman from the old Carmarthenshire pit village of Cefneithin. 'Carwyn was the best by a long way. He had an overall vision of the game and how to play it. Most coaches thought forwards were there to do their stuff in the scrum and lineout and not much else. He got all the players involved all the time. I'd never met him before [the tour began], and it didn't dawn on me just how good he was until the tour was over.'

As a method of inspiring the tour party, James would manage to get the players, from different backgrounds and from different parts of the British Isles, singing from the same hymn sheet. His first ploy on their first night in New Zealand, as Pullin remembers it, was to teach the non-Welsh members of the party a Welsh hymn. It was a formidable task that he tackled with typical enterprise by handing out sheets on which the words of his native tongue were spelled out phonetically. Perhaps surprisingly, for a hard-bitten customer from the English side of Offa's Dyke, Pullin thought it a good idea.

'One of the songs he taught us could have been the Welsh national anthem for all I knew, but it sounded good. I didn't mind all the Welsh stuff, because I always got on well with them. I can't remember, but I suppose, after being with so many of them for so long, I must have ended up with a bit of a Welsh accent.'

James imposed discipline without necessarily seeking confrontation, and he was also smart enough to tap into the expert technical knowledge of people like Pullin and his Irish front-row partner, Ray McLoughlin. 'Carwyn impressed me as a person, because he was very good at managing people,' Pullin said. 'Before the final Test, the "Front Row Union" were having a few drinks – a few too many that close to the match. Carwyn came in and said, "Time you lot went to bed."

'There were eight or ten of us. We stayed for a few more [drinks], but he made us pay for it on the training field. He was always in charge, but he would admit he didn't know the finer points of front play, so it was up to us to tell him. He'd ask for specialist advice because not many people know much about front-row play unless they've played there and even then, for some, it still takes some explaining.'

For the first time, the tour caught the imagination of the British public at large. Receptions at Heathrow for returning rugby teams were unheard of back then, and, while it wasn't quite on the scale of the Beatles, several thousand turned up at dawn one morning to welcome the conquering heroes home. The Government doled out a few gongs, and the coach was sounded out about accepting initiation into the Order of the British Empire.

James, a teacher, scholar and patriot, politely turned it down and kept quiet, rather than attempt to make any political capital from it.

It enhanced his standing amongst the Welsh-speaking *crachach* as one who put the Welsh nation first and last. How strange, therefore, that he should end up like a prophet without honour in his own land, shunned by one of the most exclusive organisations in Welsh society: the Welsh Rugby Union.

If James could weld a team together to beat the All Blacks in New Zealand, imagine what he could have done for Wales, especially when they contained so many Lions. The tide of popular opinion behind James, during the joyous months after the tour, promised to sweep him into office. However, it was one that he would have taken on his terms that he alone would be allowed to pick the team. And if that meant the abolition of the selection committee – the so-called 'Big Five' – then that would be a small price to pay for progress.

The Big Five, exalted during the glory years to an almost druidic importance, had acquired the status of a sacred cow, or five sacred cows. Sadly, too few in the WRU hierarchy had the moral courage to cast self-interest aside, abolish the selection committee and seize the opportunity of a lifetime. Instead, they thanked James for his interest and shut the door on him for good.

On his farm in the village of Aust, Pullin could hardly believe the smoke signals billowing across from the other side of the Severn. 'That put our rugby back by ten or fifteen years,' he said. 'It wasn't just very bad for Wales but for the whole of the northern hemisphere. Wales were a good side anyway, but Carwyn would have made them even better, and that would have had a knock-on effect in the other countries. It would have shown them the way forward.

'If he had been allowed to continue, the balance of power might have been different. I put it down to petty jealousy. They were obviously jealous of him in Wales, very jealous. It was a big opportunity missed.'

The Welsh coach and the English hooker joined forces at Cardiff Arms Park in January 1973 for an encore to beat them all. The Lions, reappearing almost en masse in the guise of the Barbarians for the traditional finale to that winter's All Black tour, responded to the sense of occasion with a try that has been talked about and shown in all its black-and-white glory ever since, as it will continue to be for as long as the game is played. Somehow it was fitting that the ex-Bristol Saracen should have been among those privileged to play a part in its creation, although, true to form, his intentions that afternoon were rather more prosaic.

'Three–nil – a penalty under the posts – was all we wanted,' Pullin said. 'We never went out there to play Barbarians rugby, not by any stretch of the imagination. They weren't there to play rugby either. Three–nil would have suited them, too, but we were always capable of doing something special, because that's the way we'd played in New Zealand.'

That someone from the grunt-'n'-groan department should have sewn one of the early stitches into the masterpiece, finished off by the swallow-diving Gareth Edwards, strengthened the hooker's conviction about the old Arms Park. While his compatriots dreaded the thought of going there, Pullin loved it, so much so that he makes the extraordinary confession, for an Englishman, that he enjoyed playing in Cardiff more than at Twickenham. He was in his element every time he walked through the old Gwyn Nicholls gates and down the ramp to the dressing-rooms behind the concrete slab beneath the old North Stand.

'I have never enjoyed Twickenham anyhow, not even when I was playing to be honest,' he said. 'I'd much sooner play in Wales at Cardiff, even though we usually got a good hiding there. Ninety per cent of the people at Twickenham were there because it was Twickenham. They were not really there to watch the rugby, whereas in Wales it was ninety per cent the other way.

'If you ever took one against the head at Cardiff Arms Park, a big noise would go up from the crowd, because they understood and appreciated what was happening. If you took one against the head at Twickenham, nobody would know. They wouldn't have had a clue what had happened. All they wanted to see at Twickenham was a three-quarter running in a nice try from fifty yards. But, as far as forward play was concerned, they were not really interested.'

Twickenham has long since been turned into something of a fortress, not that Pullin goes there any more. 'They are more vociferous nowadays, but when they sing that "Sweet Chariot" thing it really drives me up the wall. It's so "old school tie". If I was playing and the crowd sang that, I think I'd cringe. I used to go [to England matches at Twickenham], but it's always a busy time of the year on the farm with the sheep. I watch England games on TV, and it was great to see them win the World Cup because they'd been a good side for a few years.'

Had Wales scrapped their selection committee and given James carte blanche, England might have scrapped theirs a whole lot sooner than they did. Instead, selectors remained the bane of

Pullin's life, never more so than when he led England out against Australia in Brisbane on 9 June 1975. Not surprisingly, it brought his captaincy reign to a chaotic end. Thirty years on, Pullin revealed that he thought about taking the England team off the field as the ultimate protest against the Australian referee, the native Queenslander Bob Burnett.

Mike Burton had been sent off in the opening minutes, but Pullin knew he was on a loser before a blow had been struck. He had been lumbered with the wrong team. 'It was an awful feeling going out there as captain thinking, "This is a rubbish team I've got here. We haven't got a hope in hell." Then Burton got sent off. I thought, "That's it. This is going to be a cricket score." There were at least four people in that team who I wouldn't have picked.'

Driven to the edge of despair, Pullin was sorely tempted to abandon the philosophy that he brought to every game: 'Always look after number one if you want to get anywhere. And when you get there, don't rock the boat unless you are sure of your place. When I knew I wasn't going to get dropped and there was something worth rocking the boat for, then I'd rock it.'

That Saturday in Brisbane, he thought about turning it turtle. 'It did cross my mind to take the team off,' he said. 'I think I would have done if I'd been given a better team. Instead I knew it was a rubbish team I was out there with. It was obvious we were going to lose anyhow, but I suppose being a man short for almost the entire match gave us an excuse.

'They didn't take Stack Stevens on that trip. Then they flew [Alan] Old and [Peter] Dixon out at the last minute when they should have been there from the start. They made other mistakes, too. The selectors had this idea in their head that it was going to be an easy trip and they could blood some youngsters "for the future". An easy trip? What a joke. There is no easy trip at international level, and that business about playing for the future really annoyed me. You don't build for the future at that level. There is no such thing. If you are good enough you play, whether you're 40 or 20. You play for today, not tomorrow or next week.'

As coach, the late John Burgess picked the England team in Australia. A more democratic process operated on the South African tour three years earlier when Pullin had his say alongside those of the tour manager, Alec Lewis, and the coach, John Elders.

'I would go in and say, "This is the team I think is the best," and I'd read all the names out,' Pullin said. 'The only person we ever argued about was tight-head prop. In one case I got my way, in the other I was out-voted.'

The procedure had changed in Australia. Pullin no longer had a say. 'Burgess picked the team. I'd say, "I don't want this player or that player." He'd say, "Oh well, I do and I'm the coach." That was it. He'd already picked his team which didn't match up to anything like mine. Burgess got his way.

'My team differed in at least four positions. There was at least one glaring mistake. It meant that one of the better players was sitting on the bench doing nothing. Burgess wasn't my cup of tea. He was so Lancashire, northern-biased, it was untrue. I think he was very envious of the fact that I'd played a lot for England, and I wasn't a Lancashire man. He got rid of me as captain and Tony Neary took over . . . but I don't hold that against Neary. He was a really good player, and he'd have got there eventually, regardless of who was coach.

'At home, the captain read about the team in the papers, like everyone else. You didn't have any say at all. They didn't even speak to you beforehand. They'd say, "That's the team. Pullin's captain." There was a lot of poor selection.'

When England felt the time had come to replace him as the England hooker, Pullin was hardly chuffed at the choice of Peter Wheeler as his successor, even if he was a Lion in the making. 'He was all right around the field, but he wasn't what I'd call a good hooker,' Pullin said. 'He was adequate. If you go down the list of all-time great hookers who you'd worry about playing against, he wouldn't have been one of them. Andy Johnson would have been one, Pitzer was another and [Alain] Paco of France was a good one.'

Tane Norton, his old Kiwi sparring partner, gets a mention almost as an after-thought. 'I always knew it would be a hard game against Norton. We'd finish up more or less even. [There was] not much in it, but you weren't worried about being taken to the cleaners, whereas with the other three, on a bad day, you would have been.'

Fate didn't always deal him a winning hand. His surprising success in New Zealand and continued captaincy of England in 1974 made him the early front-runner to take the Lions to South Africa that summer. An early meeting with the honorary manager Alun Thomas, before the 30-man squad had been chosen, raised the hopes of a player hailed by Dr Danie Craven, the South African Rugby Board's redoubtable president, as the world's number one hooker. When the names were announced, Pullin's was nowhere to be found.

To his chagrin, the Lions went for Ken Kennedy, an Irish doctor, and Bobby Windsor, a Welsh steelworker then emerging as the middle man in the celebrated 'Viet-Gwent' of Pontypool. 'It was a bit of a shock when I heard it on the radio,' Pullin said with a resigned shrug. 'I thought I would have been picked, but it wasn't to be. A couple of days later, I'd forgotten all about it and got on with my life.'

He came back for one last international in 1976 and retired two years later. Like more than a few of his contemporaries, he is less than enamoured of the professional game. 'You're envious of the money they're getting, but I don't think the game is half the game it was, certainly not in my position,' he said. 'There's no such thing as scrummaging, not as we knew it. Now it's just a means of re-starting the game. They might as well throw the ball up in the air. The hooker doesn't have to do anything. The ball is put so far under his feet he hardly has to lift his leg.

'A lot of the skill has gone out of front-row play. You still need strong men. I wouldn't really enjoy it, but if you're getting paid X-thousands of pounds you would. You wouldn't say no to the money, especially as a farmer in this day and age. I don't think it's anything like the spectacle it was. It might be old age, sour grapes, I don't know. I sit down and start watching games but they are so monotonous. They do the same thing – picking up the ball and running at someone. That's the end of the game, basically.

'The big disappointment is that the good Welsh clubs – Cardiff, Newport, Swansea and Llanelli – never came in with the English and set up an Anglo-Welsh league. Let's face it, there were some bad clubs in the English League, and some of them have gone to the wall now. Look at Bristol. They've lost their ground. What they took one hundred years to build up and maintain has gone in two seasons of professionalism, which I think is criminal.'

Pullin would choose an Anglo-Welsh pair of tight-heads, Mike Burton and Charlie Faulkner (also a judo black belt), as the best props he played with or against. However, Pullin is in no doubt as to the best player of his generation, and he does not mean Gareth Edwards but another from the pantheon. 'Gerald Davies. Outstanding. Brilliant, he was. Didn't have a weakness. Gareth did. He was a great player, but, when the going was tough, he wasn't always there.

'I'll never forgive him [for] '71 – he walked off the pitch with a pulled hamstring in the first Test. We had a scrum under the posts. All he had to do was put the ball in, then either leave it to the back row or give it to the outside half to drop a goal. We were getting a hiding and a half. The ref blows up, scrum down under their posts, ten yards out, smack in the middle and Gareth buggers off.

'[There was] no one else to put the ball in. Eventually John Taylor did the job, but he didn't have a clue how to put it in. Gareth would have put it under my feet or going that way. Instead, John shovels it under their feet, they get the ball and kick it downfield. It was our best chance the whole game. We won that match, but how I don't know. It was unbelievable because they were all over us.'

The experience of being swamped did not end there. With his farm below sea level, Pullin had once been assured by his neighbours around Aust that a tidal wave hit the Severn once every 100 years. 'I remember a 70-year-old woman telling me about it, and I thought she was off her head,' he said. 'Then the farm got hit by two tidal waves in the space of ten years. There was never any warning. It hit you out of the blue.'

Just like Pullin's 'White Tornadoes' in Johannesburg and Auckland.

6

DAI THE TRY

BY THE TIME THEIR BANDWAGON ROLLED INTO THE OLD GOLD-MINING TOWN OF
Greymouth in June 1971, the Lions had virtually decided to run
with a Test back division devoid of a single Englishman. Ten days
before the start of the four-match series, David Duckham sensed
something out of the ordinary would be needed as a matter of some
urgency if he was to grab himself a slice of impending history.

In the days when the Lions made a point of going to small, out-
of-the-way places, few were smaller than the coastal venue of
Greymouth. Two of the South Island's more modest provinces,
West Coast and Buller, joined forces to justify the Lions spending a
few days in the area that had been gripped by the gold rush of the
1860s. For a thoroughbred like Duckham, drafted in on the right
wing at the last minute because of an injury to his compatriot John
Spencer, the going was less than good.

A water-logged pitch, along a strip towards the corner of his first-
half wing, presented hazardous conditions for all concerned.
Duckham, skimming over the surface, as opposed to squelching
through it, found them so much to his liking that of the Lions' six
tries in the first thirty-two minutes he accounted for all but one of
them. Five times he splattered through the mud to slide in at the
corner and five times the admirable Bob Hiller converted from the
touchline.

A sixth try, out of a total of eight in a 39–6 win – or 55–6 under current values – set a Lions record that remains unbroken, and if it wasn't quite enough to win him a place in the first Test, Duckham had served notice. He was too good to leave out, a point acknowledged by coach Carwyn James when he summoned the Coventry three-quarter at the expense of John Bevan for the second, third and fourth matches against the All Blacks. At the age of 25, Duckham had won a place among unquestionably the finest Lions back line of all time – Gareth Edwards and Barry John at half-back, John Dawes and Mike Gibson in the centre, Gerald Davies on one wing, Duckham on the other and behind them at full-back, the incomparable J. P. R. Williams.

Far from decrying him as an English interloper, the Welsh fans dubbed him 'Dai' Duckham, an early inspiration for the title of his autobiography published some years later, *Dai For England*. The famous Barbarians v. All Blacks match in January 1973 strengthened Welsh admiration for a player whose starring role in that particular match has long been overshadowed by the Gareth Edwards try. Unusually for an Englishman at Cardiff, Duckham 'felt at home' in the midst of so many Welsh Lions, his success with them at the highest level in New Zealand providing a stark contrast to his years of almost unrelenting struggle with England in the Five Nations.

His eight international seasons, from February 1969 to February 1976, coincided, through no fault of his own, with two championship whitewashes and six wooden spoons. Yet throughout those bleak years, Duckham could always be relied upon to illuminate the greyest of days with an un-English-like *joie de vivre*. With his mane of blond hair flapping behind him, he had style and elegance that would have rewarded him handsomely as a professional had he been born 30 years later.

Duckham started his England career as he meant to continue, specialising in the spectacular. He scored a 60-yard try, as one of five new caps against Ireland at Lansdowne Road, on such a cold day that he gratefully accepted the offer of thermal underwear provided, free of charge, by the RFU. It made the perishing temperatures a trifle more bearable, but England still perished that afternoon despite taking the lead no fewer than four times. 'A lot of people asked me afterwards why, as the Irish defence closed in on me, I didn't dive for the corner,' he said. 'There was one very good reason for that. The ground on that one side of the pitch was frozen solid. It would have been like diving on concrete.'

Duckham, born in Coventry on 28 June 1946, went from a

novice to an established international almost overnight, and the acclaim of a rare new talent had barely subsided than he was suffering from something that afflicted successive England teams of that era. 'We all started to get paranoid about being dropped,' he said. 'Even as an established player I felt that personally, and it did seriously undermine self-belief and conviction that we could win games, which was a tragedy because we had some outstanding players who were as good as any in the Five Nations.'

The paranoia manifested itself in some costly ways, never more so than against Scotland at Murrayfield at the outset of the 1974 Five Nations. England, fortified by back-to-back wins over New Zealand and Australia the previous autumn and a recovery launched in Edinburgh by Fran Cotton's only international try, were undone by the last kick of the match. Andy Irvine nailed the decisive penalty after Duckham had lost his bearings, chasing a touch-kick from a blatantly offside position.

It would probably not have mattered had Peter Rossborough – Duckham's full-back colleague at Coventry – not missed a number of shots at goal on a day when Alan Old, an outstanding place-kicker in his own right, succeeded with the only penalty he was asked to take. England's capacity at the time for turning victory into defeat – on that occasion allowing a 14–13 win to disappear into a 16–14 loss – was scarcely conducive to alleviating the fear of failure and curing a defeatist attitude.

For all his success as one of the outstanding three-quarters of his generation, that sense of insecurity stayed with Duckham throughout his England years. Alastair Hignell, whose first Five Nations in 1976 turned out to be Duckham's last, roomed with him before the first match of the championship at home to Wales. 'His advice was to get as much out of the experience as possible,' Hignell, now a highly popular rugby commentator for BBC Radio Five Live, said. 'Selection for England then seemed to be a reward for past performance, not an investment for the future. Accordingly, we made a point of enjoying the best hotels, the best food and the best shows in town.'

That England went through fifteen pairs of half-backs over the course of six seasons did nothing to ease dressing-room anxiety. 'Selection was very inconsistent,' Duckham said, with commendable restraint. 'That sort of policy affected our own individual confidence, and, as a result, we could never play as a team. Tactically, we were not given any real freedom to do as we liked, whereas the

Welsh three-quarters seemed to generate a freedom for themselves. I was always envious of that. We didn't have the guts to try something different.

'People complained about English fly-halves invariably kicking the ball, but that's what they were told to do. Fly-halves like Martin Cooper and Alan Old were very good players. But for injury, Old might well have played in the first Test for the Lions in South Africa in 1974 instead of Phil Bennett, which shows you how good a player he was. When the English management changed in the late '70s, so did the fortunes of the team because former players like Mike Davis and Budge Rogers were much more in touch with the squad.'

If anything, the passage of time has increased Duckham's hankering to roll the years back. 'I wish we could have our time over again,' he says. 'We bloody well beat the Springboks, which we'd never done before, and we beat the All Blacks in New Zealand, but we couldn't hack it in the Five Nations. Those were strange times when we didn't do ourselves justice.

'Even the Welsh guys would say to us, "What's the matter with your team? You've got a lot of very good players, but you don't win anywhere near often enough."'

The destabilising sense of inferiority that gnawed at English self-esteem was never more strikingly apparent than against Wales. Duckham played against them eight times and lost seven, a sequence which he broke at Twickenham in March 1974 with the only home try in a 16–12 win marking his milestone as the first English back to gain thirty caps.

It simply made their failure against the same opposition at the same venue four years earlier all the more difficult to fathom. Again, Duckham opened the scoring with a try. Another, from the debutant Harlequins' wing Mike Novak, and three goals from Hiller, eased England ten points clear at half-time. They went downhill all the way thereafter, turning a winning score of 13–3 into a losing one of 13–17, despite Wales losing Gareth Edwards to injury. The irrepressible Ray 'Chico' Hopkins from Maesteg, brought on as a replacement for Edwards, dragged his country off the ropes as if he knew he would never get the opportunity to play for them again – which he didn't. 'We just couldn't believe that we were ten points ahead,' Duckham said, still shaking his head in disbelief after all these years. 'Yet only a few months before, we had beaten South Africa.'

When England won in Auckland three years later, they had five

Coventry players in their team – Geoff Evans in the centre, Cotton in the front row and a trio who had played together in the 1st XV at the city's King Henry VIII School – Duckham, Rossborough and Peter Preece, the other centre. Apart from the demise of his home city club, then arguably the most powerful in England, Duckham's other main rugby regret was to miss the 1974 Lions tour of South Africa. A grumbling groin injury denied him the crowning glory. 'I desperately wanted to go for a whole host of reasons, not least the fact that I'd had a terrible tour of South Africa with the Barbarians a few years before,' he said. 'I wanted to go back and put the record straight. Alun Thomas [the Lions' manager] told me I was going to be picked without realising that I was wrestling with groin trouble, the same sort of injury which Jeremy Guscott struggled to overcome years later.

'My employers sent me to see a specialist in Harley Street. He examined me and said, "Do you rely on this game for a living?" I said no, I didn't and he said, "Good, because I can only recommend a complete rest of up to six months."'

J. J. Williams, the Welsh schoolteacher who first made a name for himself as a sprinter, took his place in the squad and finished up scoring four tries in the series, equalling the record set 70 years earlier by another Welshman, Willie Llewellyn. 'J. J. took my place, and there was no way I could have played any better than he did in that series,' Duckham said, 'but missing that tour remains my biggest regret.'

The long rest did little to extend his career. Dropped by England for the first time the following year, when the chronic groin condition took its predictable toll, Duckham reappeared for three more matches in 1976 before a torn hamstring against Scotland at Murrayfield put paid to his season and his international future. There would be no way back, no addition to an England record of ten tries in thirty-six matches. He reverted to centre before bidding farewell to Coventry in a match against Richmond at Coundon Road in April 1979. He was bowing out at a time when, up on Teesside, a young fellow was preparing to make his first-team debut for Middlesbrough against Tynedale at the age of 16.

Rory Underwood, an England player at the age of 20, would suffer worse deprivation than Duckham on the wing, scoring a paltry three tries in his first twenty-two matches and having to wait for the twelfth attempt to break his duck at Twickenham. Despite the early frustrations, he would eclipse Duckham's record halfway through an 11-year run of 91 Tests for his country and the Lions that yielded 50 tries, a total exceeded only by David Campese.

It took a desperate intervention from the Pom-bashing Australian to save the Wallabies towards the end of the 1991 World Cup final and deny Underwood what would have been his most famous try of all. Jingoistic claims for a penalty try, on the dubious contention that Campese had knocked-on deliberately in reaching out for the pass that would have put Underwood clear, fell on stony ground. The RAF pilot almost emulated Duckham in New Zealand two years later, scoring the Lions' solitary try in the second Test at Wellington only to lose the decider.

Duckham, whose 147 tries for Coventry put him high on the all-time list at the club if some way short of Ricky Melville's untouchable 281, left his admirers wondering how many more he would have got for England if only they had gone to greater trouble to feed him a bit more ball. 'There is no doubt he would have scored many more tries, if the players inside him had used him more,' said Bill McLaren, the BBC's inimitable commentator. 'He had a brilliant side-step, and he showed how brilliant he was for the Baa-Baas against New Zealand in '73. In a team of great players, he stood out.'

A successful businessman who runs a sports after-dinner speaking service with his wife Jean from their home in the heart of Shakespeare country in Stratford-upon-Avon, Duckham sent the Lions off to New Zealand in May 2005 with heartfelt words of encouragement in the official tour guide:

> We caught the All Blacks on the turn in 1971. They were still playing nine or ten-man rugby, while we had all the best players in Britain and Ireland well equipped to play an expansive game.
>
> New Zealand is a hell of a place to tour. Martin Johnson has made the point that the only time the mettle of our top players is really put to the test is in New Zealand against New Zealand.

Sadly, it was a test that the 2005 Lions failed on three successive Saturdays, a failure that Duckham was there to see for himself in the company of his great pal, Willie John McBride. Their friendship began more than 30 years earlier when Ireland's then captain assured a nervous, newly-wed Englishman that it would be perfectly safe for England to go ahead with their match in Dublin despite Welsh and Scottish refusals to go there in protest at the threat of terrorist action.

What concerned both ex-players about the demise of Sir Clive Woodward's Lions was just how badly they failed. 'There were some bad selection errors,' Duckham said. 'You cannot prepare a Test side in four or five matches. We had twice as many in 1971 and a far smaller squad. I wonder how many of the 50-odd players involved came back from New Zealand believing they had made a contribution as a bona fide British and Irish Lion.

'I would question whether, in their heart of hearts, they felt they had. I would also question how much genuine faith the players had in the management. We only had two managers in 1971 [Carwyn James and Doug Smith], but, my goodness, they approached the task with supreme confidence. Whereas Sir Clive kept bleating on about his Lions being the best-prepared ever, James and Smith just said, "Fear not, we are going to win the series."

'Doug even went into detail. We would win two, lose one and draw the last one. Some of us needed a bit of convincing at the outset but win the series we did and exactly as the manager said we would. For all I know, he probably predicted that J. P. R. [Williams] would secure the last-Test draw by dropping a goal.

'The last tour was very high on expectation but very low on achievement. I have talked about it at length with Willie John. Sadly, we have both come to the same conclusion – that the brand of the British Lions has been somewhat tarnished. It will not threaten the future of the Lions, but it will make those who run the Lions realise they cannot make similar mistakes over the next tour.

'The word that came back to me via a few of the players was that there were too many chiefs and not enough Indians. They had the very best coaches Great Britain and Ireland had to offer, and, naturally, they all wanted to ensure their input. As a result, coaching was so over the top that the players suffered from being fed too much information. That was the phrase which they used in private discussions.

'Maybe, as a consequence, some of them got a wee bit confused about exactly what they were meant to do and how they were supposed to achieve it. They made the mistake of taking too many players. I was under the impression that they were doing so in order to ensure they had enough to cope with injuries, but every time they lost a player, Sir Clive called up another.

'I also got the impression that a number of players had no idea what they were letting themselves in for by undertaking a tour of this magnitude to a place like New Zealand where touring is so very different to anywhere else. Mentally, some of them didn't seem to be in the right frame of mind.

'There were some bad selection errors, and the players didn't do themselves justice. Very probably nobody will ever really know why they didn't succeed. Sir Clive's refusal to acknowledge, after the event, that he had made a lot of mistakes was not to his credit. It seemed almost as if, in a political sense, he had been told not to make any such admissions by his adviser, Alastair Campbell. The saddest part of all is that the All Blacks were not seriously tested in any of the three Tests.'

In many respects, Duckham was a man ahead of his time. He issued his first warning of a player revolt as long ago as 1980, spelling out, in a way that left no room for ambiguity, that the mounting demands on the top amateurs of the time would 'probably' force them to go on strike. France, under the militant captaincy of the fearless Philippe Saint-André, threatened to do so on one occasion during the mid-'90s and the only surprise was that it took England until the autumn of 2000 to down tools in protest at the RFU's tardiness over match fees.

In Duckham's day, the only strikes were those of the clenched-fist variety administered as acts of provocation or retribution, inevitably perpetrated by one primeval forward on another. Duckham rose above all that to leave an enduring imprint on the game as one of its supreme stylists: one whose place in history can be gauged by his role, surrounded by some of game's best ever players, in two of the greatest games the world has yet seen – the Lions' series-winning epic against the All Blacks in 1971 and the Barbarians' magical win in the re-match at Cardiff Arms Park less than eighteen months later.

7

BLACKPOOL'S
BLEEDING ROCK

ROGER UTTLEY HAS PROBABLY GIVEN MORE BLOOD IN THE NAME OF SPORT THAN ANY Englishman since Henry Cooper dumped a brash young American on his not-so-smart backside at the Arsenal football stadium during the summer of 1963. Without wishing to detract from the anaesthetising effect of 'Enery's 'Ammer, the history of the World Heavyweight Championship might well have taken a very different course had the then Cassius Clay been subjected to the sort of fearful clout that Uttley had the gross misfortune to take in another part of London 17 years later.

The leather that made him the hapless victim of a violent England v. Wales match came not from a gloved fist but something far more lethal: a heavy boot in the face. The future Muhammad Ali had more than a fistful of dollars as guaranteed compensation for the indignity of landing on the bottom rope. Uttley had taken his battering for what was supposed to be the love of the game and the dubious ritual of an after-match beer with his assailant.

'Gee, you gotta have guts to play that kinda football,' former world middleweight champion Marvin Hagler said, shaking his head in a mixture of disbelief and admiration after meeting the Ireland squad before the 2003 World Cup. 'In boxing, you know the punch will come from the guy in front of you so you're prepared. In rugby you know it could come from any one of fifteen people, and a whole lotta them could be behind you. You can't prepare for that.'

The 'Marvellous' one would have marvelled at Uttley. Ever ready to put his body where some of the villains, never mind the angels, were afraid to go, he took more than his share of low blows. Some of those that hurt him the most were of the figurative variety inflicted by his own side, rather than the opposition, but no less wounding for that.

As England coach, Uttley felt snubbed by Will Carling. As coach of the Lions, he fell foul of another captain, Finlay Calder. And, as a curious way of expressing their gratitude for defending England's honour with unfailing courage, the Rugby Football Union dismissed him from his part-time role as team manager during the earlier phase of the Clive Woodward regime. They said it was an economy measure. Uttley took it on the chin and kept his dignity.

A permanent member of the Lions' Test team throughout the invincible tour of South Africa in 1974, he achieved something then which can never be repeated, if only because three-month tours and four-Test series have gone with the wind. Yet, despite that and other notable achievements – in particular the fact that he is one of the rare breed of distinguished Lancastrians to captain his country – Uttley's curriculum vitae does him less than justice. But for the odd cruel twist of fate, he could just as easily have gone down in history as the first post-war English player to captain the Lions (New Zealand in 1977), and the first English coach to win the World Cup (Twickenham 1991).

Instead he missed the former because of injury and the latter because of a tactical volte-face as mystifying as it was calamitous. While three World Cups have come and gone since then, it is neither less of a mystery nor a calamity with the passage of time.

That Uttley stood out so often as the rock defying the storms breaking all around him, in an English team all at sea for large chunks of the '70s, was worthy of one born and bred in post-war Blackpool, in his case on 11 September 1949. It was a time when Stanley Matthews, the 'Wizard of Dribble', reigned supreme, and every square inch of the 'Golden Mile' was occupied by the holiday-makers before the package holiday had been invented.

The teenage Uttley worked there one summer, something that he let slip during his first season at Gosforth. When Uttley became captain of England, Jack Rowell, then scaling the twin peaks of industry and rugby management, sent him a congratulatory telegram that said, 'Not bad for a deckchair attendant.'

Uttley discovered the brutal facts of rugby life as a naive teenager one Christmas Eve. The experience, gained while playing for Fylde's 2nd XV against Vale of Lune, almost sickened him into giving up the game. 'I can remember spitting out my teeth and saying to myself, "What am I doing this for?" It was a nightmare. I'd gone into the match [the] same as I'd gone into them all: full of the joys of spring.

'My opponent was a guy whom I won't mention by name. He was an old pro, and he'd had enough of this young buck crawling all over him. So the last thing I remembered was getting an elbow in the face. For a few days after that I wondered whether I'd go on. I enjoyed other sports besides rugby. I was a keen basketball player, and I wanted to get some fun out of whatever sport I played. [I thought,] "there have got to be better ways of spending Saturday afternoon."'

Luckily for England and the Lions, he never found one. The nasty outcome of that festive occasion at Fylde left him in painful need of a practical present ('All I want for Christmas is my two front teeth'), but there would be no diverting him from his chosen path to the top of the tree. Had that path not been strewn with obstacles, he would have doubled his twenty-three matches for England gained over a ten-year period during which annual internationals were confined to the Five Nations Championship and the periodic extra fixture against a touring team.

Uttley, the son of a director of a men's clothing shop, once described himself as 'just an ordinary working middle-class person'. His route from the deckchairs to one of the chosen few, in the most revered Lions team of all, would have taken a very different turn had he not been denied entry to the Cardiff College of Education and a place alongside the new scrum-half, Gareth Edwards. They turned the gangling Englishman down because they supposedly found him too 'reticent' at the interview.

Instead of attending arguably the finest finishing school for rugby players in the British Isles, Uttley took off in a different direction. He went to Northumberland College of Education and, more importantly, straight into the Gosforth 1st XV, where he first rubbed shoulders with the future England manager, Jack Rowell. It was not so much Rowell's caustic wit that struck Uttley as his sense of balance. 'Jack had an amazing sidestep which you would not normally associate with a second-row forward,' Uttley said, referring to Rowell's gangling, 6 ft 7 in. frame. 'For such a tall man, he had very small feet so he always looked as though he was about to fall over.'

While Rowell had to wait more than 20 years for the opportunity to be involved with England, Uttley leapt almost straight into the national team. Within days of turning 22, he was playing for his country against Japan in Osaka during a pioneering three-week tour of the Far East, under the captaincy of Budge Rogers in the autumn of 1971. A second non-Test against Japan in Tokyo four days later resulted in the visitors scraping a 6–3 victory, courtesy of two Peter Rossborough penalties. The trip ended with two matches against Ceylon in Colombo, both of which produced the predictable flood of English tries.

There were no easy caps in those days, and although having prepared him for the real thing later that season – starting with Wales at Twickenham – the England selectors duly decided to introduce another uncapped player to the second row instead. They chose Alan Brinn of Gloucester and kept Uttley waiting for the trip to South Africa in the summer of 1972. However, he ended up missing that tour because of injury, a misfortune that was to become a recurring theme throughout his career.

Mercifully, he stayed in one piece long enough to scale untouched peaks of excellence as a permanent member of the Lions' Test team, during the historic four-match series against South Africa in 1974. Few English players made the 30-man squad and fewer still won Test recognition – Uttley and Fran Cotton in all four, Chris Ralston of Richmond in one.

Pre-tour, Uttley had played every one of his eight internationals at lock. As a Lion, he made the Test team on one side of the back row with Ireland's Fergus Slattery on the other and Mervyn Davies at number 8 in preference to his English counterpart, Andy Ripley. Not content at helping create a legendary effort on the field, Uttley played a part, however unwittingly, in contributing to another off it, during the riotous aftermath of the runaway win in the second Test in the rarefied atmosphere of Loftus Versveldt.

It began with some hammering on the door of Willie John McBride's hotel room around three o'clock on the Sunday morning. Describing how he answered the door to find Uttley and Davies demanding the skipper's intervention, McBride recalled that neither was in the first, nor the last, stage of sobriety: 'Both were p****d. They told me there was a bit of trouble, and I was needed downstairs. I picked up my pipe – I never go anywhere without it, especially in times of crisis – and walked down this corridor, somewhat unsteadily, just in my underpants. The first sight I saw was

Bobby Windsor with a fire hose in his hands, and I sobered up very quickly.

'I got to the mezzanine floor, which overlooked the lobby, and there were the rest of the Lions, out of their tree, with pieces of tables, bits of chairs and other furniture strewn about. It was another of those scenes of carnage we were beginning to get used to. In the midst of all this, there was one extremely irate hotel manager.

'He said, "That's it. I've had enough of you lot. I'm going to call the police."

'I could see the next day's headlines: "Lions team thrown out of hotel" or "Drunken Lions darken rugby's name". It was a disaster about to happen. I said to the hotel manager, "Hold on a minute. I'm the captain of this team. What's the problem?"

'The guy obviously considered he had been asked a stupid question by someone trying to take the mickey out of him. He completely lost it. He said, "I've been through all this. I'm taking no more of it. I'm calling the police."

'Now I'd seen the riot police in operation in South Africa and didn't like the mental images my mind was conjuring up. I could see hordes of them rushing through the door and didn't think they'd be handing out sweets and asking these drunken idiots for autographs. So I said to the manager with what I suppose was an unprepared bout of Irish wit, "Excuse me, but if you are going to get the police, do you think there will be many of them?"'

At that, the Lions started cheering as if relishing the prospect of entertaining another South African team. Whatever the motivation for the gunboat diplomacy, it took the heat out of the ruck long enough for the hotel manager and the Lions to sleep on it. The next morning, tour manager Alun Thomas of Wales did as his predecessors had so often done down the years and observed the splendid old Lions ritual of writing out a cheque to pay for the damage.

Had an English football team been responsible for the damage, it would have caused a national scandal. By some twisted sort of logic, the rugby players got away with it because it was somehow considered to be part of touring: a ludicrous state of affairs that did not survive much longer. A little later in the tour, some of the 'piano-shifters' – a term of endearment designed to separate the forwards from the 'piano-players' behind the scrum – took their title a little too literally and shoved a baby grand down a lift-shaft.

The diplomatic immunity that had saved generations of Lions

from public exposure went with it because the incident made back-page news, not that Uttley had anything to do with it. He was, as McBride describes, 'a great man, a fine tourist and a guy who could laugh at most things' but 'not a pretty sight when he faced you at two o'clock in the morning'.

At the age of 24, the Blackpool Rock had left nobody in any doubt about his credentials as a future captain. When he assumed the leadership from Tony Neary for the start of the 1977 Five Nations Championship, it seemed as if nothing bar injury could stop Uttley claiming the ultimate prize of captaining the Lions to New Zealand that summer, especially as the overwhelming favourite had dropped out of contention in harrowing circumstances. Mervyn Davies, his great back-row colleague in South Africa, had taken Wales to the 1976 Grand Slam title when a brain haemorrhage during Swansea's Welsh Cup semi-final against Pontypool ended his career and very nearly his life.

A broken leg sustained after what *The Times* referred to as 'an ugly fracas involving several players' during Gosforth's New Year match against Richmond forced Uttley to miss the entire 1976 Five Nations tournament, delaying his elevation to the captaincy until the following season.

However, a flying start to his leadership, with wins over Scotland and Ireland, gave his Lions captaincy bandwagon a seemingly irresistible momentum only for his hopes to be dashed by another of the blown gaskets that plagued his playing days from start to finish. The selectors preferred Phil Bennett, which meant a Welsh captain as well as a Welsh coach and what was then a record number of 17 Welsh players amongst the squad of 30. Uttley had been chosen as one of the non-Welsh minority, until he ran out of time trying to recover from another bad back. Not going as captain was one thing; not going at all was something else.

A tackle on J. P. R. Williams proved his undoing. 'I remember J. P. R. coming back on the angle and thinking to myself, "I've got to tackle him." He just ran into me, and I put him down, but it really shook my back up. I thought, "I'm going to have to go off here. I'm all over the shop."' The substitutes' bench, like the mobile phone and the microwave, had not been invented at that time, which left Uttley to soldier on as best he could without a moment's thought about the risk of doing himself further damage.

A season which had promised the biggest prize of all was about to dissolve into nothing, although, in hindsight, Uttley might have suspected that someone, somewhere would make him pay a cruel price for the most fortuitous win of that season. 'We beat Ireland in Dublin because Martin Cooper [the English fly-half] danced down the touchline with his foot in touch for a rather lucky try. Despite that, I was feeling quite good as captain. There was a bit of talk about the Lions' captaincy, and I really fancied it.'

A number of senior Welsh players – Gareth Edwards, Gerald Davies and J. P. R. – had declared themselves unavailable. The Lions needed Uttley so badly that they gave him extra time after they had flown out on the first leg of the journey to Auckland. 'We trained at Twickenham on the Saturday: a nice, sunny day. Before they flew out on the Monday, they said to me, "We'll give you a fortnight to get fit."'

Jeff Squire, the Wales number 8, went instead and Uttley, to his enormous frustration, did not recover sufficiently and spent the entire summer grounded in London. 'Looking back, I'd love to have captained the Lions,' he said. 'I remember saying to Benny when he was chosen, "You've got my full support." If only I could have got out there. I think I could have made a bit of a difference.'

More back trouble forced him to miss every match during the 1978 championship, and when he finally made the long road back, for the start of what would be England's first Grand Slam since 1957, he was to be given a real kick in the teeth – as well as just about every other part of his face. Not for nothing has England v. Wales at Twickenham in February 1980 been granted a notorious place in rugby's 'black museum'.

There was a nasty mood about the old place on the day of the match. It was a mood not helped by some provocative references in Wales blaming the Thatcher government for the collapse of the coal mines and the steelworks. There also seemed to be a depressing air of acceptance that the sun was about to set on the second Golden Era of Welsh rugby and that a win at 'Twickers' would no longer be the biennial ritual it used to be.

Many people were to blame for that, not least the Welsh Rugby Union, some of whose shorter-sighted members were fond of puffing their chests out at after-match banquets and asking the rhetorical question, 'Why are we so good?' They completely forgot to keep oiling the wheels of the assembly line so that, eventually, it ground to a halt out of sheer neglect.

None of that was Roger Uttley's fault, but he was the one who got it in the neck and just about everywhere else. 'I went to drop on a loose ball and missed it as it bounced away,' he said. 'The next thing I felt was as if my head had been kicked between the posts. One side of my face was a complete mess.

'It was all opened up and swollen to the size of a football. What upset me was the feeling of disfigurement in what was then an amateur sport, supposedly played for fun. I only had to look in the mirror to ask myself, "Is it really worth all this?"

'When I got home, one of my sons thought I had gone to fight a war somewhere. I wouldn't have said so at the time, but I don't mind admitting now that I was frightened against Wales. It got to the stage when you didn't know where the next boot or punch was coming from.

'There was a horrible atmosphere throughout the whole game, and it started when we were standing there during the national anthems. Physical violence is a very nasty, messy business, and you cannot go out onto a rugby field with a licence to maim.'

Bill Beaumont, England's captain that day, saw the mess for himself: 'Roger's nose had been split wide open, and there was blood pumping everywhere. There is always a problem when people hype up a game too much. At the end of the day, it is still only a game – not a declaration of war.'

The blow that connected most forcibly, which Wales lock Geoff Wheel claimed was an accident, made such a mess of Uttley that he required plastic surgery that involved 'sand-blasting' part of his face. Steve Smith, his fellow Lancastrian and England's scrum-half that afternoon, has never forgotten the incident. 'Roger's face looked like a rugby ball after one of the Welsh forwards had had a good old welly at it,' Smith said. 'They had to put 16 stitches into him, although we reckoned no one could tell the difference. It's like the old one about the football manager warning his team, "Unless you lot buck up your ideas, I'll be bringing in some new faces." And one player says, "Can I have one please, boss?"'

The 1980 Grand Slam provided a fitting finale to Uttley's career, as well as a searing test of his ability to keep going in punishing conditions. Torn rib cartilage during the last match against Scotland at Murrayfield raised his pain threshold to new heights, but he soldiered on to the very end as though nothing much had happened. The Slam had arrived in the nick of time.

By the end of that year, Uttley had hung up his boots at the age of 31. He had been left no option but to quit by the state of his back. Nigel Melville's first match for Wasps, at Rosslyn Park on

Saturday, 6 December 1980, was Uttley's last, bringing him to the end of a bumpy road a week before he had been due to play for the North against the South-west on Merseyside.

As one career ended, so another began with England and the Lions. Just as his only Lions tour as a player had concluded with a series victory, so his only tour as a coach produced the same winning outcome. However, to describe his role in the 1989 victory over Australia as a happy experience would be to stretch a point, in view of the difficulties that Uttley encountered as assistant coach in his dealings with the captain, Finlay Calder.

It all stemmed from a clash of Anglo-Scottish styles. Uttley favoured the English mauling game, whereas Calder preferred the ruck as a more effective means of winning the Test series. England hooker Brian Moore was in the thick of it, as the relationship between the Scottish captain and the English coach deteriorated.

'It was obvious from the start that neither Finlay nor the Scottish contingent rated him [Uttley] at all,' Moore said. 'The Scots were very dismissive of him, and the breakdown of the relationship had a crude and completely unnecessary conclusion at the end of the tour. With some of the Scots as ringleaders, we bought putters for each member of the tour management. With a disgraceful act of churlishness, they came back with a putter for each of the hierarchy, but Roger's was demonstrably cheaper and worse than the others. I believe it was a studied gesture. It could hardly have been otherwise.'

If the '74 Lions had symbolised the time of Uttley's rugby life, his experiences in Australia 15 years later provided a stark contrast. 'There was a fair degree of anti-English feeling on that tour. I never even got a mention, apparently, in the official tour report. To be successful, you've got to work with other people to achieve a common goal for the common good, and that was all that concerned me on that trip.

'I had the feeling that Calder had no respect and not a great deal of time for me as the tour wore on. J. J. [John Jeffrey] was all right. Derek White was a nice guy. The Hastings brothers were fantastic, and I had no problems at all with "Geech" [Ian McGeechan]. It was just Finlay. I found it a bit unsettling.'

Nine months after the tour, when the 1990 Five Nations Championship reached its staggering denouement at Murrayfield, Uttley, according to Moore, had been 'keenly looking for revenge after the slights he had suffered at the hands of the Scots in the previous year's Lions tour'.

Yet again, Uttley found that fate had kicked him in the teeth. As Calder and the whole of Scotland celebrated the ecstatic climax of a Grand Slam success achieved by an ambush of the hitherto imperious English in Edinburgh, Uttley trooped back south of the border 'tae think again'. Once he had dusted himself down, he fixed his gaze on the greatest goal of all; one which would provide some compensation, if not atonement for the lost Slam.

A World Cup in England offered the players the chance of a lifetime and their coach the challenge of taking them where no European team had gone before. Whatever happened, there would be no second opportunity. A true blue amateur in accordance with the game's Corinthian spirit, Uttley was a part-time coach who, come hell or high water, would be returning to his proper job as director of physical education at Harrow School first thing on the Monday morning after the final. Winning the World Cup would be a poor excuse for turning up late.

To claim the reward of a home final appearance meant negotiating a hazardous route that would require a victory against France in Paris in the quarter-final, followed by a game against Scotland at the dreaded Murrayfield in the semis. With those two matches successfully negotiated, Australia were waiting for England in the final. If nothing else, the Australians could at least count on the enthusiastic, if misguided, support of the vanquished Scottish team, whose appearance at Twickenham made it clear that they had not come to adopt a position of neutrality. They took their seats garbed in Wallaby green and gold.

Beneath the Scottish players, in the bowels of the old West Stand, the Sassenachs were in the dressing-room going through a few last points in the fraught moments before kick-off. One was hammered home above the rest – that whatever their fate, nobody should give any less than his best so there could be no regrets. Uttley recalled that the players were told, before they went out, 'Whatever you do, don't come off at the end saying, "What if?"'

The history book shows that England lost 12–6, and the what ifs will be asked for as long as people reminisce about that match. Perhaps they should have put an asterisk in brackets behind the score to signify what it didn't show: that the Wallabies won the 1991 World Cup going backwards and that the hosts lost it because of a radical shift in tactics away from the might of their forward pack. For every single player, with the notable exception of Jason Leonard, the chance had gone forever and the passage of time has hardly eased the harsh verdict that England should have won the World Cup 12 years before they did.

Uttley can see that now with an almost cruel clarity. 'It was a missed opportunity to have struck a big blow for England, the British Isles, Europe and northern-hemisphere rugby. We failed. I look back on it with a tinge of regret, but nobody thought we would get anywhere near the final. We started from a very low base and spent four years building the whole thing up, getting the players fitter and educating them to play the game that was required. We had a strong pack of forwards, a decent back row and workmanlike half-backs. We had, maybe, one and a half decent centres, we were iffy at full-back – with the best will in the world – and we had Rory Underwood on the wing, so what were we supposed to do?

'[Rob] Andrew was a great footballer, and we gave him his head. I can't accept the fact that people were critical of the style England played. It hurt very much when the likes of Geech started talking about England killing the game. That was after we had screwed them to the floor.

'When we got to the final, all the supposedly great Australian footballing side did was kick the ball and tackle. Our biggest problem when it came to playing to our strengths was that we didn't have enough intuitive footballers. I can remember saying, "Let's go out and play football." We talked about that a lot. We wanted to play keep-ball, which is what sides do now – keep the ball, shift the point of contact and kick your points when they make the mistakes.

'Nobody expected us to get to the final. Getting there meant getting through some huge emotional games, like [the ones against] France and Scotland. It was a case of thinking, "Look, we've been through all that. Let's be bloody-minded about this. How are we going to do this in some detail?" It was a mistake I made. We should have adopted a more ruthless approach.

'Instead the feeling was, "We've got to the final now, let's go out and enjoy it and play football." We should have been saying, "Right, we've got over these hurdles. Now we've got the biggest one." What, in actual fact, didn't happen was that we didn't re-set the final goal, which was to win the World Cup. That didn't become an end in itself; it was simply part of the continuum of developing English rugby. That's why it was a great opportunity missed. I would hold my hand up to that quite easily. As time goes on and you see how difficult it is to get yourself back into this situation, no matter how good you are, then you've got to say we slipped up badly.

'We should just have kept doing what we were good at: the likes of Dean [Richards] taking the ball up [and] Rob putting the ball into the corners behind the opposition, forcing them to kick it out so we got the lineout. The silly thing was that we'd spoken – and I'm not trying to shift any responsibility off myself or Geoff – about devolving responsibility back onto the players. It is they who have got to make decisions. As coaches, we cannot go out there and play for them. We had to encourage them to make judgements and decisions on the field.

'Half-time only lasted for three minutes, which made it very difficult to make any major tactical changes. In retrospect it was wrong. We should have just stuck to our guns and said to the lads, "Stuff the football, let's go for the result." There is no denying it was a bad day. We sorted them out, we had the possession, we had the opportunities, but we played it all in the middle of the pitch.

'All I can say in defence is that it was a very stressful time. That quarter-final in Paris was one of the most intensive atmospheres I have ever experienced. At the end, their coach [Daniel Dubroca] blew up at the referee. Tunnel vision can be very dangerous, unless you have someone standing out looking in who can say, "Have you thought about this, that and the other?"'

Come what may, Uttley knew he would be back at Harrow School that Monday morning. 'That was the other thing: I was retiring. Very few get the chance to finish with a World Cup final, and I wanted to enjoy it. In retrospect, that was a mistake. I suppose you soften the blow by saying nobody expected us to get to the final so we did pretty well. But it could and should have been far more than that.'

Two years before the World Cup, Uttley found himself in the faintly ludicrous predicament of having to put Harrow School before England. When Will Carling made his debut as captain against Australia in the autumn of 1988, the coach had to leave the team's hotel and rush back to the school to supervise one of Harrow's matches. Uttley's attendance had been insisted upon by his own headmaster, former England international Ian Beer, then a member of the RFU's more senior ranks and on his way to becoming president.

On the Saturday after the World Cup final, Uttley watched Harrow win at Eton on the playing fields that, according to most historians, did not actually exist during the time that the Duke of Wellington spent at the school in the late eighteenth century, thereby casting doubt about the staging of any dummy run for the Battle of Waterloo. Whereas the world had watched his team play the previous week, his first match as the former England coach drew a crowd of precisely two hundred and twenty-one and five dogs. 'I found it very hard on the Monday morning,' he said. 'Very depressed. So near and yet so far. I whacked a little black ball around the squash court for half an hour. A few lengths of the pool and I felt better. Basically, a case of alcoholic poisoning!'

Coaching England had been far from plain sailing. In Argentina the previous year, his method had been called into question by Carling, the team captain, and Moore, his influential lieutenant. Two years earlier, Uttley had intervened to save Carling's reign ending almost before it began, when he launched an assault on a past England number 8 and selector who would ascend to the presidency of the RFU – Welshman Derek Morgan.

Carling claimed he had overheard Morgan complaining about an aspect of his performance and the team's. 'I was drunk, as was usual in the early days,' Carling said. 'I turned to Morgan and said, "Christ, what the hell do you know about selection? You never picked me as a student, even though I was playing for England. Explain that logic to me." I had him by the throat up against the wall. Roger Uttley had to pull me off. All very embarrassing but symptomatic of my relationship with most rugby alickadoos.'

The Carling–Moore criticism in Argentina hurt Uttley. 'It annoyed me intensely. I liked Will a lot when we first met. I was looking forward to working with him, but he was a complex character. I found it difficult at that stage to relate to him. He sort of ignored me.

'It came to a head after the third match of the tour played in a football stadium. There was a tunnel under a moat for the players to get to the dressing-room, and I waited there at the end of the game. Will was plainly not amused, and when I asked him what the trouble was, he told me to "F*** off". He and Mooro were in tandem at that stage. There were other moments when Will wouldn't speak to me.'

By the sound of things, it was probably just as well. Carling's attempt to change the coaching personnel did nothing to reconnect the pair on speaking terms. Dick Best, then coach of Harlequins, had been following the tour as part of his job with a travel company, and the move to bring him into the fold produced a perfectly understandable response from Uttley. Not to put too fine a point on it, he felt insulted.

'Will said, "How about if Dick takes us for one session?" I said, "If that's what you want, I'm out of here." It never got beyond that, but I knew then that things were difficult. All I wanted was to see England do their best. I was just doing my bit. I found it difficult to deal with Will. I remember being in a lift with him in the team hotel in Buenos Aires and again at breakfast. There was hardly a word between us.'

Carling claimed that his motives were simply 'to provide the best possible coaching for the England players, regardless of personnel and egos'. With a World Cup on the horizon, some sort of rapprochement had to be reached if two of the leading lights in the whole production were to be on any sort of speaking terms, however limited.

'When we got back we had a meeting in London, near Piccadilly in a coffee bar, for a chat. We both knew that we had to work this out. I said I knew I wasn't the perfect coach, but that I wasn't there to entertain them. It wasn't up to me to provide new and exciting drills, which is what they seemed to want. The way you progress in this game is by having a variety of drills which you continually work at so you improve. You do not constantly interrupt it to reintroduce things for amusement's sake.

'I enjoyed all the other guys – the likes of Jon Webb, Simon Halliday, Rob Andrew: all great lads. I enjoyed coaching England, certainly early on, and I enjoyed working with Geoff Cooke, who did a great job in taking the whole country forward. The great sadness came with getting into situations like I had with Will. He was enormously talented in so many ways.

'But he did make himself unpopular with other people. Everybody thought he was selfish and that he looked after his own interests. The whole thing got out of hand at one stage. What goes around, comes around. I have seen him since, and there is no problem. I think he has grown up a lot.'

Six years later, in September 1997, when professionalism demanded a full-time coach to run the England team, Uttley reappeared on the national stage in the new guise of part-time team manager under Clive Woodward. Ironically, by returning to the fray as part of the new chain of command, the rugged old Wasp, with his battle scars, succeeded Jack Rowell, whose reluctance to abandon his prosperous career as a captain of industry dropped him out of the running.

Uttley's alliance with Woodward lasted less than 18 months. An incident in Cape Town, before the last Test at the end of the infamous 'Tour to Hell' in June 1998, confirmed the suspicions that they were not exactly working hand in glove. When the coach pulled his entire squad out of their cramped three-star hotel in Newlands and took them into the finest hotel in Africa, a few miles away, the manager was just about the last to find out.

The following January, he had become one of thirty-four victims of a cost-cutting exercise at the RFU spearheaded by chief executive Francis Baron. Woodward, told of the decision early that morning, insisted on driving to Harrow School to break the news to Uttley man to man, face to face, even if they did not see eye to eye. Years later, Woodward spelt out the ruthless thinking behind the sacking: 'We could not become the best in the world with part-time people, divided in their attention, regardless of how talented or respected they were.'

There was never much love lost between them, and yet it was utterly Uttley that in a moment of crushing personal disappointment he should think of England first and himself last. With typical generosity, he offered to lend his services free of charge, and he was more than willing to do the same seven years later, during the hiatus caused by Woodward's sudden resignation. Nobody should have been the least bit surprised at Uttley's gesture. Old warriors never quit, and he was among the bravest of the brave.

As an old Lion, he followed the 2005 New Zealand tour from afar with increasing despair. 'It was badly thought out from the word go,' Uttley said. 'You have the best logistics ever, you have the most money ever and then you produce a side which plays like that. To go out there and lose the series 3–0 was a bit of a disaster. The whole selection policy seemed strange, and that is being kind. Playing Jonny Wilkinson out of position in the first Test, for example, seemed illogical. I just felt sorry for all the thousands of supporters who went down there.'

8

HEART AND SOUL

ON THE FIRST SATURDAY OF MARCH 1982 A CROWD OF 60,000 – ALONG WITH SEVERAL million watching on television – witnessed a rare event at Twickenham. England beat Wales in successive home matches for the first time since the end of the Second World War. A rarer event, which went completely unnoticed, took place in the vicinity of the home dressing-room during the hubbub which followed the final whistle.

After 11 years of yeoman-like service for Queen and country, Fran Cotton knew the quickest route down the stairways of the old West Stand to the players' inner sanctum. Instantly recognisable by his jaw jutting out like the prow of a battleship, he steamed along the corridors of Headquarters at a rate of knots safe in the knowledge that no door had ever been slammed shut on him before.

His natural bonhomie, fuelled to overflowing at having witnessed an English win, made him all the more unsuspecting about what lay round the corner. Cotton had seen off some very tough hombres and survived some fearsome moments in the line of national duty, but he had never before been hit by Air Commodore R. H. G. Weighill and the full weight of the International Rugby Board's regulations on amateurism.

Both forces conspired to stop a speechless Cotton in his tracks, before he could get as far as opening the door to the dressing-room. Rules were rules, and the Air Commodore was a stickler for them.

Cotton had been branded a professional and, therefore, had no right to be fouling the premises; he had to hop it or risk a major diplomatic incident.

Absurdly, the rules declared him guilty of trespass. For the heinous crime of writing a book about his career and earning a bit of filthy lucre for his trouble, one of the sport's more noble servants had fallen foul of the draconian regulations that perpetuated Union hypocrisy. The whole episode made an ass of the IRB's laws governing amateurism. Fran had worked himself to a frazzle down the years in the finest Corinthian spirit. Yet, all of a sudden, there he was, excommunicated like those union players who had exercised their democratic right in a free world to join the paid ranks of rugby league. The difference was that Cotton had never taken a penny for playing the game itself.

Nothing could have been further from his mind as he strode towards the dressing-room that he had left only the year previously, because of retirement at the age of 33. Most of all, he was anxious to indulge in some hearty back-slapping with his Sale colleague, fellow Lancastrian, long-time friend and new England captain, Steve Smith.

'I was delighted because England wins over Wales were pretty infrequent in those days,' Cotton said. 'So, straight after the match, I walked towards the dressing-room to congratulate my old mate, and I got three-quarters of the way there when I was stopped by R. H. G. Weighill. He said, "What are you doing here?"

'I said, "I'm going to see my mate Smithy."

'"You are most certainly not," he replied. "You must leave at once."'

Rather than make a scene, Cotton swallowed his pride and turned on his heel. Union's paranoia about professionalism ensured that the cold war against rugby league outlived the collapse of the Berlin Wall and the disintegration of the Soviet empire, a fact that meant that Cotton was at least in good company. For example, the Welsh Rugby Union ordered David Watkins out of the old Cardiff Arms Park when the Wales and Lions stand-off had gone there to have a few photographs taken for his autobiography.

Some years later, the same Union excelled themselves in small-mindedness, refusing to let BBC Wales interview Jonathan Davies during a home international simply because the former Wales captain had gone north to ply his trade with Widnes. None of that was of any consolation to Cotton as he waited, season after season, for reinstatement: 'I was banned, and I stayed banned for 12 years. It was crazy. Thank God they revised it eventually.'

By then, the Air Commodore had retired from the RFU. Bob Weighill, an international in his own right who had captained England against France in 1948, was a thoroughly honourable man whose job was not to question rules so archaic that they had been framed in Victorian times but to ensure that they were enforced. He was shabbily treated by the Lions during their tour of New Zealand in 1993 when they gave him a childish cold shoulder for implementing the rule that prevented Wade Dooley, the England lock, from rejoining the tour as a player after flying home for his father's funeral.

The Board was never slow to hit the soft targets, but when it came to exposing those who had taken money for playing the game they failed lamentably. While Cotton, Gareth Edwards, Barry John, Phil Bennett, Bill Beaumont and a host of other luminaries were *persona non grata* for writing a book, the International Rugby Board turned a blind eye to allegations swirling around the 1989 tour to South Africa by a World XV drawn from several countries but mainly the British Isles and in particular Wales. The manager, none other than Willie John McBride, said, 'Everyone in the outside world said the players were all being paid, but I had no evidence to suggest that. Nor has anything been uncovered since, and I know that a lot of people have spent a lot of time looking for evidence.'

Clearly, McBride had never read Robert Jones's book entitled *Raising the Dragon*. Had he done so, he would have found the evidence in black and white. Jones, one of a group of Welsh players involved in clandestine preparations for a trip that was to cause the Welsh Rugby Union huge embarrassment, was honest enough to admit that the attraction of the tour went beyond a free trip to South Africa. 'There was also the issue of the money being offered,' he wrote. 'It was not a massive amount by the standards of modern professional players' salaries, but, by the standards of the amateur game or my own salary at the time, it was a colossal amount – more than two years' pay. An amount like that, I knew, would make a huge difference to my family's life.

'A lot of people – Thorby [Paul Thorburn], Mike Hall, Bob Norster and several others – had signed up to go. Those who hadn't been invited had obviously not been told exactly how much was on offer, and, when they found out, they started asking how on earth I could turn down that sort of money . . . it certainly made a big difference to me financially.'

And while all that was going on, Cotton was into the seventh year of a life ban, not for slipping a brown envelope furtively into his pocket before going out to play but for writing a book and taking the proceeds. It never occurred to the Unions – or maybe it did – that they were eliminating very able people who had a real contribution to make for the good of the game, a point underlined by Cotton's subsequent achievements as manager of the best Lions tour of the last 30 years – South Africa in 1997 – and as a leading figure within the RFU-cum-International Board.

How strange that his achievement in fulfilling just about every major role that rugby union had to offer should have started at Central Park, Wigan, one of the oldest shrines to rugby league, located – as it used to be before its demolition – just a few miles away from his birthplace in the village of Golborne where he was born on 3 January 1948. The family were steeped in the game and Francis Edward was seven years old when his father, a professional with St. Helens and Warrington, took him to see the most prolific try scorer rugby had ever seen, union or league.

Brian Bevan, hollow-cheeked, balding and apparently held together by bits of sticking plaster, looked at times as though he had seen a ghost. He played like one: a will-o'-the-wisp Australian who joined the Royal Navy as a stoker during the Second World War and ended up in Britain at the end of it. His total of 796 tries over 19 seasons gives some idea of the trouble that so many of his opponents had in attempting to lay a hand on him, before he gave them all a break by hanging up his boots at the age of 38.

The impression he left on a wide-eyed Cotton in the 'hen pen' at Central Park was every bit as indelible as the one he himself left on the union game. 'The first match I saw was Wigan against Warrington, and Brian Bevan was the reason my father took me because he was probably the best winger of all time. When he trotted out, I could not really believe what I was seeing.

'This guy had a bald head, no teeth and bandages wrapped round his knees. He looked more like a pensioner than a superstar. For 20 minutes he never touched the ball. Then someone gave him a pass in his own 25. He beat half the Wigan team and scored under the posts. I was hooked. He will always be right up there with Billy Boston and Tom van Vollenhoven as the best wings I have ever seen.'

Cotton's first visit to London was not to Twickenham but to Wembley, and not for any of Warrington's three Challenge Cup victories there during the '50s but for one of the most controversial FA Cup finals of all time. Never one to put all his footballing eggs in one basket, he divided his schoolboy loyalty, for one season only, between Wigan rugby league team and Bolton Wanderers. By pure chance, that season ended in May 1958 with another of Cotton's heroes, Nat Lofthouse, scoring both goals in Bolton's 2–0 win over the Busby Babes – or, to be more accurate, those who had survived the Munich air disaster three months before the final.

Lofthouse's second goal, when he bundled United goalkeeper Harry Gregg, ball and all, into the net, would never have been allowed today. As an 11 year old lost among a crowd of 100,000, Cotton saw little of the action, but he could always say, without fear of contradiction, that he was there. 'They still argue about that goal, but, as my hero, Lofthouse could do no wrong, which, given his physical presence, is probably what you would expect a prop forward to say.'

During his first year at Newton-le-Willows Grammar School, Cotton's sporting career took a decisive twist. After dalliances with rugby league and soccer, he found his true *métier* in the front row of the scrum. His imagination had been fired by another local hero of the '50s, Brian McTigue, the Wigan and Great Britain prop who played like 'a bull elephant running amok' according to the British manager, Tom Mitchell, during a famous Test win over Australia at the Sydney Cricket Ground.

Within months of leaving school, Cotton had made his first-class debut at the age of 18 for Liverpool against Birkenhead Park. He was in the Lancashire squad at 19, and the first time he went to Twickenham was to play for England Under-25 against Fiji at the age of 21. He made the journey to the team's pre-match base at the Lensbury Club in a 'battered old Beetle'. The Lensbury was a bit of a change from Central Park: '[It was] all very grand for a lad from Wigan. You suddenly realised you were in a different world.'

If it came as a culture shock, he disguised it remarkably well. Twickenham was so far removed from the heartland of rugby league that it might as well have been on a different planet – from a socio-economic perspective, at least – and yet Cotton bridged the gulf so completely that he turned it into a home from home. His England career stood the test of time for ten years, no mean feat during a decade when a never-ending number of players passed through the international side – here one minute, gone the next.

The 1971 Five Nations Championship began in predictable

fashion. England had been, in Cotton's words, 'stuffed in Cardiff'. The incumbent tight-head prop, Keith Fairbrother, survived for two more games before the selectors decided the time had come for another change and sent for the one who was to become known as 'The Chin'.

International teams then were not so much announced as muttered in a fashion that would have given the great American showman Phineas T. Barnum a fit. Once the Press Association had been informed, the word dribbled out, and the interested parties would invariably learn of their fate, for better or worse, from a journalist. The latter was true in Cotton's case: 'I was asked to take a phone call in the students' union bar at Loughborough from the *Leicester Mercury*. I was so thrilled that I smashed the phone down on the receiver and started running round the room. I could not have been more delighted had I won the pools. It was a truly fantastic moment.'

The outcome of his debut in the annual Calcutta Cup match was to prove rather less fantastic, despite the fact that Scotland had not won at Twickenham since 1938. Peter Brown's conversion of Chris Rea's last-minute try ensured that the Scots would not be reminded of that particularly unpleasant fact again, and, just to let the Sassenachs know that it was no flash in the pan, they gave England another 'rare auld pasting' at Murrayfield the following Saturday, in a game that was supposed to celebrate the RFU's centenary.

The following season, when they changed both props – Stack Stevens for David 'Piggy' Powell at loose-head and Mike Burton for Cotton on the tight-head side – England were whitewashed and only saved themselves from a repeat three years later because Dougie Morgan, the Scotland scrum-half, missed two late penalties. The following year, under the captaincy of another outstanding Lancastrian, Tony Neary, they made no mistake and lost the lot.

'You always went into the England dressing-room in those days,' said Cotton, 'looked around and thought, "What are some of these guys doing here?" We never picked our best team. There were always far better players out of the team who, for some strange reason, couldn't get in. Even the Welsh lads were amazed at some of the teams we picked.

'All sorts of crazy things were happening. They dropped "Nearo" for the 1977 season and he was world-class. New Zealand at Twickenham in 1978 was a classic example. We went in with no tight-head prop and a strange pair of second rows [Cotton had been dropped and replaced by Barry Nelmes of Cardiff with John Scott switched from number 8 to lock the scrum with Bill Beaumont]. We had no scrum and no lineout. Surprise, surprise – we got stuffed. Admittedly, the players were scattered across the whole country. It wasn't an easy job, but that did not excuse the huge number of mistakes which were made. I felt so frustrated because they kept making the same mistakes over and over again. Selection was pretty poor throughout the '70s.'

Small wonder, then, that during those years hardly a Lion was seen anywhere in England beyond the confines of Longleat Safari Park. Throughout the winning tours of New Zealand in 1971 and South Africa three years later, the largest of the four home countries provided the smallest number of Test players with never more than three in any one match. Cotton was one of them, in spite of England's poor performances at that time, which made his recognition as the best in Britain and Ireland all the more satisfying.

In 1974, for the tour of tours, he proved himself as truly a man for all seasons in the most demanding arena of all. Few can claim to have propped at the very highest level on either side of the scrum and mastered the very different technical requirements of each position. Cotton went as the reserve loose-head to Sandy Carmichael of Scotland and ended up playing all four Tests as the number one tight-head instead of Mike Burton.

Early injuries to both allowed Cotton to seize the opportunity, which he never let go, ensuring he was infinitely more successful in playing terms than in his off-pitch role as choirmaster. He had been appointed on the basis of a reputation of being able to organise a sing-song, earned largely while playing for Lancashire. In next to no time the Lions had adopted as their battle-hymn that famous old Lancashire number 'Flower of Scotland', which Billy Steele, the Scotland centre, introduced years before the Murrayfield faithful adopted it as their anthem.

'We always sang it on the coach going to matches, and we wouldn't get out until we'd finished,' Cotton said. 'I remember, when we pulled into the stadium at Pretoria for the second Test, the bus came to a halt outside the front entrance and all the police standing around waited for us to get off. Nobody moved until we'd finished the last verse. So we sat there for two or three minutes singing our heads off. They must have thought we were mad.'

There were times when others thought they really were. Like the manager of the Union Hotel in Pretoria, who feared that his establishment was about to be burned to the ground, a not unreasonable conclusion considering that a group of Lions in an alcoholic haze had lit a fire in the lobby. He wasn't the only hotel manager upset at the state of his premises after having had a Lions team to stay. The 1968 Lions wreaked damage on a consistent scale during their tour of South Africa, so much so that they became known as 'The Wreckers'. The title was made all the more unacceptable by the fact that they never got round to wrecking the Springboks, failing to win any of the four Tests. If the '74 Lions could not quite match the off-field behaviour of their predecessors, it wasn't for a lack of effort on certain occasions.

One prank made headline news that, ironically, served only to increase the mystique of the Lions. When some of them had been caught running around in the 'altogether', a half-baked explanation was offered as an imaginative attempt to cover up the episode. It was said that their passion for scrummaging was so great that they often did it late at night in the nude. It struck some of the Springboks as not entirely implausible. After his Natal team had been beaten by the Lions, Tommy Bedford, the home captain, was quoted as saying, 'These Lions are so keen on scrummaging, they even practise late at night without any clothes on.' Presumably, that made it rather easier to slip the binding . . .

Then there was the day they checked out of their hotel in East London (South Africa) after beating Border, and Tommy David, the Wales flanker from Pontypridd, discovered that his bedroom furniture had been rearranged in a way that ensured it a good airing on the canopy above the hotel's entrance.

'We had an almighty rollicking from the manager,' Cotton said. 'Those sort of schoolboy pranks were all part of the rugby culture in those days. The tour manager or the liaison man from the South African Rugby Football Union would pay the bill for the damage, and we'd move on to the next stop.'

The tour being the stuff of legend, the Lions came home to an ecstatic reception at Heathrow airport. It might not have been anywhere near the scale of the reception that greeted England's return from Australia with the World Cup, but it was the first time any rugby team had captured the public imagination sufficiently for several hundred fans to greet them in such a way.

The Welsh contingent went home to civic receptions, and those from the smaller, valley communities were paraded around before an adoring public in a pony and trap. Back home in Lancashire, Cotton found a no less heartfelt expression of northern approval for what he had done: a large offer to return to the game that in his boyhood he would have been only too willing to play for nothing.

'It was the only serious offer I had from league – £16,000 to sign-on, which was a fair bit of money, especially in those days. I considered it all right, but it came at a time when I didn't need the money. There was talk of the England captaincy, and I had a hell of a lot going for me. I thought, "I'm enjoying all this. Why change?"'

There was still much to be done: like trying to beat Wales, to put one over on the pair of fellow Lions whom he considered the greatest players of his generation – Gareth Edwards and J. P. R. Williams. The mind can only boggle at what they would have been worth today, in a professional game where the law demands that flankers stay bound to the scrum until the ball is out, an imposition that wing forwards never had to worry about in those days.

'Gareth was out of this world. I have never seen a scrum-half dominate like he did behind a good pack. Give him good ball on those hard surfaces and he was phenomenal. The Lions never lost when Edwards played. He was the best player I have seen by a street. Apart from being incredibly quick, he was also incredibly strong. He had all the skills and a tremendous tactical appreciation of the game. He was undoubtedly the superstar of the tour.

'J. P. R. was the most competitive man I have ever met in my life. Training, drinking, playing – his attitude was always the same, and that rubbed off on everyone else. If you were trying to score a try against him in training, he wouldn't think twice about putting you in the front row of the stand. That's the way he was. Telling him to take it easy was a complete waste of time. If you did, he wouldn't have known what you were talking about.

'Any trip to South Africa always guarantees you a severe physical examination. The Springboks made a few mistakes during that tour, but trying to target J. P. R. was the biggest one of all. The harder they tried to hurt him, the stronger he came back at them. People often ask me about the hardest scrums I've faced. I always tell them that it was in practice with the '74 Lions against a certain Welshman.

'He was always a thorn in England's side because he had a habit of scoring tries against us. You just had to admire him and doff your cap to an all-time great player. He had a total self-belief, and that was what made him the player he was. As a counter-attacking full-back, he and Pierre Villepreux of France were out on their own. J. P. R. would have been fantastic in today's game.'

Convinced that no job on a rugby field was beyond him, the doctor from Bridgend was never slow to dabble in the murky world of the front row. For a full-back who often gave the impression of being a one-man panzer division, nothing was too much trouble. However, he pushed his luck far too far by scrummaging against Cotton. If nothing else, it presented 'The Chin' with a heaven-sent opportunity to give him his come-uppance.

'J. P. R. had done some scrum practice during the '71 tour and got away with it. We practised virtually every day in '74, and when we were a prop short one morning he volunteered to stand in. It wasn't a case of poor technique but no technique at all! He went flying straight out of the scrum, and I could hear him muttering something like, "Things have improved a bit since 1971." We had earned his respect.'

Then established as a giant of his trade, Cotton went to New Zealand with the 1977 Lions only to find his fight to win another series undermined by Edwards' refusal to make himself available and, more pointedly, by the Welshman with overall responsibility for on-field strategy. John Dawes, captain during the celebrated previous tour six years earlier, returned as coach with Phil Bennett, another Welsh great, in charge of the troops.

The majority of the squad (seventeen) were Welsh – at least two too many because it meant there was no room for accomplished internationals like Scotland centre Jim Renwick and England wing Mike Slemen. Dawes, who had succeeded Clive Rowlands as Wales coach after captaining the Lions to victory on the previous New Zealand tour, left much to be desired, certainly as far as Cotton was concerned.

'John was a disappointment as the coach. He seemed to be going through a peculiar stage of his life. His attitude was, "You are Lions. You ought to know what you are doing." He was a complex character, and I couldn't work him out. I doubt whether John really came to terms with having been so successful as Lions captain in '71.

'I don't think he distanced himself enough from the players. We lacked a little experience in certain positions, particularly at scrum-half. There is no doubt in my mind that had Edwards gone on that tour we would have won the series. We had a very good pack, but we needed stronger characters among the backs: someone to tell the forwards, "Look, we'd like the ball ten seconds earlier without you lot putting the polish on it." I enjoyed "Benny's" captaincy, but sometimes he would get himself a bit down. He could have done with more support from the management. We didn't have the same unity of purpose as we had in '74. The weather was awful, chucking it down three days out of four, and there were one or two moaners. You've got to take it as it comes and make the best of it, but we didn't have enough of those boys. We never had that unswerving focus necessary to win a series.'

Cotton's role as an immovable cornerstone of England's 1980 Grand Slam made his selection for a third Lions tour that summer a formality. Alas, his participation was to end before the first Test. In high drama against a SAR Federation XV – popularly known as the 'Proteas' – in the old Dutch colonial town of Stellenbosch, he was led from the pitch complaining of chest pains. Fears that he was suffering a heart attack were not exactly allayed by his subsequent transfer from the local hospital to Groote Schuur Hospital in nearby Cape Town, where Dr Christiaan Barnard had performed the first heart transplant.

'I had a problem in a previous match in Potchefstroom where I got an infection in my leg. I stayed behind, missed the next match in Bloemfontein and knew that the game after that in Stellenbosch was my last chance of getting a Test place. I should never have played, but I thought that if I didn't I wouldn't get picked for the Test, so I made a totally irrational decision.

'Suddenly, during the first half I had these chest pains, and I became disorientated. Allan Martin [the Welsh second row] came up, took one look at me and called the physio. I was taken straight to the local hospital where they gave me all the jabs they give you when they half-think you've had a heart attack. They took blood samples and did tests, then a doctor came up and said, "I think you've had a heart attack."

'I could not believe what he was saying. They sedated me, gave me more injections to thin the blood and transferred me to Cape Town. I was still in my Lions tracksuit because I didn't have any clothes, and when they wheeled me into the hospital who should I bump into but Dr Barnard. He said, "Hello. What's the problem?"

'I said, "I think I've had a heart attack."

'So he said, quick as a flash, "Don't worry. If you need a new one, pop upstairs and we'll fix you up with one!"

'It sounds funny now but it wasn't at the time. They did more tests and found out that I was suffering from pericarditis, an infection of the sack around the heart. The relief was enormous. After that, it was a case of rest, but those were unquestionably the five most traumatic days of my life. I was 33, had been married a couple of years and we'd only just had our first child. You can imagine the turmoil back home when the Lions tracked down my wife, Pat, and gave her the news.'

His international career had one match to run, against Wales in Cardiff at the start of the 1981 Five Nations. England replaced him in that game by sending for the undertaker, otherwise known as Austin Sheppard, the substitute prop, who ran – and still runs – his family funeral business in Bristol. A pulled hamstring – something more readily associated with thoroughbreds than the donkeys of the front row – had forced Cotton into an early exit, and by Monday morning he had phoned the chairman of selectors, Budge Rogers, with news of his retirement.

'I pulled the damned hamstring trying to drive Maurice Colclough over the Welsh line. The other front-row players were not amused. A pulled hamstring meant you had been training; that you considered yourself to be a highly tuned athlete. I'd had so many injuries. I propped against the All Blacks for the North when we beat them at Otley with one good shoulder, and, luckily, I could tuck my outside arm across my chest in the scrums without anyone realising anything was wrong.

'In hindsight, I think I was wrong to stop playing completely. I wish I'd gone on playing for Sale for a couple more seasons, but at the time I'd had enough. I was so fed up that I left my England kit in the boot of the car for three months.'

It turned out to be a blessing in disguise. Free to devote more time to his family and his job, he proceeded to make as big a name for himself in business as he had in rugby and earn a fortune into the bargain. It had been a long haul from his early working days with the National Coal Board, above ground as a mine-management trainee rather than down the pit as his father had done before rugby league provided an escape route.

After a spell as a schoolteacher, he took the plunge into the business world as national sales director for a sportswear firm that went bust two years later. That proved to be another of those blessings in disguise. 'I thought it was a bit of a disaster, until the person who took the company over asked me to help run it,' he said. 'That enabled me to gain invaluable experience without any personal risk.'

Reunited by then with two of his fellow England colleagues, Steve Smith and Tony Neary, the trio struck out on their own with the launch in August 1987 of Cotton Traders, a retail leisure wear business. 'We bought the product and sold it on to the consumer. As luck would have it, we were first into the rugby leisure market. It just took off.'

Before long, they literally put their shirt on England, with effect from the 1991 World Cup. It was a new jersey designed for the tournament and also for exploiting the growing market in replica rugby tops. When the RFU refused to let the England team wear the new strip for the Five Nations Championship that followed the World Cup, Cotton's company sued for breach of contract, serving a writ for £20 million on each of the 57 members of the Union. The complainant was not at that time one of the 57, which spared him the intriguing dilemma of whether to serve a writ on himself.

'At that time, our ten-year deal had run for six months,' he said. 'We had made a massive investment. Once the RFU refused to see us, the only course of action was the legal one. Within 24 hours of issuing the writ, we were down at Lincoln's Inn thrashing out a deal with the RFU's legal people.'

Five years later, the American giant Nike bought the company out of its contract for a reported £3 million. Cotton could have retreated to a life of luxury, but, instead of putting his feet up for the rest of his life, he chose to keep working, continuing to give the RFU the benefit of his wisdom, free of charge. 'I like work, and I enjoyed my role with the RFU. What was I going to do? Play golf? I'm not a golfer. As it turned out, our contract with the RFU was an excellent piece of business. It was also good business for the RFU, because they made a heck of a lot more money in the long run.'

Financially secure, he channelled his energy into one more Lions tour, managing the victorious 1997 series against the Springboks with a winning mixture of no-nonsense authority and good humour. In tandem with the coach Ian McGeechan and the Lions management they used some lateral thinking to pick three English players – John Bentley, Nick Beal and Will Greenwood – none of whom had appeared in the Five Nations Championship a few weeks earlier. Bentley, reclaimed from rugby league, spent the following season at Newcastle untroubled by any England demands, whereas Beal would become a member of their 1999 World Cup squad. Greenwood had to wait for Clive Woodward to succeed Jack Rowell as coach before winning his first cap.

Ieuan Evans, the mercurial Welshman, who was then nearing the end of a distinguished career, had been widely touted for the captaincy, until the Lions decided that the sight of a beetle-browed Martin Johnson knocking on the Springbok dressing-room door would send out a more menacing statement of intent. Few understood the psychological advantage of that better than Cotton, who was tough enough for his life-long pal Steve Smith to joke that a suitable epitaph on Fran's gravestone would be: 'What are you looking at?'

His only real spat as Lions manager was with a player who was not considered good enough for the tour: Will Carling. For all his unprecedented success as captain of England, Carling's one Lions tour – to New Zealand four years later – had been a comparative failure, which might have explained why he never embraced the Lions concept as representing the pinnacle of a British or Irish player's career.

When Carling appeared at the Lions' hotel during the tour, Cotton ordered him to stay away. It was another indication that the relationship between them was still poor, after it had deteriorated rapidly some months earlier. 'Early in January that year, we selected a group of 60 players, because we were in the midst of some turmoil over contracts,' Cotton said. 'We needed to know for certain that they were available, rather than wait until the end of the championship in April to start talking to their agents.

'A number of English players, particularly three-quarters, were not on that list. Phil de Glanville, the England captain, was one. Carling was another. We sent the list to the relevant Unions so we could get addresses. Shortly afterwards, I went to London to attend the Rugby Union Writers' Club dinner at the Café Royal. During the course of the evening, Colin Herridge – the former RFU treasurer – came up to me and said, "I have seen your squad."

'As a big mate of Carling's, he had probably by then tipped Will off that the squad was about to be made public and he wasn't in it. A few weeks later, I'm driving to the Scotland match at Twickenham, on the Saturday morning, when I hear on the radio that Jon Holmes, Carling's agent, has said his man is not available for the tour. I presumed that to have been a pre-emptive strike: a damage-limitation exercise on behalf of his client.

'Carling had never come up to me before in his life, but he sought me out in the bar of the Hilton hotel before the after-match dinner. He starts talking and I said, "I've heard you are not available for the tour. Is that right?"

'He says, "It's going to be a high-profile tour. The only way I'd do it, really, is if I could do it my way."

'I said, "What do you mean?"'

'He then said that he would need to be in charge. I said, "What I'll do is make sure we talk about it at the next meeting of the Lions selectors in Birmingham next Sunday. I'll come back to you."'

'On the morning of the meeting, a friend of mine said, "Have you seen the *Mail on Sunday*?" In it, Carling said that he was not available for the tour even though he had been offered the captaincy. So now I hit the roof, because that had compromised the whole selection process. I had to explain my conversation with Carling to the other selectors and that I was bringing it to this meeting for discussion.

'The answer would have been "no". They didn't want him as the captain. They didn't want him as a player because of his track record in New Zealand in '93 where he just didn't perform. As he put it, touring with the Lions didn't suit him. Fair enough. There was no way Ian McGeechan would have wanted Carling.

'Will was pretty expert in his PR, but it was very arrogant to say he would only go as captain. I was very annoyed by the whole incident, and I let him know it. He was questioning my integrity and the integrity of the selection process. That brought about the rift between us. The next time I saw him was in the City Hall in Cardiff at the dinner after the Welsh match some weeks later. I went back with my wife to the hotel, walked into the disco and there's Will straight in front of me. He had been enjoying the night with the rest of the lads.

'He said, "Look, I'm not happy about this. Not happy."'

'I said, "What are you not happy with?"'

'He said, "All this stuff in the press that I asked to be captain."'

'"Well, that is the truth," I replied.'

'Then he got on his high horse and said, "I believe you are going to be England team manager next year. If you are, I'm not playing."'

'I said, "First of all, I don't want to be team manager, but if you don't want to play, that's your decision."'

'He said, "I'm so annoyed. If I'd been there [at the Lions selection meeting], I'd have bloody well hit you."'

'I said, "I promise you one thing. If you had done, I would have hit you straight back." And that finished the conversation. I guess it was also the end of the relationship, but there was no way I was going to be threatened or intimidated. It had been pretty heated, because everyone else had walked away.

'Will was a great player with a fantastic record as England captain, but he was also a very complex man. I never got to know him well enough to understand him. I was trying to create a unity of purpose within the '97 Lions, and he was not considered worth a place in that environment. He'd had too much of his own way. Maybe he had a problem with the reins being given to someone else, as they had been to Gavin Hastings in '93.

'He would love to have been Lions captain. It was the only thing missing from his CV. He was very disappointed in '93 when Gavin got it. Gavin was better suited at pulling a disparate group of players from four different countries together.'

The sequel to that row was provoked by Carling's visit to the Lions' hotel in Durban. Cotton asked him to keep away and made the request via the former captain's fellow Harlequin, Jason Leonard. Told that the manager didn't want to see him 'hanging around', Carling described it as 'an extraordinary remark to make and quite insulting'.

Cotton's sole concern was ensuring that no extraneous element interfered with the business of winning the series. 'It was never meant to be insulting,' he said. 'Don't forget, we were playing the Springboks that Saturday. For Will to deposit himself in the hotel was totally against what we wanted at the time, in terms of total focus on the Test. As manager, I could not have let it go. It had to stop.

'It wasn't a personal thing, just that we could not afford to allow outside people bringing in any outside influences. Carling had been coming into the team hotel and having meals. We didn't want him coming into our official functions. I spoke to Jason and asked him to have a word. Jason said, "I've had a word. He won't be coming back."'

From Cotton's standpoint, it had been worth the hassle. A second successful tour of South Africa – a distinction that he shared with McGeechan – put him right up there in the Himalayas of rugby, amongst the few Lions of England able to survive at such a rarefied altitude. Not bad for a miner's lad from Wigan.

9

PIE AND CHIPS

BILL BEAUMONT'S BOYHOOD DREAM HAD ALWAYS BEEN TO WEAR THE RED ROSE, BUT when he did it was never as he imagined. His burning childhood ambition was to open the batting for Lancashire at Old Trafford, to stride forth beneath the hanging baskets of the old pavilion and out into the middle to give them what for with his whirling bat.

He could have tilted his cap at a jaunty angle just like Cyril Washbrook, a Test selector when England recalled him to face Australia at the age of 41 during the summer of 1956. Like a true Lancastrian in his country's hour of need at Headingley, he reached the crease with England in crisis at 17–3 and proceeded to make 98.

Beaumont, born in Chorley on 9 March 1952, was four at the time, but he would learn all about Washbrook and the other flannelled heroes of the day – like Brian Statham – because cricket was in his blood: Lancashire County Cricket. His uncle, Joe Blackledge, had played for them, and, what's more, he had captained them for a whole season, which meant that he called the shots even if he didn't play as many as he would have liked.

Joe decided when Statham needed a break and presided over a batting order headed by Geoff 'Noddy' Pullar, the incumbent England opener. Joe had been appointed as Lancashire's last amateur captain, which entitled him to be called 'Mr' on the scorecard. He replaced another England opener, Bob Barber, who had decamped south to Warwickshire and who, as a professional, was not entitled to be called Mr.

Uncle Joe was in the throes of holding a crumbling team together when his ten-year-old nephew was taken along as a special treat for his first glimpse of county cricket: Lancashire v. Hampshire, Old Trafford, Saturday, 16 June 1962 on the first day of a three-day match. The Beaumont family has seen many unforgettable sporting occasions and made a few off their own bat, but this, most definitely, was not one of them.

Mr Blackledge did not, as they say in cricketing parlance, trouble the scorers unduly. 'I was hoping to see my uncle get a few runs,' his nephew recalled. 'Instead he ducked into a bouncer from a fast bowler called Butch White and got laid out. Cricket was my great love, and I remember going with my dad to Blackpool to watch Lancashire play the South Africans in the summer of 1960 when I was eight and then, a few years later, seeing Richie Benaud win the fourth Test for Australia at Old Trafford.'

The bouncer which did for his uncle Joe sounded typical of Lancashire's luck during a summer of largely unremitting failure, as suggested by their final league position: second from bottom. *Wisden Cricketer's Almanac*, the cricketers' bible, declared:

> By general consent within the county, Lancashire experienced the worst season in the club's history. The summer was especially unfortunate for J. F. Blackledge, the newly-appointed captain. It had been hoped that he would be able to call upon the advice of [Ken] Grieves, the senior professional but Grieves went into business. Nevertheless, Grieves has accepted the captaincy for 1963.

The early lesson in sporting politics sailed over the young Beaumont's head or perhaps, like Cyril Washbrook, he deliberately ducked inside the line and allowed it to pass through to the keeper as if sensing that he would have to deal with enough short-pitched stuff during his rugby career, both on the pitch and in the committee room.

At such a tender age, he was too busy playing and watching sport in his native north-west. Few boys can have been privileged enough to have had such an eclectic upbringing. If he wasn't watching Lancashire at Old Trafford, it was Wigan when Billy Boston was in his prime or Blackburn Rovers, almost as big a childhood passion as Lancashire County Cricket.

When Rovers went all the way to Wembley in 1960 for their first FA Cup final since the '20s, the result moved the young Beaumont to tears. 'I sat in front of the television in me Blackburn shirt and watched the whole game,' he said. 'We lost 3–0 to Wolves, and, at the end, I cried.'

What happened that day reduced one of the Blackburn team to a similarly anguished state. Dave Whelan broke his leg that afternoon, long before anyone had invented anything as simple as a substitute – the same Dave Whelan who went on to amass an even bigger fortune than Beaumont as the head of his own sportswear business.

The Beaumonts and the Blackledges were steeped in sport. As well as his Uncle Joe, Beaumont's father played rugby union for Fylde. Despite that, William Blackledge, jun., grew up keeping wicket in summer and goal in winter, a sporting all-rounder in the mill town of Chorley, where his contemporaries included Paul Mariner, a local likely lad who went on to score goals for Arsenal and England.

And then one day while visiting his grandparents, he bumped into another young fellow with the most famous football name of all, Stanley Matthews, jun., who was being given some coaching for his A levels. With the family business beckoning, young Beaumont could afford not to let studies affect his pursuit of sporting excellence: 'Deep down I expected to end up working in the family business so there was no great incentive [to study hard].'

Beaumont was introduced to rugby while he was a boarder at Cressbrook Preparatory School in Kirkby Lonsdale in the Lake District. Originally a prop, he then underwent a staggering metamorphosis and resurfaced as a fly-half who boasted a career drop-goal tally of one, not that anyone beyond the school paid a blind bit of notice.

When he left Ellesmere College in Shropshire at the age of 17, Beaumont had a vague idea of ticking over at Fylde Rugby Football Club in between summers for Chorley Cricket Club. The notion that he had it within him to captain England and the Lions had not occurred to him. Nor had it occurred to anyone else, because as far as Lancashire Schools were concerned W. B. Beaumont did not exist.

It suited laid-back Bill down to the ground. His father paved the way for his arrival at Fylde RFC, informing the secretary by letter that his son had finished his school career at full-back but, being a bit short of pace, would probably find his proper niche somewhere in the pack. English club rugby in the late '60s and early '70s was not sufficiently well organised to be called chaotic. Fylde, on the Lancashire coast, was no different.

Remembering his initial time with the club, Beaumont said, 'Nobody had a coach in those days. The captain was the coach. That's how it was, and everyone accepted it. There was a massive difference in fitness and attitude between the lads in the fifth and sixth teams and those in the firsts. Like most of the others, I just wanted to play for a bit of fun at the start.

'We used to train twice a week, on Tuesday and Thursday nights. Then, every Thursday night, we'd give ourselves a treat. After training, it would be straight down to the local chippie to see how much we could eat. A pie and chips were obligatory – the more, the better.

'Modern coaches and nutritionists would have had a fit if they had seen us. When I was captain of England, my Friday night routine would be to settle down, at home with my wife Hilary, to a prawn cocktail followed by a steak and a bottle of wine.'

Just over 100 Englishmen have been given the ultimate distinction of captaining their country. None of them can have started their senior career at a more humble level. Beaumont's take-off point was so far down the scale that he made those who started at the bottom seem as if they were halfway to the top. Few have made a steeper climb to the dizzy heights of Twickenham than Beaumont from Fylde's 6th XV.

The new boy played one match for the sixths – away to Burnage, a junior club in Manchester – at full-back. The club did not take long to come to the conclusion that the experiment was not worth repeating. Redeployed in the back row for the following Saturday, Beaumont impressed someone, somewhere that he was worthy of a rapid promotion.

They stuck him in the thirds, and the future captain of the Lions finished his first season at Fylde in the 2nd XV. The advent of the 1970–71 season brought a rethink, with some people at the club clearly unconvinced about the local lad's worth as a second-team lock. On the basis that he was not big enough, they demoted him to the thirds with instructions to learn his trade as a prop. It was in this position that he made his first-team debut fully 15 months after joining the club and then only because of a front-row shortage.

When the penny finally dropped and the teenager began growing into a real lock, he made his first second-row appearance for Fylde against New Brighton at the age of 19 and soon he would be ready to go places. The 'donkey' was up and running. The following year, in 1972, he made his Lancashire debut in the County Championship against Cumberland and Westmorland, fortified by some old-fashioned advice from his second-row partner, Richard Trickey of Sale. 'Don't try anything fancy,' Trickey told him. 'No sidestepping or selling dummies or trying to drop a goal. Just stick your head up the prop's backside, shove like a lunatic and contest every blasted lineout no matter where the ball is meant to be thrown. Just remember you are a donkey, and behave like one.'

Within two seasons, the young Beaumont had brayed his way into the England Under-23 ranks and beyond to a national trial, which proved to be another eye-opening experience as well as an eyebrow-raising one. Pleased to find himself chosen among The Rest, Beaumont discovered that not everyone knew who he was, including his captain that day, the Bristol flanker Dave Rollitt. The 'Grey Fox', as he was known, did not mince his words when he bumped into Fylde's finest: 'And who the hell are you, may I ask?'

Had he been a sensitive soul, Beaumont might have jacked the rugby lark in there and then. 'Hardly a vote of confidence when even your skipper hasn't a clue who you are, but he did add that, since I had been selected for an England trial, I couldn't be "completely useless".'

Rollitt wasn't far off the mark. Beaumont made a good enough impression to be named among the substitutes for the opening match of the 1975 Five Nations against Ireland in Dublin. Roger Uttley's withdrawal through injury and Beaumont's subsequent promotion from the bench meant that he had won his first England cap at the age of 22. It was some feat for the lad who had started out some five seasons earlier as the last line of defence for the Fylde sixths.

Two years later, shortly after marrying Hilary, he was a Lion, postponing a Majorcan honeymoon in order to join one of the less auspicious expeditions to New Zealand by the team whose acronym sounded like the capital of Lebanon: BIRUTT (The British Isles Rugby Union Touring Team). Summoned to join the tour, after his fellow England lock Nigel Horton had broken a thumb, Beaumont wondered what he had let himself in for.

'Instead of feeling over the moon, I was heartbroken,' he said. 'I remember wondering why on earth I had agreed to travel. I had just got married, my honeymoon had been postponed yet again and I experienced the same empty feeling that had marked my return to boarding school as a youngster.'

His sense of foreboding would not have been helped by the advice proffered to him upon arrival at the Lions' lair in Christchurch. He would find out soon enough that the tour management left much to be desired, which was perhaps what his fellow Lion, the wonderfully unconventional Willie Duggan, had in mind when he greeted Beaumont with the immortal words, 'If you have any bloody sense, you'll get on the next plane back home.'

During a New Zealand winter of incessant rain, Beaumont rapidly discovered that the Lions were not all they were cracked up to be, at least not the 1977 variety, under the less than perfect coaching direction of John Dawes. To Beaumont's chagrin, the Lions had knackered themselves on the training ground in the run-up to the second Test in Wellington: 'There was no way anybody would have been fully recovered in time for the Test match. Dawes came in for a lot of criticism for that session, and Fran [Cotton], as hard and conscientious a trainer as you could wish to meet, accused him of literally burning out the Test team. It was no wonder the selected players looked lethargic when they went down 16–12 in the Test.

'I was determined to demonstrate I was worthy of my place in the squad, and although blokes were dropping like ninepins, I willed myself to keep going. I was staggered to discover Fran had been left out of the Test team but then I couldn't understand why they had taken Phil Orr as a loose-head rather than Ian McLauchlan in the first place. Trevor Evans got the vote at openside ahead of Tony Neary, another selection I couldn't understand because "Nero" proved to be the missing link from the pack when he was eventually included for the final Test, by which time it was too late.'

Far from making up the numbers, Beaumont went straight into the Test team and stayed there for the last three matches of the series, marking his debut with a win at Christchurch. The Lions lost the series 3–1: an unhappy end to an often unhappy tour. A kind of siege mentality had been bred: an introspection not helped by the bickering over media relations with the honorary coach, Dawes, and the honorary manager, George Burrell.

Beaumont felt the tour suffered from 'weak management' and cited as an example the snubbing of a social event after the second Test: 'A dance had been organised in our honour at a local rugby club, but the players decided they wanted to stay at the hotel and celebrate in their own way. We had previously accepted the invitation, and I thought it very discourteous of us not to turn up. That was an occasion when the management should have put its foot down and insisted that we attend a function that people had put a lot of effort into organising.

'You have to meet-and-greet and enjoy the country you're visiting. We didn't do that. We erected barriers rather than breaking them down, and, as a consequence, we ended up being very insular. A siege mentality set in of the nobody-likes-us-but-we-don't-care sort. You can't do that because the pressure just keeps building up. The media criticise you as poor tourists, which tends to get a sort of "sod you" reaction. John could have handled it better.

'There was one occasion when the management had planned a closed training session, but, when we arrived, a crowd of mainly youngsters had turned up to watch. John was all for driving off there and then, but Fran Cotton stood up, said he couldn't believe what we were doing and led us all off the bus to train in front of them. We should have been encouraging those kids.'

A wet winter, even by Kiwi standards, did nothing to lighten the mood, nor did the hotel facilities that invariably fell a long way short of five stars. The players had plenty of time to brood over a growing awareness that they were not exactly living in the lap of luxury, while the New Zealand Rugby Union raked in a fortune from their efforts on the field. Small wonder, therefore, that when Australian entrepreneur David Lord went round the rugby world attempting to sell his ultimately doomed idea of hijacking international teams – much the same as Kerry Packer had done to Test match cricket a few years earlier – he found no shortage of players willing to sign on the dotted line.

A fully-grown Lion, Beaumont returned home to be made captain of England. At that time, rugby was still relatively small beer, so much so that the new skipper had something of a shock when he arrived for a business meeting in London to find several rugby journalists – five instead of the usual two – waiting for a chat. It did not take Beaumont long to realise that leading England was far from a bed of roses.

He learnt, to his cost, that English selectors had a habit of picking if not the wrong team, then certainly the wrong pack, which was what they did against Graham Mourie's All Blacks in November 1978. They picked a number 8 at lock (John Scott), a specialist loose-head prop (Barry Nelmes) at tight-head and a number 8 (Roger Uttley) who had only just returned to the fray after long-term injury.

Having paid the inevitable price in cold figures – England lost 16–6 – Beaumont did not have to wait much longer to realise that advice from the selectors on matters of strategy was best taken with a pinch of salt. Not unusually for Lansdowne Road, a stiff wind was blowing down the pitch when England played there in 1979, which prompted a debate between the skipper and some senior players as to what to do for the best in the event of winning the toss.

They supported Beaumont's 'gut feeling' about playing into the wind. 'The selectors intervened and told me to play with the wind if I won the toss. I called correctly and decided to follow their instructions. We lost the game 12–7, the players were unhappy, and I vowed never again to be a selectors' lackey.'

This policy brought some spectacular results for the North in the shape of their 21–9 'stuffing' of the All Blacks at Otley and for England later that same season in the glittering form of the Grand Slam. Winning it meant beating Wales at Twickenham in a match with a sour atmosphere that put rugby to shame. It was the infamous occasion that ended with Wales, reduced to 14 men following the early sending-off of Paul Ringer for an allegedly late tackle, scoring the only tries but losing 9–8 to Dusty Hare's late penalty.

The pre-match hype spread far beyond rugby to embrace political issues, at a time when the South Wales coal miners were in the throes of fighting for their livelihoods. Those were the winters of discontent, and the industrial bitterness from the picket lines overflowed into a game of rugby.

'That sort of stuff didn't help, and we realised the week before the match that it was going to be pretty nasty,' Beaumont said. 'There was a lot of aggression on and off the field, probably more than I ever experienced. For once, we had a decent team – one good enough to win, but we didn't play particularly well that day.

'I don't think any of us involved in that match is able to look back on it with any satisfaction. In retrospect, you wonder whether you acted in the right way. I remember telling the players not to believe anything they either read or heard.'

Fat chance. The die had been cast, and at the end Dai was downcast at what the Welsh, with some justification, as yet another example of injustice at the hands, or more accurately the feet, of the

English. Beaumont couldn't help but be aware of the smell of rancour coming from every pore of Twickenham that day and must have been tempted to equip his team with gas-masks.

'The usual happy atmosphere you associate with rugby internationals was missing that weekend, and the theme of poor, oppressed Wales having to take on the English bully-boys was very much in evidence. There were cheap shots going in all the time, and Dusty Hare was the victim of a blatantly late tackle quite early in the game. Sadly, that was a foretaste of what was to come. Scrums were going down on a regular basis, but it was little wonder considering the way the front rows were charging at each other like rutting stags.'

Dave Burnett, the Irish referee, read the riot act to both teams, leaving neither in any doubt that the next offender would go. Paul Ringer's late tackle on the English fly-half, John Horton, was mild compared to some of the more gruesome incidents that had preceded it, but if the referee was to retain credibility, the Welsh flanker had to walk. And walk he did: out of the match, out of the ground and, as far as the Lions selectors were concerned, out of the tour of South Africa at the end of that season. Rightly or wrongly, his hopes of making the tour vanished in that moment, and yet Wales almost survived without him. They won the battle 2–0 on tries but lost the war because Hare kicked a late penalty winner after Wales had missed all five of their shots at goal. It was an extravagance that helped rescue one of Beaumont's Lancashire pals, Steve Smith, from permanent embarrassment.

The Sale scrum-half had almost thrown it away, allowing the Welsh hooker Alan Phillips to charge down an attempted clearance that sent Elgan Rees sprinting over. Hare's pressure kick repaired the damage, and, a few minutes later, England reached the sanctuary of their dressing-room, which, in the skipper's words, 'resembled an army field hospital'.

In a typically friendly gesture, Beaumont went into the Wales dressing-room. So many bridges had been burned that finding his way there was no mean achievement. 'I got a muted reception but then they were understandably gutted to have battled so well with just 14 men and been beaten in injury time. I had been looking for Geoff Wheel [his opposite number] because he had run off the pitch at the end, and I hadn't had a chance to shake his hand.

'Ironically, most of the Welsh players were great mates of mine. I went into their dressing-room and went round the individuals I'd been on tour with as Lions – Pricey, Allan Martin, Jeff Squire and a few others. I just said, "Look, it's been a shit game, lads. Let's make sure we get together for a few jars later on."'

He sought Ringer out at the after-match dinner in the West End, not to reopen hostilities but to say he was sorry for what had happened to him. The only surprise was that nobody else had been sent off. 'If it had happened today with all the television cameras and the tougher disciplinary procedures of the modern game, a few more than just Ringer would have gone off.' At that same dinner, Beaumont had been approached by the Lions manager, Syd Millar, about the captaincy and sworn to secrecy that he would be the first Englishman for half a century to lead the Lions. Douglas Prentice had been the last in 1930.

Back in the Five Nations, the wounded Welsh circled the wagons, their mood not helped by England's progress towards the Grand Slam, their first for 23 years. They clinched it in some style when John Carleton scored a hat-trick of tries in the last game against Scotland at Murrayfield.

For the Lions tour of South Africa an Irish manager plus an Irish coach – Noel Murphy – militated against an Irish captain, no matter how impressive Fergus Slattery's credentials were. As it turned out, Slattery made himself unavailable as did Tony Neary, another leading flanker, which left the tourists seriously short of a specialist on the openside of the scrum.

Ringer was another non-starter, the Lions selectors having declared him *persona non grata* because of what had happened at Twickenham. Beaumont had strong views on the matter, adamant that the Welshman had paid his dues and that the decision to punish him further was wrong. Clearly, the skipper had no say in the selection of the 30-man squad.

It was equally clear that he had not been consulted on the travel arrangements. The Lions flew economy, which may or may not have sharpened the collective sense of free enterprise that enabled them to circumvent some of the draconian amateur regulations. To supplement the daily allowance of £3, the Lions generated funds for the tour kitty from ticket sales and personal appearances at supermarkets. It was a commercialism that was clearly in breach of the rules, but, as usual, the authorities turned a blind eye when it suited them.

Beset by injury from the first minute of the first match when Stuart Lane of Cardiff became the earliest casualty, the Lions lost the series 3–1. Typically, Ray Gravell gave it his all, even if that made him lucky to stay on the pitch during the match against the Orange Free State at Bloemfontein when the bearded Wales centre from Mynydd-y-Garreg (the Rocky Mountain) hit the opposition fly-half de Wet Ras so hard and so late that the South African must have felt he had run into the entire mountain.

'I laid him out: broke his shoulder,' Gravell said. 'It was a bad tackle, a sending-off offence, but it had the desired effect. The crowd went mad. Billy Beaumont said, "Grav, what have you done?"

'I said, "Billy, I've got him a late one, early!"'

Only seven Lions stayed fit long enough to start in all four Tests – Clive Williams, Peter Wheeler, Graham Price, Bill Beaumont, Jeff Squire, John O'Driscoll and Maurice Colclough, who was to repeat the feat in New Zealand three years later. He did so despite an accusation levelled at him more than 20 years later by the tour manager Willie John McBride that when it came to handling the 'rough stuff', he 'wasn't up to it at all'.

Rodney O'Donnell suffered the worst injury: a dislocated neck against the Junior Springboks that ended his career, after the Irish full-back had won a place in the first Test ahead of his Scottish rival, Bruce Hay. O'Donnell could safely lay claim to being the most superstitious Lion of all time, a point which he emphasised after being discharged from hospital in a neck brace: 'Wouldn't you know it,' he said. 'I get hurt tackling number 13, I was 13 days in hospital and this damn contraption has 13 holes in it . . .'

His superstitions extended far beyond not walking on any line in any pavement, anywhere in the world. Any combination of numbers could send him up the wall, as happened when he was allocated room 418 in the Lions' hotel in Johannesburg. 'I can't have this one,' he told Millar, the perplexed manager. 'The numbers add up to 13.'

That was nothing compared to the elaborate routine he insisted on going through before getting into bed. John Hopkins, who covered the tour for the *Sunday Times*, described it with commendable detail. 'First every picture in the room had to be straight, the telephone resting squarely on its cradle, the lights out, the bed covers turned back. Then he would charge at his bed like a high jumper, approaching it at a trot in a curving run.

'At the last minute he would leap backwards into the air, doing a Fosbury flop, and, if he had judged it correctly, he would land on the bed hitting the bottom sheet without first touching the top sheet or blanket. Once safely in bed, he thrashed his feet around half a dozen times, and once that was done he could go to sleep. If, however, anything went wrong, he had to start the whole procedure all over again.'

Beaumont approached bedtime in a more conventional manner, which was just as well otherwise a sizeable chunk of the tour profit might have gone on replacing broken springs. At twenty-eight, the captain of England and the Lions was in his prime and looking forward, not unreasonably, to three more years at the top, including a second tour in charge of the Lions, to New Zealand.

His long-term plan was to bow out after England's trip to South Africa in 1984. The gods decreed otherwise, and Beaumont would not be the first to appreciate the hazards of looking too far ahead. His great pal and fellow Lancastrian, Fran Cotton, had been forced to retire the month before Beaumont took a 'mighty whack' to the head during the Calcutta Cup match at Twickenham in February 1981.

He staggered on without quite being sure where he was, delegated responsibility and resumed normal duty for the rest of that Five Nations Championship. Beaumont thought nothing more of it until he took a worse blow in Béziers during a pre-season tour of France with Lancashire. This time he had to take a longer count and ended up in hospital to learn, for the first time, of the grim possibility of being disabled.

'The alarm bell began to ring,' he said. 'The symptoms were a bit worrying – slurred speech, a tingling sensation in my tongue, pins and needles. After the X-ray in France, the specialist there said I had the neck of a 60 year old. I was only 30. I knew there was a problem.

'I'd seen a neurologist earlier and once he had pieced it all together, he decided, "Enough is enough." I was experiencing symptoms I had never experienced before, including impaired vision, slurred speech, pins and needles, and a tingling tongue.'

He shrugged it off and carried on, celebrating his OBE in the New Year's honours by leading England out against Australia at Headquarters on 2 January 1982, a fixture which has gone down in Twickenham folklore as the Erica Roe match. When she did the streak to end all streaks, Beaumont was in the middle of the pitch trying to make himself understood to the increasingly distracted group of players who had been huddled around him.

Beaumont was in full flow, with Erica bouncing around the pitch in the background, when Peter Wheeler interrupted him. 'Billy, you're going to have to look at this,' he said. 'Some bird has run onto the pitch with your arse on her chest . . . !'

Back in the bosom of the team, so to speak, a fortnight later, England drew with Scotland at Murrayfield without anyone having the foggiest idea that their captain had played his last international. A week later, when Lancashire played against North Midlands in the County Championship final at Moseley, not even the captain realised that he had just played his last game of rugby.

Another blow to the head brought the old sickening sense back, and, for once, Beaumont for all his guts could not play his way through the concussion. This time something had to be done, and events moved swiftly. A series of neurological tests forced Beaumont to miss the home match against Ireland, much to his annoyance.

A further consultation with another neurologist, Dr Ray Lascelles, at Manchester Royal Infirmary, left him facing the stark truth. 'There was a risk that if I carried on playing I could end up paralysed and in a wheelchair for the rest of my life,' Beaumont said. 'There was no choice to be made. The Lions were going to New Zealand the following year and my big plan had been to try to be the first guy to captain them on two tours, but, once I realised there was a danger of brain damage if I continued, I had to retire. I had no option.'

Smith succeeded him as captain of England, not that the burden of shouldering responsibility for the national team had affected his irascible nature. When Beaumont rang to wish him well, the Sale scrum-half could not contain himself. 'Crikey, Bill, you shouldn't complain. After five hours of tests, the doctors have proved that you do have a tiny brain inside that big, dull head of yours. Who would have believed it? Mind you, having found a brain, you've gone and damaged it . . .'

If Beaumont had one regret, it was about how the players had fallen foul of the blazers and what he called 'the old feudal system'. Tens of thousands of spectators paid tens of thousands of pounds to see the players play, and yet the players 'lived in fear' of the officials and selectors. They wielded too much power so that any player who spoke his mind was liable to find himself excommunicated from the team.

The grandees of the game queued up to pay fulsome tribute to Beaumont. John Burgess, the late Lancashire and England coach, described him as the best thing to happen to the game for years, which did not prevent the Rugby Football Union from ostracising the ex-captain. His 'crime' was to keep the proceeds from a ghost-written autobiography.

Throughout his years on BBC television's popular *A Question of Sport* programme, Beaumont had been paid a fee of £2,100 for each series. Half the money had been donated to the RFU's charitable trust, the other half to his local club Fylde. The game had done very well, thank you, out of William Blackledge Beaumont, and, with a growing family, it was time to think that charity began at home.

His grandfather offered him some sound advice, posing the rhetorical question, 'If, ten years hence, your backside is hanging out of your trousers, would the RFU buy you a new pair?' It helped make up his mind to publish and be damned, even if it did mean breaching the archaic regulations on amateurism.

As Beaumont put it, 'From having been, in their eyes, the best thing since sliced bread when I was leading England, I was now a dirty professional who had demeaned himself by taking the money.'

He, along with many distinguished colleagues, remained in that preposterous state of limbo until the International Rugby Board, the sport's governing body, deigned to end the farce at their annual meeting in April 1989 and reinstate those whom it had cast out. Beaumont made his return as team manager of Fylde, and six years later he had joined the RFU in the newly created role of national member, a move which coincided with the sport going open.

The momentous decision, taken at the Ambassador Hotel in downtown Paris, opened a Pandora's box that threw the English game, in particular, into a state of near anarchy. The power struggle between the RFU and the club owners – a new breed of multi-millionaires, often with no rugby background – unleashed convulsions on a weekly basis.

The interminable squabbling had such a destabilising effect on the game that the most sacred of cows, the Five Nations Championship, was in some danger of disintegrating. Relationships between England and the Celtic countries, none too cordial at the best of times, almost ceased when the RFU broke ranks with the three other home Unions to negotiate its own television deal – a five-year contract for £87.5 million that included an almost 25 per cent slice for the major clubs in the hope that it would keep them on-side.

England had gone off on their own after their request for a larger cut of the television cake – based on the not unreasonable claim that they had more clubs to support than the other countries – had fallen on deaf ears. Some at Twickenham at that time wanted out of the Five Nations anyway, on the basis that England and France needed to be keeping more exalted company.

That they considered forming an alternative Five Nations with New Zealand, Australia and South Africa showed to what extent they had been blinded by their own arrogance, and the shameless disregard they had for the old tournament itself. Ireland, Scotland and Wales found themselves fighting for their very existence. In order to ensure their survival, they threatened to expel England unless they agreed to share their television money.

Despite that crisis being resolved by the RFU signing a ten-year accord with what was then the Five Nations, another larger crisis developed over television money in January 1999 when England were kicked out only weeks before they were due to open the championship against Scotland at Murrayfield. Diplomatic relations between the Celts and the English had broken down, and it took someone of Beaumont's stature to broker an 11th-hour reprieve.

It was done in time-honoured rugby fashion over a pint and a pie in a pub called The Drum and Monkey in Glasgow, a venue which only added to the stupidity of the whole charade. Allan Hosie, the former international referee whose insurance business was based in Glasgow, had donned the black cap to announce England's expulsion but had left a glimmer of hope by suggesting that he could perhaps avoid a doomsday scenario for all parties by talking to someone like Beaumont.

While some on the RFU committee proposed challenging the legality of the ban through the courts, the former captain duly shot straight up to Scotland in the company of RFU chairman Brian Baister, another voice of reason who had also worked tirelessly against the hawkish elements in the committee room. Beaumont restricted himself to a shandy, and the negotiations resulted in enough concessions being made on the money issues for Hosie to lift the ban, which was very sporting of him considering that the alternative would have been the destruction of the championship and very little money for anyone.

Whether England should have called their bluff and pushed their brinkmanship over the edge into the expensive hands of the lawyers is another matter entirely. Beaumont and Baister did the sport a great service, but, sadly, their intervention did little to improve English standing among the Five/Six Nations club. They repaid Beaumont by blackballing him from the chairmanship of the tournament, which, if nothing else, illustrated the depth of the antipathy towards England and that too many Celts held a grudge.

There can never have been a more ideal candidate for the chairmanship of the Six Nations than Beaumont. Even allowing for the old prejudices, his election in a contest against the very able and personable Frenchman Jacques Laurans ought to have been little more than a formality. Scotland and Ireland ganged up against the Englishman, which negated his support from Wales and enabled Laurans to come home at a canter.

For Beaumont, the vote felt 'like a stab in the back'. That the Irish delegates Syd Millar and Noel Murphy were men he had fought alongside in the trenches for the Lions made it all the harder to bear. They had been mandated by the Irish Union to vote for the French candidate. 'When I asked why they had voted against me, the explanation was simple,' Beaumont said. '"We trust you Bill, but we don't trust England." So, despite our friendship, I was guilty by association of a crime they clearly felt very strongly about. I was an Englishman.'

Another Dublin ambush lay round the corner. As one of the RFU's two delegates to the International Rugby Board, Beaumont had brought his considerable influence – or what was thought to be his considerable influence – to bear in support of England's bid to host the 2007 World Cup. They based the bid on a radical plan designed to give it more of a global dimension by including 36 countries instead of 20 and introducing a secondary level Rugby World Nations Cup to be run concurrently.

Of the 19 International Board votes at stake, excluding the RFU's two, they gained one – from Canada. Instead of standing on their own and insisting that every match be played in their country, the French promised Wales, Scotland and Ireland a pool each, which at least spared the Celts from having to support England, no matter how good their bid. Once all the horses had been traded, the margin of their defeat – 18–3 – added up to humiliation.

Not for the first time in his life, the manager of the 2007 Lions flew home with three words uppermost in his mind: funny old game . . .

10

THE WORLD-BEATING
WELSH REJECT

WALES HAVE NEVER BEEN AVERSE TO PICKING A FEW UNLIKELY LADS OVER THE YEARS
and wrapping them up in the famous red jersey without always
asking too many questions about ancestry. Had they delved into the
case of Brett Sinkinson, a central figure in the 'Grannygate' scandal,
they would have discovered that the New Zealander's grandfather, a
slaughterman, came from Oldham not Carmarthen.

Few prospective Welsh internationals would have sounded more
improbable than a young fellow from Yorkshire, who believed that
at any minute Everton Football Club would present him with the
chance of achieving the only ambition that mattered. And, on top
of all that, he was attending a Royal Navy school in Anglesey. For
that reason alone, Clive Woodward was perfectly entitled to play for
Wales as a schoolboy, just as Ryan Wilson (later Giggs), born in
Cardiff but brought up in Manchester, could represent England
schoolboys at football. As a ten-year-old boy whose imagination
had been fired by England's World Cup triumph over West
Germany at Wembley in 1966, Woodward wanted to be what Giggs
became.

Nobody will ever know whether he would have been good
enough. Woodward, sen., an RAF officer concerned lest his son's
obsession with soccer interfere with his education, transferred him
to HMS Conway, a naval school in north Wales, where the sporting

143

curriculum put the emphasis on rugby to the point where football was taboo.

Consequently, when recognition of his footballing prowess arrived, the call came not from Everton but from the selectors of Wales Schools. In 1974, they invited the 17-year-old Woodward to take part in a trial at the opposite end of the country where he would go head-to-head with Gareth Davies, a Welsh-speaker from the Gwendraeth Valley, who was destined to follow such local heroes as Carwyn James and Barry John.

Davies won the nod and went on to play for Wales at senior level, then the Lions. Woodward blazed the same trail in the white of England, but, 30 years later, he still felt that he had been victimised because of his nationality. A schools cap for Wales would not have prevented him playing for England at senior level – as Stuart Barnes showed years later – but in Woodward's case it might conceivably have changed the course of world rugby history.

Some thirty years ago, the tortuous journey by road from one end of Wales to the other took hours longer than it does today. 'The drive seemed to go on for days,' he said. 'I was in my last year at school in upper sixth, and one of the selectors drove me down. I'd been in isolation from the age of 13 at this ridiculous boarding school where they never sent boys to take part in trial matches. I had no way of knowing how good I was because I was playing in this crappy school in North Wales.'

The 'crappy school' has long gone, like their frustrated pupil's hopes of a Welsh cap, but, for a while at any rate, the teenage Woodward thought he might just succeed in spite of the system. All four half-backs involved in the final schools trial in Cardiff that day would go on to represent the Lions: Davies and Terry Holmes on one side, Woodward and Alun Lewis – 'quite a fat kid' from Caerphilly – on the other.

'I got there and people said, "Who's this kid?" I had raw, natural talent, and when I began to run the ball, I remember this kid Lewis saying, "What are you doing that for? This is a trial." The guy who brought me down said that not many boys from North Wales got picked and, as far as he knew, nobody who was English. They wouldn't pick me.'

He went back to Anglesey suspecting that his fate had been sealed not by the way he ran but by the way he spoke; it seemed that he had been discriminated against. 'The selectors were obviously impressed, and near the end of the day the head coach called me over. "You, Woodward. Where did you really learn to run and play like that?" he asked in a thick Welsh accent.

'"HMS Conway, sir, in Anglesey," I replied after a moment.

'"Yes, I know that. But Conway is a boarding school. Where are you really from, Woodward?"

'"From North Yorkshire, sir. Dad's in the air force there."

'"Are you English then?"

'"Yes, sir. Why? Is that a problem?"

'With that, he turned and marched straight back to the other selectors, leaving me quite perplexed as to what had just happened. This kind of not-so-subtle discrimination had been going on for years and was apparently accepted as part of the landscape. When I finally understood, I was truly shocked. What difference did it make where I was from? I could play rugby, I was qualified to play for the Welsh schoolboys because my school was in Wales. So what was the issue?

'Anyway, I got my own back playing for England Colts against Wales at Twickenham a year or so later. We hammered them 9–8!'

The next time he ran into Wales, again at Twickenham on 16 February 1980, it ended in the same score. A shameful match studded with gratuitous violence, far worse than the late tackle for which Paul Ringer got his marching orders, proved to be just another chapter in a saga of controversial matches against Wales that would take their rejected schoolboy from the heights of ecstasy to the pits of despair as player and coach.

As luck would have it, Woodward's arrival as an international centre coincided with England's long barren run ending in a Grand Slam. Tony Bond's wretched luck in breaking a leg one hour into the first match against Ireland at Twickenham allowed the new boy to make his bow as a substitute sooner than he could have hoped, less than a fortnight after his twenty-fourth birthday.

By the end of his first season after leaving Loughborough, he had achieved the double whammy of a Grand Slam and selection for the Lions tour of South Africa that summer. In those days when nothing seemed too much trouble, he soared into the Test team only to come back down to earth with more of a thud than a bump. Unlike Icarus, Woodward's crash came about not because the sun melted his wings but because he conceded a try on one wing in the pouring rain of Port Elizabeth on Saturday, 28 June 1980.

Unfortunately, it cost the Lions the third Test and with it the series, but, then, Woodward was never one to do things by halves.

The fateful moment followed a long diagonal punt from Naas Botha, which brought the Springboks some relief after having been under the cosh. However, it ought not to have given them the platform to win a match that, at that point, they were losing.

Woodward made two mistakes. He 'side-footed' the ball into touch in his own 25, then turned round to take up a defensive position never suspecting what would follow. Gerrie Germishuys, South Africa's left wing, and Theuns Stofberg, their flanker, seized the opportunity in a flash. As the rival packs trudged back for the lineout, Germishuys took a quick throw to Stofberg, who drew Woodward as the last line of defence, before putting his wing on a clear run to the corner. Botha added insult to injury by kicking the conversion. The South Africans praised Germishuys for his 'great presence of mind', although that was not exactly what was going through Bill Beaumont's mind as the skipper watched the series disappear down the plughole.

'I can remember it clearly,' Woodward said. 'Botha kicked the ball over my head . . . I had no option but to kick it out. I just tapped it out instead of booting it over the stand. I turned my back. They scored and we lost 12–10. It had been a wonderful year, way beyond my wildest dreams, but I was gutted by that one error. I got dropped to the bench, which I was fuming about. All the players were saying there was no way I should have been dropped.'

With time to recover and resume their dominance, the Lions should still have won the Test and prevented the series from being decided, in the words of John Hopkins covering the tour for the *Sunday Times*, by a try 'executed with the speed of a cat burglar'. Lions coach Noel Murphy likened it to 'a bad dream', a sentiment with which Morné du Plessis concurred. The Springbok captain's verdict that 'the better team lost' was of no consolation to the Lions and, in particular, their right wing.

Beaumont knew Woodward the player, warts and all, and that he could be 'a bit of a drifter', which was the skipper's euphemistic way of saying that he was prone to the odd lapse of concentration. 'He was a real maverick who could win a game or just as easily lose it, depending on whether or not the ploy he attempted was successful,' Beaumont said. 'He always wanted the ball. The only problem was that you were never too sure what he was going to do with it. Sometimes you would want to hug the guy and then, the next minute, to kick his backside.'

For the record, Beaumont did not give him a hug that day at the

Boet Erasmus Stadium for 'slipping into drift-mode', at least not that anyone noticed. For all that, Woodward had made his mark on the tour and a lasting impression off it, with his new Celtic friends, as an all-round good bloke. He and Gravell made an odd couple: an erudite, elegant Englishman joining forces with a self-proclaimed Welsh nationalist from Mynydd-y-Garreg, his native 'Rocky Mountain' in west Wales.

Gravell looked like a latter-day Owain Glyndwr in size-ten boots, and there were times when the opposition could have been forgiven for thinking that he was the reincarnation of the Welsh chief, born in the fourteenth century, who conducted guerrilla warfare against the English invaders. If 'Grav' could give a nasty-looking French forward more than a playful punch in the shoulder as they lined up in the tunnel at the Parc des Princes before his debut there in 1975, imagine what he was capable of doing to an Englishman.

Peter Wheeler, the England hooker who had been made responsible for the rooming list and the pairing off of the Lions two by two, put Gravell and Woodward together; it was no more than was to be expected from someone with such a mischievous sense of humour. Almost a quarter of a century later, when Gravell introduced his wife Marie to his old English friend in Brisbane during the 2003 World Cup, Woodward told her, 'I roomed with this man – and survived!'

Gravell, a broadcaster-cum-actor whose c.v. includes being cast by Louis Malle for the legendary director's film *Damage* starring Jeremy Irons and Miranda Richardson, has kept in constant touch since the tour. 'Clive is a gentleman, very laid back, or at least that was the impression he gave me in South Africa all those years ago,' Gravell said. 'I'd be bouncing around the room half-mad, and I'm sure he thought I was nuts. He'd laugh, but there were never any problems. No bickering, no quarrelling, just a genuine friendship. I called him "Woody" long before everyone else did, and when they moved him to the wing I'd say, "Woody, I've seen better wings on a blackbird."

'He'd come straight back at me, "And I've seen better centres in a box of chocolates."

'We hit it off from the start, even though we came from different backgrounds. I am a Welsh patriot, unashamedly so. I'm not a separatist, but I am a strong believer in maintaining and supporting our own identity. Clive and the rest of the English boys on that tour respected the fact that I was proud of my language, and that's the great thing about the Lions: four different nations putting any historical or political differences aside and fighting for the same cause.'

Tony Ward, the mercurial Irish fly-half whose goal kicking almost won the opening Test, after he had become one of the earlier replacements during a tour plagued by serious injury, found Woodward a 'kindred spirit'. 'When the game was broken and loose he'd do anything, and that's what appealed to me about him. A lot was made of that incident in the rain at Port Elizabeth, and I suppose, looking back, it was amateurism at its best.'

Astonishingly, for someone who was third-choice goal kicker for his club – behind Dusty Hare and Paul Dodge – Woodward topped the points chart from the second match until the penultimate Saturday. Ollie Campbell, the Irish fly-half who eventually overtook him, said, '[Woodward was] a natural kicker with such a lovely, smooth style. Even when he miskicked, the ball was always very close to the target. I couldn't believe he was so far down the list of kickers at Leicester.'

With typical modesty, Campbell forgot to mention that he had gone out of his way to offer a few tips aimed at improving Woodward's technique. It may sound rustic by Jonny Wilkinson's standards, but his Irish colleague taught him that kicking was all about getting the run-up correct. Woodward also pre-empted Wilkinson with his habit of talking to the ball once he had reached the address position (four steps back and one to the side), something that was unusual in 1980.

By no stretch of the imagination did any of his Celtic friends imagine then that they were rubbing shoulders with a visionary who would win the World Cup one day, not least because the World Cup did not exist until 1987. Neither Gravell nor Ward, who almost drowned when the vicious currents of the Indian Ocean swept him out to sea off Umhlanga Rocks near Durban, noticed any blinding shafts of insight from Woodward the strategist.

The signs were there at the time, even if they were, perhaps, imperceptible. However, his strategical nuance was later clearly illuminated by the shining light of his seven years as England's head coach. In hindsight, Woodward saw a lack of preparation as a key factor in the Lions' failure. It was an observation of an amateur past from a professional present and not intended as a criticism of the all-Ireland management-coaching team of Syd Millar and Noel Murphy. He felt that they failed to tap into the expertise readily available from the interested spectator and much-admired Leicester coach Chalkie White.

'I think they made a huge mistake,' he said. 'We had Syd as manager, Noel as the coach and that was it. On that trip we had an awesome pack of forwards, but I think we also had an awesome back division. All the coaching was done with the forwards. There was no coaching of the backs, and yet Chalkie White was sitting in the stand watching every session.

'I kept saying, "This is the guy we need. Why don't we ask him to get involved?" We had a better back division than the Springboks, but instead of being coached we were left largely to our own devices. Chalkie was never asked to help or even consulted, which was ridiculous. A coach looking after the backs would have made a significant difference to the end result.

'I had three key mentors as a player: Earl Kirton, who coached me at a young age at Harlequins; Jim Greenwood, who did the same during my four years at Loughborough; and Chalkie. When it came to back play, none of the coaches involved with the Lions, in my time, were anywhere near the standard of those guys.'

What Gravell admired most about Woodward was his ability to laugh at himself, not that he had much option after the Wales v. England match at Cardiff Arms Park in January 1981, when Wales scraped a fortuitous win because England's Leicester centre gave away a late penalty in front of the posts. Woodward fell for one of the oldest tricks in the book: the dummy pass from the base of the scrum, as perfected by Brynmor Williams and subsequently outlawed by the IRB.

Gravell said, 'It takes a big man to tell a story against himself, and he told me in great detail what happened to him when he went back to work in England on the Monday morning.' By then Woodward had been promoted to sales manager of Rank Xerox, and his working week started with a major piece of business to be done in Derby with Rolls-Royce, one of his company's biggest clients.

'Woody goes in with his team and one of them says to the security guard, "Did you see the big match on Saturday?" The guard didn't recognise Clive so he says, "Too right I did. What about that prat Woodward? And the sales guy says, "I know. What a pillock!"'

That match, he conceded years later, was the beginning of the end of Woodward the international player. His career gradually declined over the next three years, before his final exit from Twickenham as a player on St Patrick's Day, 1984. By then, he had still been considered good enough for a second Lions tour. However, New Zealand in 1983 was everything that South Africa three years earlier wasn't. For Woodward it was a 'bit of a nightmare'.

With typical candour, he confesses that his selection was a mistake and that it all went rapidly downhill from there. 'Being brutally honest, I shouldn't have been on the trip,' Woodward said. 'I was picked on reputation, and that was wrong. I was nowhere near my best. I didn't play for England at all that season because of an operation on my shoulder, except for the last game against Ireland, and I didn't think I played very well that day.

'The four centres on the tour were myself, [Robert] Ackerman and the two Irish guys [David Irwin and Michael Kiernan]. With due respect to all of us, we were not the most talented four centres ever sent on a Lions tour. I went out and tried my hardest. They were looking to me, but I just could not perform at my best.'

Needless to say, he failed to make the team for any of the four Tests. Judging by what Willie John McBride had to say more than 20 years later, he made roughly the same impression on the manager as he had on the Test team. In the freemasonry of rugby, and more especially Lions rugby, no legendary figure can have made a more pointed attack on an individual player. In blasting a hole through the Mafia-style *omertà* that decrees that what goes on tour, stays on tour, McBride gave his out-of-sorts English centre both barrels. 'Clive Woodward didn't count,' he said. 'He never contested a place for the Test side and really, in many ways, didn't want to know about the tough stuff. Yet he had been on the previous Lions tour and should have been one of the key guys on tour. However, he wasn't near the Test team at any stage because he seemed disinterested and played as though he was. Why? That's Clive.

'Of course, Clive has been an extremely successful English manager with the intelligence to know that his success is based on having a strong team around him. As he said when he was approached about coaching the 2005 Lions in New Zealand, he would want to take his back-up team with him: key men like Andy Robinson and Phil Larder.

'Clive has successfully convinced the RFU to pour millions of pounds into the senior squad, and by winning the World Cup he has proved he was right, but, unfortunately, none of the other home unions can afford to put that sort of money into their national sides.' Not much more than faint praise there for an achievement unique in European terms.

Woodward accused McBride of breaking a golden rule, before going on to suggest that the Ulsterman had been somewhat less than the perfect manager. 'When you are in a privileged position, as he was, it is wrong to criticise players publicly, for whatever reason. I know things about players during my seven years with England which I would never, ever divulge. I would never write anything negative about any player. You are not there as a manager or a coach to make money out of selling books.

'He was probably referring to the couple of occasions when I had to see him for the antics we got up to. Maybe he hasn't forgotten that. I remember going out a few times with two or three colleagues and getting back late. I won't name my colleagues. You never know, it might get me into trouble with the management!

'There was no one on that '83 trip to look after the backs. You question why Willie didn't have anyone there to help the back division. Instead, he was standing on the touchline smoking a pipe making critical comments about a situation which, with any vision or foresight, he could have possibly fixed.

'Instead, he seemed neurotic about the media, which was something I never understood. It was all very negative, and it made for an incredibly negative trip. Willie just seemed to want to circle the wagons and shout 99 [the famous emergency call invented by McBride's 1974 Lions as the signal for everyone to get stuck in, ideally into the nearest opponent].'

Off the pitch, it wasn't exactly a bundle of laughs, either. New Zealand's obsession with rugby and their intolerance of losing British teams can make an escape from the subject very difficult, and few British teams lost as consistently as the 1983 vintage, black-washed from the top of the North Island to the bottom of the South.

'In South Africa they wanted to beat you, but you got the impression that they were genuinely pleased you were there. When I went to New Zealand you felt the hostility. You'd go into bars late at night, and you felt as though someone was going to fight you, whereas in South Africa they wanted to buy you a beer and put their arm around you. In New Zealand they wanted to beat you on the pitch, and they also wanted to beat you off the pitch. It got very heavy at times. There were times when you had to look out for yourself.'

By then, Woodward's international days were numbered. As a player, he took his leave of Twickenham for the last time nine months later in depressingly familiar fashion, retreating to the sanctuary of the dressing-room from the scene of another defeat by Wales, when England managed nothing more thrilling than five Dusty Hare penalties. It also marked the end of the road for two more Tigers: Peter Wheeler and Nick Youngs.

Woodward took off for Sydney, returning five years later to work his way up the coaching ladder via Henley, London Irish and Bath until England used a bit of uncharacteristic lateral thinking to make him their first full-time coach. Ian McGeechan had originally been offered the position and had wrestled with his conscience before deciding against taking the post on the basis that as a Scot, albeit of the Anglo variety, he couldn't quite come to terms with coaching the Sassenachs.

Woodward started without an office to call his own and finished seven years later at the head of an empire. Nobody wins the World Cup without a bit of luck and Woodward's guaranteed him a second tilt at history, after the 1999 tournament had ended in Jannie de Beer's fusillade of five drop goals for South Africa during the quarter-final in Paris. Had someone been screaming out for the job it might have been very different, but the absence of a credible alternative persuaded the power-brokers at the RFU to stick with him through to 2003.

There was a good deal of anguish along the way to the World Cup victory. For a while, the perennial failure to close out a Grand Slam raised serious reservations about Woodward's ability to win the matches that really mattered, like the game against Wales at Wembley in April 1999 when Lawrence Dallaglio instructed Wilkinson to kick to the corner and set up the platform for a try rather than go for goal. Three more points would have guaranteed English immunity from the Scott Gibbs extravaganza, which gave the old tournament an unforgettable finale in the last minute of the last match before the Five Nations became the Six.

Losing one Grand Slam decider was careless but two more in the next three seasons – against Scotland at Murrayfield in April 2000, where, inexplicably, they kept trying to run the ball during a second-half tempest, and against Ireland at Lansdowne Road in October 2001 – demanded some very severe soul-searching. Significantly, Martin Johnson had been absent due to injury on both occasions.

Other events during 2001 had already tested Woodward's self-belief to the limit before the latest Grand Slam debacle. Despite England's outstanding form that season, the Lions snubbed him so

TOP LEFT: Carl Aarvold in classical pose, cutting a swathe through the New Zealand defences during the 1930 Lions tour.

TOP RIGHT: Aarvold the defender during one of his finest internationals, going low to bring down France wing Adolphe Jauréguy at Stade Colombes in April 1929. Aarvold scored two of England's four tries in a 16–6 win.

ABOVE: Two English captains of the Lions immediately before the final Test at Wellington in August 1930. Carl Aarvold, extreme right, had taken over from Leicester lock Doug Prentice, extreme left, as the acting tour captain.

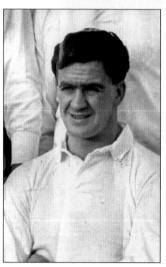

TOP: Brian Black, a South African Rhodes Scholar who played for Blackheath and England, challenges Hugh McLean, the All Black in the all-white, during the Wellington Test in 1930. A pilot officer during the Second World War, Black was killed on active service in 1940.

ABOVE LEFT: Jeff Butterfield of Northampton, Yorkshire, England and the Lions – a master centre likened in those Twickenham winters of long ago to 'a lightning flash across a sombre sky'.

ABOVE RIGHT: Lions sunning themselves at Eastbourne in May 1959 before leaving for New Zealand. Clockwise from front left: Bev Risman, Jeff Butterfield, the guitar-strumming Alan Ashcroft, Ronnie Dawson, Peter Jackson and, with the shades, Haydn Morgan.

TOP LEFT: 'Nijinsky', aka Peter Jackson, who scored more tries for the Lions than any other English player despite making only one tour. His wonderful collection of scores for Old Edwardians, Coventry, Warwickshire, England and the Lions included a match-winning masterpiece against Australia at Twickenham in February 1958.

TOP RIGHT: England on the day that they made history, at Twickenham on 20 December 1969, by beating South Africa for the first time. Back row (from left): K. Kelleher (referee), R. F. Johnson (touch judge), David Duckham, Peter Hale, Bryan West, Peter Larter, Keith Fairbrother, Tony Bucknall, 'Stack' Stevens, Ian Shackleton, Nigel Starmer-Smith, Mike Titcomb (touch judge). Front (from left): John Spencer, John Pullin, Bob Hiller (Capt.), Mike Davis, Keith Fielding, Bob Taylor.

ABOVE: Another historic moment at Eden Park, September 1973. Captain John Pullin is mobbed after his country's first Test win in New Zealand. (Photo courtesy of the *Auckland Star*)

TOP LEFT: John Pullin, scourge of the All Blacks for England and the Lions, with a furry friend on his farm beside the Severn at the height of his career in the early '70s.

TOP RIGHT: Some of the greats taking it easy on the beach in Durban, July 1974, during the most memorable Lions tour of all. From left: Gordon Brown, Phil Bennett, Bobby Windsor, Mike Burton, Gareth Edwards, Fergus Slatter, J. J. Williams and, in the foreground, J. P. R. Williams.

ABOVE: Clive Woodward making a break for Manly in what must have been an explosive Sydney club match, judging by the initials on the ball. He spent four years there in the mid-'80s, which was long enough for him to be invited to join the Australian squad by their then coach, Alan Jones.

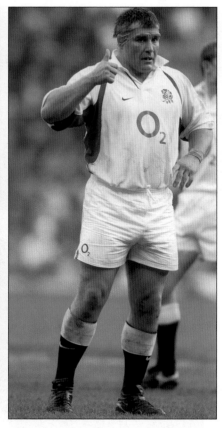

TOP LEFT: Jeremy Guscott, a Lions match winner in Australia in 1989 and again in South Africa eight years later, going through the gears during England's 34–20 win against Scotland at Murrayfield in March 1998. Neil Back, another outstanding English Lion, watches him go. (Photo courtesy of the *Daily Mail*)

ABOVE LEFT: Jason Robinson's magical try on his Lions Test debut, against Australia at The Gabba in Brisbane, June 2001. Chris Latham, one of the best full-backs in the world, is left snatching at thin air as Billy Whizz manages to stay just inside the touchline. (Photo courtesy of the *Mail on Sunday*)

TOP RIGHT: The most reassuring sight for England and the Lions in any tight corner anywhere in the world – a thumb's up from Jason Leonard during his 101st international, which was against Scotland at Twickenham in March 2003. Before retiring, he pushed the world record for the most caps to 114. (Photo courtesy of the *Daily Mail*)

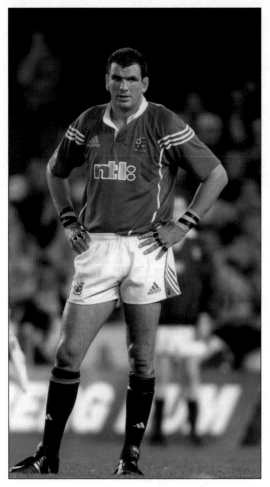

TOP LEFT: A rare sight: four English captains, all outstanding Lions at various times, enter the arena against Italy in Rome, April 2002. From left: Matt Dawson, Jason Leonard, Lawrence Dallaglio, Martin Johnson. (Photo courtesy of the *Daily Mail*)

TOP RIGHT: Matt Dawson, one of the rare English breed to have gone on three Lions tours, takes on the Australian back-row hunters George Smith and Phil Waugh during the World Cup final. (Photo courtesy of Andy Hooper at the *Daily Mail*)

LEFT: For once in his life, Martin Johnson can only stand and stare as the opposition notch up the points during the fateful second Test against Australia in July 2001. (Photo courtesy of the *Daily Mail*)

TOP LEFT: Martin Johnson, back in Australia two years after captaining the losing Lions series against the Wallabies, relishes the supreme moment in English rugby history. (Photo courtesy of Andy Hooper at the *Daily Mail*)

TOP RIGHT: A master of his craft at work during the World Cup final. Lifters Richard Hill (left) and Trevor Woodman help Johnson to reach the ball just a few inches above the highest Australian jumper. (Photo courtesy of Andy Hooper at the *Daily Mail*)

ABOVE: Lawrence Dallaglio, a winning Lion against South Africa in 1997, on the podium in Sydney. Alongside him are Trevor Woodman and Jason Robinson. (Photo courtesy of Andy Hooper at the *Daily Mail*)

BRITISH ISLES RUGBY UNION TOUR
SOUTH AFRICA 1968

TOP: Brian Moore, aka the 'Pit Bull', in full, snarling flow during England's Grand Slam clincher against Wales at Twickenham on 7 March 1992. A Lions' Test winner in Australia three years earlier, he replaced Kenny Milne of Scotland in the 1993 series in New Zealand and retired after the World Cup two years later. (Photo courtesy of the *Mail on Sunday*)

ABOVE: The 1968 Lions outside their hotel in Cape Town featuring a young Willie John McBride and an even younger Gareth Edwards.

completely that there had to be more to it than met the eye: of course, there was. In their wisdom, the Lions committee chose Graham Henry, an outsider, after deciding that no British or Irish coach was up to running the show; Woodward was not even considered worthy of an interview.

Donal Lenihan, the tour manager, and Woodward were old adversaries. The baggage built up between them over the years would probably have been heavy enough to bring one of the carousels at Heathrow airport to a standstill. The 'animosity' – a word the Englishman has used to refer to their relationship – went back to a few clashes during the volatile immediate post-professionalism period when Woodward was coaching London Irish and Lenihan managing the Ireland squad. The row was about the Premiership club signing two of that squad: Conor O'Shea and Gabriel Fulcher. The fallout from that conflict increased Woodward's suspicion that he had effectively been blackballed by the Lions, although, during the period that led to Henry's selection, there had been some ambiguity over Woodward's job description with the RFU, which had briefly changed from coach to manager.

The lack of an approach, however perfunctory, still rankles. 'It annoys me intensely. I was coaching the number one team, and we were on a massive roll. You'd have expected a phone call at the very least. That goes back to the history between me and Lenihan. In the early days of professionalism we [London Irish] were targeting players from Ireland, and he was getting pretty stroppy about it.

'I was public enemy number one. London Irish didn't get on that well with the Irish Rugby Union anyway, and having an English coach in charge of the club provided the cocktail for a lot of heated discussion. It was a complete reversal of my later role with England. Donal would ring me and say they were holding a training session the next day and he'd need the international players so you had to get pretty aggressive. He was doing his job, I was doing mine.'

Woodward was in Johannesburg halfway through England's drawn series against the Springboks in June 2000 when news reached him that Henry had got the Lions job. 'I was livid,' he said. 'I have nothing against Graham. I like him a lot, in a way, but a British or Irish person should have been in charge. I'm not saying I should have been given the job, but I'd like to have been interviewed. Graham Henry learnt a huge amount from that trip. To give him that experience and the job he's got now . . .'

A trip of unrelenting intensity bordered at times on the mutinous, never more so than when Matt Dawson turned his tour 'diary' into a full-frontal attack on the Lions management. With a sense of timing that was unfortunate, to put it politely, Dawson's thoughts were published in the *Daily Telegraph* on the day of the first Test. Within hours of the paper hitting the streets, the Lions had outclassed the Wallabies to win by a street, which made the thoughts of their reserve scrum-half appear infinitely more unfortunate. After spending the night playing second fiddle to the untouchable Rob Howley, Dawson had to face the music.

He escaped with a reported fine of £5,000 and got off lightly. The Lions management considered sending him home for what they, understandably, regarded as a clear case of disloyalty. Woodward, who followed the tour as a television pundit, was adamant about the course of action he would have taken had he been in charge.

'I would have sent him home,' he said, 'and I've told him that, too. What Dawson did was totally out of order. When it happened, I phoned Graham Henry and gave him my full support. England had clear rules to cover this sort of thing. The Lions didn't. They were all doing their own thing on the tour with Henry writing a book.

'Graham wasn't used to working with several coaches. One coach wanted 45 minutes with the players, the next coach wanted the same time, and suddenly you had a three-hour session. The coaches felt good, but the players were in bits. The Lions in Australia made so many mistakes off the field, and they lost to a pretty poor Australian team.'

Dawson wasn't the only dissenting voice to air his grievances in public when he ought to have bitten his tongue until after the tour. While Dawson spouted forth before the series began, Austin Healey had waded in just before the end with an epistle for *The Guardian* ghosted by the former Wales captain turned journalist, Eddie Butler. Whether he gave it the Shane Warne treatment with a bit of Muttiah Muralitharan chucked in for good measure is another issue, but the Lions management had only themselves to blame when the column boomeranged back onto the front page of the *Sydney Morning Herald*. It had slipped clean through their vetting system.

Henry was aghast at the motivational ammunition that came, free of charge, with Healey's description of Justin Harrison as 'a plank'. By the end of that fateful day, the 'plank' had become a national hero, stealing Keith Wood's throw to Martin Johnson at the front of a lineout that was close enough for the Lions to have mauled their way over. A try would have given Jonny Wilkinson an attempt at a conversion to win the series. Healey had just done for the really interesting player-column what Colonel Sanders did for the Kentucky chicken.

'They [Dawson and Healey] were both wrong in what they did,' said Woodward. 'It was a fundamentally unhappy trip and that tends to be reflected by what happens on the pitch. The Test matches were awesome, and the atmosphere at the second one in Melbourne, with the roof shut, was the best I have ever experienced. But that was probably the weakest Australian team I had seen for six years. I recall being in Brisbane after the first Test, and I was in the hotel gym when the Wallabies came in to do their recovery session. I kept out of their way, but I can see them now. They looked a beaten team, and I remember thinking, "There's no way back."'

Well, they found one. More to the point, the Lions found one for them when they gifted Joe Roff an interception from a Jonny Wilkinson pass, during the second Test in Melbourne. It turned a stupendous series on its head and allowed an Australian team nowhere near as good as the World Cup-winning one of two years earlier to get off the ropes in a classic example of what W. C. Fields meant when he entitled his famous film *Never Give a Sucker an Even Break*.

Within two months of the resumption of the new European season, England had contrived to lose another Grand Slam in a match postponed from the previous March because of the foot-and-mouth epidemic. The before and after quotes offered a classic example of Woodward at his contradictory best. On the Friday he had been at pains to spell out why the match was more important than the following month's skirmishes with Australia and South Africa, saying, 'we are playing for the Grand Slam and Grand Slam teams go down in history'. Keith Wood's famous try did for them at Lansdowne Road, a failure that shook Woodward more than any other, even if his pre-match view had shifted to put the result in a softer perspective: 'So we've lost one game in fourteen? Big deal!'

In hindsight, he blamed the Lions and the demoralising effects the tour had on a few of his players: 'I reckon it took us over 12 months to recover from that Lions trip and get everyone back on track. The tour impacted hugely on England. Iain Balshaw went backwards as a result of it. Ben Cohen went backwards. Quite a few others went backwards, too.'

Woodward and his 'accident investigators' had had no shortage of practice in analysing England's shortcomings, but they came up with an answer to the problems and put England on their unstoppable road to the World Cup in Sydney two years and one month later. Woodward had always put the emphasis on entertainment and style, doing so with a panache that changed the face of English rugby, ridding it of its stodgy old conservatism and replacing it with a sense of adventure.

The desire to please produced a naivety that certainly accounted for two of the lost Grand Slams, and the penny took a long time to drop. It took his lieutenants a long time to convince him, but, after the loss in Dublin, Woodward put pragmatism above everything else for the first time since his appointment in September 1997. His country, without a major sporting success since the football World Cup of 1966, responded in vast numbers to his success at the rugby equivalent by bringing central London to a standstill, and his Queen rewarded him with a knighthood.

The boy whose parents sent him to a rugby-playing school in north Wales to cure him of his obsession with soccer had made history in a way he never intended. His schoolboy heroes were largely footballers renowned for their lavish skills and a penchant to enjoy life to the full off the pitch. 'All my idols in those days were footballers,' Woodward said. 'Real characters like Stan Bowles, Tony Currie, Frank Worthington. I liked that lot, and it was because I loved football that I was sent off to school in Wales.'

In a sense, Woodward had gone one better than the only other English footballing knight to have won a World Cup. Whereas Sir Alf Ramsey had the good fortune to win it in the summer of 1966 without having to go further afield than Wembley, England's rugby team won it in grand manner, beating the holders Australia in Sydney, at the end of a long night that, for sheer drama, outstripped anything produced during the four previous Rugby World Cup finals.

The southern-hemisphere monopoly of the Webb Ellis Trophy had been broken in the southern hemisphere. It would all have been comparatively routine if only Ben Kay hadn't fumbled Matt Dawson's pass when all it required was a stride or two and a flop over the line. A try at that point of the match and England would surely have won comfortably enough in normal time, without Elton Flatley dragging Australia level with two penalties that surely stand supreme as the greatest pressure kicks of all. They enabled the Wallabies to take the prolonged final to the last 29 seconds of extra time before Jonny Wilkinson's drop goal rescued not just England but the tournament from being plunged into the farce of a drop-goal competition. For Woodward it was as if all those cruel Grand Slam twists had merely been a means of testing his resolve and belief that he really did have the organisational flair to create the chain of command that would destroy every Antipodean notion of the stereotyped English player.

Along the way, Woodward had changed the face of English rugby by changing its attitude. He made mistakes because he wasn't afraid to make them, which meant doing all those un-English things like picking young players. Eventually, he found the perfect balance between style and substance, and if, in the earlier days, there was too much of one and not enough of the other, he got it right when it mattered most. By then, he could trust Martin Johnson, Lawrence Dallaglio, Wilkinson and many more to show the world how they had transformed the image of English sport from jolly good losers into hard-nosed winners.

Woodward immediately vowed to win the World Cup a second time and challenged his players not to retire, only to find that some would follow the peerless Johnson's lead in getting out at the top. Three severe Test beatings in Australasia during June 2004 left no doubt as to the enormity of the reconstruction work, and by the following September the head coach and Johnson's replacement as captain had quit within 48 hours of each other. In August, Dallaglio went to Woodward's home in Devon to tell him of his decision, only to learn that he was not the only one who had made up his mind to quit. Dallaglio confirmed his resignation as captain from a first-floor banqueting suite at Twickenham on the first Tuesday of September, and by the Friday of that week Woodward had given his reasons for doing likewise as head coach from the same venue.

He blamed the Premiership clubs for refusing to release their England players for more training days, but his abrupt departure – facilitated by an escape clause in his four-year contract – raised another question. After more than a few wheels had fallen off the World Cup chariot, might it not have been a case of realising the full extent of the rebuilding operation?

Despite retiring from the England set-up, he still had a significant part to play in the story of Lions rugby. With a delicious sense of irony, it left him with one last adventure in the sport: leading the Lions into a battle of wits against the New Zealander who had preceded him. Graham Henry knew only too well, from personal experience, that a Lions tour is an unforgiving arena for a losing head coach and that history tends to pass a harsh judgement. Precisely how unforgiving, Woodward would find out all too soon.

There had never been much love lost between them. The aforementioned bad blood between Woodward and Lenihan conspired to leave the coast clear for Henry to take charge of an outstanding Lions squad in 2001, featuring many England players who within the next two years would prove themselves second to none the world over.

A harsh training regime at the end of an unrelenting domestic and European season made for an unhappy tour, something that Woodward frequently referred to when spelling out how he would right the wrongs that he believed his *bête noire* had made in Australia. While Henry's lot finished up as the most fatigued Lions of all time, Woodward planned the 2005 Lions on a scale grand enough to ensure that none of them would be overworked.

The best of British and Irish deserved nothing but the best, which meant taking 45 players and no more doubling up two to a room. Every player would have a room to himself and every comfort provided, not least in the shape of a specialist management team of 30 and a chartered 737 put at their disposal for all internal flights in New Zealand.

The whole operation cost between £7 million and £10 million, a touchy subject with the Lions committee at the outset and one which became touchier still when it emerged that they had presided over arguably the most expensive failure of any Lions team. An expedition which started with a last-minute draw in Cardiff against a scratch Argentinian team deteriorated all too rapidly into a 3–0 rout by the All Blacks.

Under Brian O'Driscoll's captaincy, the team was, as Woodward constantly reminded everyone, 'the best prepared in Lions' history'. If this was true, it invited speculation as to how much worse they would have fared had they not been quite so well prepared. That they had too many players and not enough matches before the Tests in which to do them all justice was only one part of a flawed concept.

Woodward's policy of trying to turn the clock back almost two years to recreate what he had achieved at the World Cup meant compromising his basic principle of always picking on form, never on reputation. By the time he saw the light and made wholesale changes in a forlorn attempt to repair the damage, it was too late. The All Blacks, 21–3 winners in a polar storm in Christchurch in the first Test, had completed the clean sweep in Auckland a fortnight later by winning the third and final Test 38–19, despite being some way below par.

The Lions produced their best for the second Test in Wellington only to suffer their worst beating of the series, 48–18. They lost, not by a street, but by a gulf – an aggregate margin of 67 points over the three matches. For every Lions try, the All Blacks scored four and a try-count of 12–3 could easily have been worse. Remembering how his Lions had lost to the last throw of the last Test in Sydney, and how the subsequent abuse had forced him to give up his job with Wales, Henry made enough capital out of the try-count to enjoy the last laugh. 'The 2001 tour was a blessing for me,' he said. 'I thank the people for the ribbing because it pushed me back to New Zealand quicker than I intended. The Lions' series in Australia finished at seven tries each. I'll repeat that – seven tries each and some great rugby. I don't know what the try-count was in this series. I've lost count . . .'

Woodward's last great hurrah, before leaving rugby for football, turned out to be one calamity after another, starting with Lawrence Dallaglio's dislocated ankle in the opening quarter of the opening match and ending with a Test record that, judged on simple statistics, made it the worst ever Lions tour of New Zealand. The man who won the World Cup will always hold an exalted place in British sport, but a finishing sequence of seven straight Test defeats between June 2004 and July 2005, including five against New Zealand (the first two with England), did nothing for his reputation.

Nor did his decision to hire Alastair Campbell, whom the All Black management accused of 'spin doctoring'. Hired as a 'media consultant', Prime Minister Tony Blair's former director of communication gave a team-talk to the Lions squad during the build-up to the Wellington Test immediately before Woodward announced the team. Regrettably, the 2005 Lions will be remembered for too much spin and not enough substance. A verdict of misadventure on a grand scale.

11

STUFFED BOOTS
AND BURGERS

FOR 20 YEARS, JIM TELFER KEPT HIS OWN COUNSEL ON ONE OF THE MOST contentious selection issues of any Lions tour – the appointment of Ireland hooker Ciaran Fitzgerald as captain for the 1983 series in New Zealand and the omission of Peter Wheeler, his English counterpart. Telfer had suffered along with the rest of the foot-soldiers in 1966 when selection blunders pushed the Lions off down the slippery slope to an All Black whitewash. Alun Pask, the accomplished Wales number 8 from Abertillery, had been so widely touted for the captaincy that his choice had been considered by many to be little more than a formality. This was especially the case, as the Scottish captain, Mike Campbell-Lamerton, scarcely met the single most important criterion of any Lions skipper – that he had to be good enough to command a Test place strictly on merit.

The selectors, in their infinite wisdom, chose the Scottish army officer, a decision which was bound to end in tears. The first Test, a comprehensive 20–3 beating at Carisbrook Park in Dunedin, proved one too many for Campbell-Lamerton. 'I'd rather die than go through such an experience again,' he told the illustrious New Zealand journalist Terry McLean, who reported that the captain 'spilled tears when he reached the dressing-room, so deep was his mortification'.

The Lions turned to a Welshman from Gwent to replace

Campbell-Lamerton: not Pask but David Watkins. The Newport stand-off had no idea why the selectors wanted a quiet word with him on the touchline of the training pitch. 'My first reaction,' Watkins recalled, 'was, "oh, shit." Does this mean I'm out of the Test side?' He continued, 'They told me that Mike Campbell-Lamerton was standing down and that they wanted me to captain the team. Mike said, "You are the life and soul of the team and the right man for the job."'

The 1983 Lions did not have to change their captain, but there were enough parallels to evoke ominous memories for Telfer. As in 1966, alarm bells rang over the choice of the 30-man squad, and this time Telfer, no longer one of the troops slogging it out at the front, had been put in charge of the whole shooting match as the honorary assistant manager and coach.

The 2005 Lions went to New Zealand armed with as many coaches as an Inter-City 125. As head coach, Sir Clive Woodward surrounded himself with six coaches, plus two fitness coaches and one kicking coach. Telfer did it all on his own – hard enough when the going is good, impossible when it is not. By the end of the tour, history had repeated itself in the depressing form of another whitewash.

The granite Scot, who might have been chiselled out of the Cheviot Hills where his father served as a shepherd, took it on the chin with typical stoicism, refused to complain and put it down to experience. Winding down towards retirement 20 years later, he decided that enough time had elapsed to break his long silence. In part-confessional mode, he tackled the taboo subject with characteristic candour in response to being asked about any regrets during the course of an international career that spanned five decades to encompass four Lions tours, one Grand Slam, one World Cup semi-final and the most recent of Scotland's Five Nations titles in 1999, courtesy of English extravagance against Wales at Wembley.

'Oh yes, there are some regrets,' he said before identifying the biggest. 'The Lions defeat in 1983. That was a big watershed for me, a big disappointment. I had no assistant coach, and not taking Peter Wheeler was a big mistake. He'd been with the Lions in South Africa three years before. He would have been a lieutenant who I could have trusted. We nearly won the first Test and we were only beaten 9–0 in the second. You never know what influence someone like Wheeler would have had on those games. I have never told anyone this before.'

So Fitzgerald's appointment was a mistake? 'In hindsight, it probably was,' Telfer said. 'We were carried away by the euphoria of Ireland winning the Triple Crown earlier that year. You have to be dispassionate picking a Lions squad. Ciaran was a great captain for Ireland, but captaincy of the Lions is different. You have to have a captain who is good enough to play in the 1st XV.'

The alternative hooker, Colin Deans, was an established international in his own right; he was a player at the top of his game as he would prove the year after the tour as an integral member of Scotland's Grand Slam team. When the Lions picked him, he had proved himself in the Test arena over a five-year period, playing in twenty-nine of his country's thirty-one matches since his debut against France in February 1978. Yet the moment they chose Fitzgerald as skipper, Deans knew he was doomed to a place in the midweek team.

Telfer had a vote on team selection on that ill-fated journey through the New Zealand winter but not the casting vote that would have ensured that the coach got the team he wanted. That he should be given the players that he wanted was a not unreasonable request bearing in mind that the coach is ultimately held responsible for his team's results. Willie John McBride, as the honorary manager, and Fitzgerald, as captain, also had votes on the three-man panel. Every attempt to promote Deans failed. 'I got on well with Willie John, but I got out-voted 2–1,' Telfer said. 'Simple as that.'

The choice of captain had been based, naturally enough, on that year's Five Nations Championship. Scotland began with Roy Laidlaw and finished with Jim Aitken. England changed skippers halfway through a dismal campaign, switching from Steve Smith to John Scott and collected the wooden spoon due to their inability to win a single match.

Wales stuck with Eddie Butler all the way through the tournament, not that the Pontypool number 8 was ever in the frame, which left Fitzgerald. Ireland's Triple Crown and a share of the title with France made him, in McBride's words, 'a strong contender to skipper the Lions because he'd shown his leadership qualities. One other man would have been an obvious Lions captain: Peter Wheeler of England. But England had finished bottom of the championship, and with Ireland winning it there seemed little reason to ignore Fitzgerald's claims.

'Furthermore, when Ireland beat England 25–15 in Dublin, Fitzgerald had taken three strikes against the head from a pack that included Wheeler, so how could we justify taking Wheeler ahead of Fitzgerald? Colin Deans of Scotland was the other candidate, and he was playing well, but, in terms of the Lions party, England's demise during the season was seriously bad news. [Mike] Slemen, [Paul] Dodge, [Steve] Smith, Wheeler, [Phil] Blakeway, [Jim] Syddall and [John] Scott could all have expected to make the tour but, in the end, none of them did, although Smith did join us late on as a replacement.'

Whether the selectors had made a mistake in picking a captain first and a hooker second, only they know. When the party was announced on the Monday following the last round of the Five Nations, its most conspicuous absentee was all at sea, nursing the remnants of a hangover as he and his wife Margaret headed for home by boat from Dún Laoghaire through some appropriately rough water towards Holyhead.

The issue of poor selection dogged the Lions almost from beginning to end, rearing its head with virtually every setback. The first, against Auckland at Eden Park in the second outing of the tour, marked the advent of an 18-year-old butcher's boy called John Kirwan, whose first notable act was to hare out of nowhere and prevent a certain Lions centre from completing the apparent formality of falling on the ball in the in-goal area to claim a try. Clive Woodward never saw him coming, but, then, he wouldn't be the last.

Beating the All Blacks was hard enough without what McBride called this 'anti-Ciaran Fitzgerald thing in the English section of our own media. They had wanted Wheeler there as hooker and captain. They couldn't accept Fitzgerald, especially after Wheeler had been omitted in favour of Deans. But this was our media being anti, so no prizes for guessing what the New Zealand media picked on straightaway.'

The critics were not the only ones who found it hard to take. Two English Lions, in particular, found it hard to believe. Bill Beaumont considered Wheeler the best hooker he had ever played with 'by a mile. In the modern game he would have been a fantastic player because he had great hands. Brian Moore won a lot of caps, but he wasn't in the same league as Peter.'

Moore, Wheeler's successor for England and the Lions, made his unique concoction of competitive ferocity, psychological warfare and an acutely developed motivational sense go a very long way. In the eight years from 1987 until his retirement after the World Cup

163

in South Africa, the 'Pit Bull' snapped and snarled his way through sixty-four Tests for England and five more for the Lions. When he came to take stock of his career and put it all into context, Wheeler's omission baffled him as much then as it had done in 1983. 'I am still incredulous that the Lions kept choosing Ciaran Fitzgerald as their Test hooker and left Colin Deans out of the side,' Moore said. 'Deans was the better player by an almost immeasurable distance.

'Even more incredibly, they left Wheeler out of the party altogether, which was a disgrace. That gave me an insight into the political in-fighting and the trade-offs which go on among the home Unions: a factor in the selection of the 1993 party when Jeff Probyn was left behind in favour of one inferior Scot and another severely inferior Scot.'

At the time when the Lions selectors decided he was no longer up to scratch, Wheeler had played seven Tests for the Lions in a row – all four against the Springboks three years earlier and the last three on the previous series against the All Blacks in 1977 when he displaced Bobby Windsor. The middle man in the fearsome Pontypool front row, Windsor had been an automatic member of the invincible team in South Africa in 1974 and his removal in favour of the Londoner from South Norwood undermined a lifelong friendship with his club captain Terry Cobner, who had emerged from the pack as the unofficial forwards' coach. 'The Duke' never forgave him.

In retrospect, England's tardiness to make Wheeler their captain patently did him no favours when it came to extending his association with the Lions. More than 18 months elapsed between Beaumont's enforced retirement in February 1982 and Wheeler's belated elevation in November 1983, the new leader achieving the rare distinction of kicking off with a win over New Zealand at Twickenham. For the seven matches in between, the job had been shared between Steve Smith and John Scott.

Wheeler wrote about the RFU's reluctance to appoint him as the England captain in his autobiography:

> Only the selectors know why they chose as they did. I feel that there may have been some antipathy towards Leicester because we tended to take an independent view of matters dear to the Rugby Union's heart. I have also heard that Budge Rogers, the chairman, regarded me as akin to a 'professional' because of my contact with the Adidas company.

By then the first rumblings of revolution were rolling around the rugby world. More and more of the game's top players came to the conclusion that they were being taken for a ride. Considering the increasing demands heaped upon them to justify the rapidly rising commercial value of the international game, it was surprising that the penny had taken so long to drop.

The power-brokers on the home Unions were not smart enough to realise that they could only push their amateur servants so far. It never occurred to them that there was something fundamentally wrong about a strictly amateur sport accepting hefty sums from sponsors and television and then expecting the players to give up more of their spare time to keep pace with the game's burgeoning profile. The players were not asking to be compensated for time away from work but a few modest signs that someone appreciated their sacrifices. Instead, they were always liable to be sent the occasional invoice over some unauthorised expense that could just as easily have been written off without falling foul of amateur regulations that had been framed in Victorian times.

Wheeler, born in Croydon on 26 November 1948, was in the vanguard of those players driven by a sense of injustice, even if it did bring him a reputation for being something of a barrack-room lawyer. 'You'd just entertained 70,000 people at Twickenham, and they sent you a bill for 30 quid for your wife's hotel bill,' he said. 'There were other insensitivities of that sort. Nobody was looking for large sums of money. I always said that the two parties who needed to be looked after were your family and your employers. They were having to bear the brunt of amateur players having to do more and more squad training, but they were never looked after. The least you could do was to bring your wife to the match, have a good weekend and look after your employers with a couple of complimentary tickets.

'The RFU were not very good at adapting to professional attitudes. It was a case of trying to get them to do the simple thing to ease the burden of the players. There were some stupid little issues. For example, we used Mitre balls for our club matches but Gilbert balls for our internationals. In training we had six old Gilbert balls that, aerodynamically, were a totally different shape. So I asked the RFU, "Why can't we have six new Gilbert balls for training?" The answer was always, "We'll get you some new balls next time . . ."

'I felt I was in a position to make some points a bit more forcibly than others, but you are never aware who you are upsetting. The

RFU never come out and confront you. Of course, it was a great honour to play for your country. Your family were delighted and so on, but, once the World Cup came along, professionalism was bound to happen. The commercial pressures manifested themselves in a couple of ways, like the boots business.'

Rumours of Welsh players breaking the amateur rules by accepting cash for wearing a certain make of boot had been rife for some time. It took an Englishman to blow the lid off the scandal and open a veritable Pandora's box in the process.

Mike Burton probably changed the face of rugby more than any other front-row forward in the history of the sport, never missing a trick to shatter the old stereotype of the prop forward as a dim-witted fellow whose dull intellect did not allow him to run and pass at the same time. An adopted son of Gloucester, he used the strength of an ox and the cunning of a fox to become a master of his grunting trade as the anchor man of the scrum. Off the field, he was clever enough to turn himself into a millionaire as a pioneer of the corporate hospitality business.

He did it all despite a distinctly disadvantaged start to life. The product of a romance during the final months of the Second World War, Burton never knew his father – an American serviceman. Growing up in Maidenhead, where he was born on 18 December 1945, his uncle fired the boy's passion for soccer, taking him to watch Arsenal at Highbury, where, as luck would have it, his first match turned out to be a deeply poignant occasion. It was the last time that the famous 'Busby Babes' of Manchester United played in England before so many of them perished the following week in the Munich air disaster.

'Football crowds were impeccably behaved in those days, and, even when the ground was bursting at the seams, they always made room for lads like me to get a vantage point almost right on the touchline,' Burton said. 'I remember watching Duncan Edwards in the kick-about before the start. I could see to the level of his knees. He chipped the ball with his toe, it bounced ten yards away and immediately bounced straight back to him. I can see him doing it now as clear as crystal, even after all these years. I'd never seen anyone do that before. It was like watching magic. My mouth was wide open with amazement.

'That was all I could talk about all that weekend and at school on the Monday. And then, on the Wednesday, I heard that the plane had crashed, and so many of that team I'd watched a few days earlier were dead. I remember reading all about it in the *Daily Mirror*. I cried and the other kids cried. It was dreadful. When I think how good sport has been to me, I think of the day I saw Duncan Edwards and remind myself that he never played in England again.'

Had his mother not married a lorry driver from Gloucester when her son was 13, Mike Harrop the 'Gooner' would never have had the chance to reinvent himself as Mike Burton the Lion. By a happy quirk of fate, the new family relocated to the Gloucester suburb of Longlevens, a famous nursery for the Cherry and Whites at Kingsholm.

'I went to Longlevens School, and they put me straight into the rugby team,' Burton said. 'They put me in as a prop, and I never moved from the day I began until the day I finished nearly 20 years later. It was the making of me.'

When he muscled his way into the England team at the age of 26, joining John Pullin and the Cornish prop Stack Stevens in an all-West Country front row against Wales at Twickenham, the boot manufacturers were wooing rugby's leading players in what would escalate into a full-frontal assault on the amateur regulations.

Burton, flattered that anyone should give him boots, wore them for two seasons without, he swears, receiving a penny. Subsequent events would suggest that during that time he worked hard on acquiring a commercial savvy second to none: 'When we finished training with England at the Lensbury Club in London, we'd find all these reps waiting in the car park. Some of them were famous athletes, like John Cooper and Derek Ibbotson, each working for different sportswear companies. They'd say, "We have a very nice range of boots. Would you like to wear them?"

'When someone is being nice to you, it's not easy to be rude. I was just a prop from Gloucester, who'd never been given anything in his life. We'd always had to buy our own boots, and here were these chaps giving them to us for nothing, all out of the boots of their cars.

'What we didn't realise then was that they were getting free advertising for their products in front of a BBC television audience of six or eight million for every international. I found out later that to advertise something like that on prime-time ITV would cost you something like £30,000 for eight seconds.'

The penny was bound to drop, and, when it did, the boots came stuffed with fivers or, in Burton's case, tenners. France v. England at the Parc des Princes on 2 March 1974 turned out to be a landmark date; it marked just one in a long series of illicit deals that ultimately left the International Rugby Board no alternative but to declare the sport open in Paris 21 years later.

To be strictly accurate, the deal that would have had Burton, to name but one, drummed out of the game for life was done not in the French capital but at Versailles, famous as the venue for the signing of the treaty after Germany's defeat in the Great War. How fitting, therefore, that Burton's illegal 'treaty' of Versailles should have been with a German company successful in cornering a global sports market with their distinctive footwear. England were staying in Versailles when Burton was made an offer that he did not refuse. 'Two or three players were in a room trying on boots when I walked in. The rep who was doling them out handed me a pair. "Try these," he said.

'I said, "I'd never, ever wear a brand new pair of boots. They've got to be broken in."

'He said, "These are very soft leather. Go on, try them and see."

'He gave me the box, and I went into the bathroom. I sat on the toilet with the seat down to try them on and discovered that there were five £10 notes in the boot. I tried them and went back into the room.

'"How are they?" says the rep.

'"Absolutely perfect," I said.

'I wore them the next day. When I ran out for the kick-off, I was astounded to see that both teams wore Adidas boots. That was my first experience of boot money. I understood that [both teams wearing the boots] was sending a subliminal message to millions of viewers. I'd suspected some players were getting something when I wasn't, but that didn't bother me. It wasn't important to me at the time. I just wanted to play and see how far I could go.

'When I first played two years before, I remember a famous England player taking a pair from one rep and a different pair from another rep. He wrestled with his conscience as to which pair he should wear and ran out that Saturday with two different boots: one on each foot. Very clever because he must have got double the rate.

'It was all hush-hush. Once I started to know the score, I got £50 every game after that for wearing Adidas boots. We used to go to their headquarters in Poynton and get promotional kit. That was the start of the professional era. I did try to get them to up the ante, but you had to be careful not to push it too hard. You knew that they held the whip hand, because if they had gone to the RFU we'd have been for the high jump.'

Wales's leading players of the time, whose success in the Five Nations and overseas with the Lions gave them an infinitely higher profile than their English counterparts, had their own boot deal, but it was Burton, in the finest publish-and-be-damned tradition, who broke ranks with the publication in the early '80s of his autobiography. For a few days, it rose high enough on the news agenda to contend as a sort of subsidiary scandal to the main event: the disappearance of the Labour Minister John Stonehouse. For Burton, then in the early stages of his hospitality business, it was all grist to a golden mill.

'At one stage, when I was being pilloried over the boot furore, the phone rang in my office, and the voice at the other end said, "Hello, John Stonehouse here. I just want to say thank you for taking some of the heat off me." I was beginning to wonder when I realised it was a mate with a sense of humour.'

Like Queen Victoria, the RFU was not amused. The scandal demanded decisive action and the Union rose to the occasion by summoning Horst Dassler, the head of Adidas, from the company's headquarters near Nuremberg to the East India Club, one of their favourite London establishments. The Club was a historic venue redolent of the time when Britannia ruled the waves and half the globe seemed to be painted red.

Waves of a different kind had been made when Herr Dassler strode up the steps to appear before the Union's investigating committee under the chairmanship of the president J. V. Smith, a grain merchant from Minchinhampton in the Cotswolds, who had played on the wing four times for England in 1950. Burton knew him well, having been involved in periodic scrapes with the 'law' during his career. There was, for example, his sending off in a County Championship semi-final at Bristol, which he followed with a theatrical bow to the RFU blazers assembled in the committee box.

'I knew J. V.'s style because I had appeared before him many times on disciplinary panels. He was one of those proper chaps who would chair meetings in a very formal, clipped style, "Right, make your statement." When the top man from Adidas walked in, you could imagine J. V. saying, "Right, Mr Dassler, what have you got to say?"'

Not very much. Dassler was in no mood to shop any of the players by name nor give any details about payments. 'He was quite amused by these quaint little chaps,' Burton said. 'By the time it was all over, he was almost patting them on the head. What he did tell them was that rugby football accounted for less than 0.25 per cent of his company's global sports business, which rather put it into perspective. It was a laugh a minute.'

Curiously, the man who had lifted the lid on the whole business did not renew acquaintance with the RFU hierarchy. They had already declared Burton *persona non grata*: banned for life for writing a book and keeping the proceeds, along with the rest of those who had committed a similar offence. The boot-money issue brought the game into widespread disrepute and made a mockery of the sport's amateur principles, but no action was taken against Burton, presumably on the basis that a second life-ban would have been a bit much.

Instead, the RFU contented themselves by imposing a ban on any manufacturers' trademarks appearing on the boots worn by their players at international matches. It did not prevent them from using their ingenuity to circumvent the ruling, and one imaginative player resorted to an almost ballet-like pose to ensure his boots were given maximum exposure.

'The soles were made of fluorescent yellow, and, on one occasion, a famous try was scored when the player in question cocked his legs in the air and did a can-can dance on his back. Everyone knew the name of the manufacturer,' Burton said. 'Before the match, you looked around the dressing-room and saw various players working like fury, blacking out the stripes on their boots.

'As a married man with three children, the money came in handy. We didn't get anything in those days. Maybe some free beer at Kingsholm: a barrel amongst the players, and that didn't make much impact on the social budget. It wasn't as if your wife could share in that, not unless she was going to turn up early and drink six pints before the match was over.'

Burton, though, did have his moments when the RFU picked up the tab. The most hilarious centred around the 'Captain's Room' at the Hilton hotel where the players spent Saturday night/Sunday morning after attending the dinner following a Twickenham international.

'On this particular occasion, we retired to the Captain's Room, which was so grand that it looked like two or three rooms put together. It was all very convivial. When I walked into the bathroom and sat down on the sheepskin cover of the toilet there was a telephone beside it on the wall. I picked it up, and this chap in a foreign accent said, "Room service."

'Amazing, isn't it, how those blokes are always Spanish or Portuguese. Anyway, I ordered 24 beef burgers. The guy from room service said, "24 beef burgers?"

'"Yes, please."

'"You like gherkins?"

'"Yes, we'd like gherkins. And chips."

'"Chips?"

'"Yes."

'"You mean french fries?"

'"Yes, french fries."

'Ten minutes later there was a knock on the door of the Captain's Room. When it opened, it was like one of those scenes from a hospital, with all these trolleys being pushed down the long corridor into the room. They had a couple of waiters in tow, and, when the trolleys came to a stop, they whipped the silver covers off. Underneath [were] 24 beef burgers, gherkins and chips. Fran Cotton was one of the first to dive in. He nudged past Alec Lewis, the chairman of selectors: "Thanks very much, Alec. Just what we need."'

Once the chairman of selectors had sized up the situation, he turned to the other prop in an accusing manner and said, 'Burton, is this your doing?'

An invoice arrived on the doormat of his home two days later with his two complimentary tickets for the next match, which showed him that the RFU had put the assistant secretary, Lieutenant Colonel Dennis Morgan, on the case. 'I had a bill for 50 quid, so I went to see the Lieutenant Colonel at the first available opportunity,' Burton recalled. 'He told me that the Air Commodore [RFU secretary Bob Weighill] wanted to see me. The Air Commodore said, "I'm waiting for a reaction."

'I thought, "Reaction to what?"

'Then he said, "You obviously ordered those beef things."

'I denied it, and that was the last I ever heard of the episode.'

Within a fortnight of the RFU closing the file, Burton had received the biggest accolade of his life. He had been picked by the Lions for the tour of tours to South Africa, starting in May of that same year, 1974. What's more, he had made the elite 30 at a time when competition for places had rarely been keener. The British and Irish game was about to reaffirm its superiority over the southern-hemisphere sides, after the series win in New Zealand three years earlier.

It had taken Burton a mere seven matches for England to justify recognition at the highest level alongside his Lancastrian sparring partner Cotton. The English pair were chosen in tandem with the formidable Scottish duo of Ian 'Mighty Mouse' McLauchlan and Sandy Carmichael, the brave Glaswegian who had been battered by the Canterbury 'butchers' during the previous tour.

The '74 Lions, managed by Alun Thomas of Wales, had been put in the hands of two Ulstermen from the green glens of County Antrim who both played for Ballymena. The captain, Willie John McBride, was making his final expedition as a Lion. It was his fifth tour and put him beyond the reach of everyone else in terms of Lions longevity. The coach, Syd Millar, had played seven Tests: the first against the All Blacks in Wellington in 1959, the last against the Springboks at Port Elizabeth nine years later.

'Willie and Syd were the best managers of men I ever came across,' Burton said. 'Willie didn't suffer fools gladly, but he was a wise man who understood us all. At different times during the tour, he made allowances for us being boys. Syd had the capability of putting us through pain, because he had the track suit and the whistle. If you'd had a few beers the night before, he wouldn't treat you like a naughty schoolboy, but, by God, he would hurt you on the training ground the next morning.'

The Gloucester prop had played against McBride once before: at Twickenham in February 1972 when Ireland beat England 16–12. On the flight from Heathrow to Johannesburg, he began to get to know McBride the man, biding his time before being summoned upstairs for a motivational chat: 'He was sitting in the bubble of the Jumbo, and I was ushered up with a couple of other players who he didn't know that well. It was his way of introducing himself without being formal about it. He said to me, "We've seen you play, Mike. We've watched what you do, and, you know, it might come to a bit of this."

'At that point he held his hands up and leant back like the Marquess of Queensberry in a boxing pose. I said, "That's OK, by me."

'He said, "I know. That's why we have selected you."

'By the time he'd finished talking to you, you couldn't wait for the plane to touch down in South Africa and start looking for the Springboks. I was in awe of him. Mentally, he had built a pack to beat South Africa. He had put that winning culture into the minds of the 16 forwards before we landed. There was some doubt before we left as to whether some would be good enough to be Lions. Every man came back as a legend.'

They left knowing full well that many back home thought that they should have given South Africa a wide berth in protest at their reviled apartheid regime. Demonstrations outside the team's London headquarters forced McBride to take the bull by the horns and address the issue within the privacy of the Lions' inner sanctum.

'He got up and asked someone to close the door,' Burton said. 'He referred to the protests and how he had gone to meet Peter Hain, one of their leaders. Then he said to us, "I am going on this tour with an open mind. If anyone has any political objection to going, or if anyone doesn't feel happy in his own mind, you can leave the room, and we'll carry on. But if you want to stay with us, then you stay now. Now is your opportunity." And he left the silence hanging there. Nobody left the room. Then he said, "I was very impressed with all of you today: the way you applied yourselves on the training field." You just knew this tour was going to be special.'

It turned out to be more special than Burton imagined. Their early rout of a mixed-race team called The Leopards gave him an insight into what would make the Lions invincible over the course of a series of 26 matches that included four Tests.

'We so dominated the Leopards that they only won one scrum all match,' Burton said. 'Every time they put the ball in, we shoved them off it, except for one. In the dressing-room afterwards, Syd said to Willie, "How did we lose that one?"

'"I don't know," said Willie, "but the significant thing was that every time we dropped our knees and drove, nobody slipped – nobody lost his footing. In that respect, it was perfect. But you're right, Syd. We did lose the one . . ."'

That none of the front row on duty that day made the Test team was another indication of the Lions' awesome strength. Burton, the leading tight-head until he injured himself, had to be replaced by Cotton, who had gone as the reserve loose-head. Ken Kennedy, the Irish hooker, played second fiddle to Bobby Windsor and Carmichael to his compatriot, McLauchlan.

McBride's Lions were so good that the outstanding English back-row pair of Andy Ripley and Tony Neary also failed to make the Test team. 'There were some marvellous forwards: players who, like me, were out there to win and refused to be distracted from that focus,'

173

McBride said. 'Windsor, Uttley, Slattery, Ripley, Ralston, Neary, McLauchlan, McKinney, Kennedy, Davies, David, Cotton, Carmichael, Burton and Brown. Each man deserved a medal . . .'

Some of those medals would have been earned for fighting their corner at the Boet Erasmus Stadium in Port Elizabeth against Eastern Province in what would have been another Canterbury had the Lions not been ready to get as much of their retaliation in first, during a series of punch-ups that gave birth to the famous – or infamous – '99' call. McBride sat that match out but still gave the team-talk, sensing that Hannes Marais, the home-team's captain, would want to land a psychological blow before the first of the four Tests.

'He [McBride] said, "They've got the same colour of jerseys as Canterbury in '71,"' Burton recalled. 'Then he stopped for a pause and said, "Remember that." I couldn't remember it because I wasn't on that tour, but everyone had read about Canterbury and I thought, "Bloody hell, this is going to be some game . . ."

'So we steeled ourselves for what was to come. I stood at the front of the lineout, the Mouse [Ian McLauchlan] stood at three and Bobby's throwing the ball in. My job was to look after Gareth Edwards, who was captain that day. As the ball came in, I stepped back and this Basil de Coning ran from ten yards on his own side, through the gap and the ball was in the inside centre's hands when he poleaxed Edwards.

'Edwards never complained but he did look at me. I realised then it was my responsibility not to let it happen again. At the next lineout, I saw this bloke take off, and he was going to kill Gareth. As he got level with me, I hit him right under the chin. He went round my straight arm like a Catherine wheel and landed on his back. Edwards leant over him and said, "You all right now, Basil?"

'I thought, "He won't do that again." And then all I could hear was Bobby shouting out, "99, 99, 99." Whenever there was a fight of any sort we fronted up, but it was never part of any pre-match plan. It was a spontaneous reaction. That was the one thing the Boks could never understand and one of the reasons they lost.'

Burton, never one to back off when there was a 'bit of notoriety' flying around, stuck his chin out when the Australians went 'the biff' at the 'Battle of Brisbane' the following year and duly became the first Englishman to be sent off during an international. Having retired, after helping Gloucester beat Leicester to win the 1978 English Cup final, he then set about launching himself into a new business.

For Twickenham's first big match the following season, Burton hired an old London double-decker bus, drove it into the north car park and entertained his first clients to a champagne reception, a bite to eat and a ticket to the match. 'Afterwards, I'd walk round with a couple of England players,' he said. 'I had what people demanded, and I was the first man into it.'

International rugby, Wimbledon, the Grand National – nothing was too much trouble. He also won a contract as an official travel agent for the 2007 World Cup worth millions of pounds. The fat kid, who once marvelled at Duncan Edwards, probably made a mental note of something else at Highbury that winter's afternoon in the late '50s: there wasn't a hospitality box to be seen.

12

REVOLUTIONARY ROB

ON TUESDAY, 5 SEPTEMBER 1995, SIR JOHN HALL BOUGHT A FAMOUS BUT AILING OLD rugby club and turned it into a subsidiary of the Newcastle United Sporting Club. Up until that point, Gosforth had been chugging along in their own quiet way. Supported by a few hundred diehards, the club clung to the fading memories of two Twickenham finals in the distant '70s, which hardly equipped them for the brave new world of professionalism.

Rugby union had declared itself an open game nine days earlier – open in the sense that it was no longer restricted to true-blue amateurs – and Sir John had gone bursting out of the blocks before some of his dithering competitors had got round to checking their spikes. Typically, his entrepreneurial skills had swept him ahead in a game about which he knew nothing other than that it was played with an oval-shaped ball.

On Thursday, 7 September, Rob Andrew was behind his desk, in his capacity as the associate director of a commercial property company in the City of London, when he took the call that would change his life. Freddy Shepherd, chairman of Newcastle United FC, introduced himself and got straight to the point. 'We've just bought Gosforth,' he said, 'and we want you to run it. Can we talk as soon as possible?'

The next day, Andrew met Shepherd and Douglas Hall, who was Sir John's son and a fellow director. They were en route to the

Magpies' match at Southampton that weekend so it made sound business sense to stop overnight and meet the prospective manager of their new rugby operation. The deal was hammered out over dinner at a restaurant in Westminster.

Andrew, not content to retire on the strength of the drop goal with which he had eliminated the holders Australia from the quarter-finals of the World Cup a few months earlier, had been planning to play for one more season as England's fly-half while pursuing a commercial property career with excellent prospects. What Messrs Shepherd and Hall put to him over the dinner table that night changed all that and a great deal more besides. From that evening onward, Andrew's life would never be the same again. In offering him a five-year contract worth £750,000, Sir John Hall's powerbrokers had chosen exactly the right man to become rugby's prototype professional.

They sold him a vision that money could not buy: the challenge of building a professional rugby club from nothing into something worthy enough to fit into Hall's concept of the 'Geordie Nation'. Andrew had decided to accept the offer well before the dessert tray came into view. He was not about to renounce the offer of a lifetime. 'I'd pretty much made up my mind by the time I left the restaurant,' he said. 'It was all finalised the following week.'

While Andrew joined Wasps for the journey to Bath the next day as though nothing had happened, Gosforth travelled to Birmingham for a Second Division match at Moseley without the faintest clue that their fate was in the process of being put into the custody of a Yorkshireman renowned for having a safe pair of hands. The club's largely conservative membership, wary of a sport that seemed to be careering into the arms of the nouveaux riches after decades of amateurism, greeted Hall's takeover with a mixture of anxiety and trepidation.

Like it or loathe it, Gosforth RFC had had its day. On Tuesday, 12 September, Sir John addressed the members of his newly acquired club in their clubhouse at Kingston Park, outlining his dream of turning what was then little more than a field with a fancifully named grandstand and a bit of terracing into a 10,000 largely all-seater capacity stadium. Money, he declared, would be no object.

Andrew confirmed his formal acceptance, studiously ducking a bombardment of calls about a report in the *Daily Mail* about his imminent appointment as Tyneside's rugby equivalent of Kevin

Keegan, who was, at that time, going great guns with Newcastle United at the top of the Premiership. 'Squeaky', a nickname that had stuck from his early England days in reference to his clean-cut image, did his best to carry on as normal. He turned out for Wasps that Saturday as though nothing had happened nor was about to happen.

Those who poured scorn on the Newcastle offer pointed to the visit at Twickenham that November of the World Cup-winning Springboks and wondered why, in that event, would Andrew give up what was left of his England career? The archaic regulations governing player transfers in-season meant that nobody on the move could play for a period of 120 days, which would make it rather awkward for Andrew to combine managing a new club in the north-east with playing for England.

He recognised, earlier than most, that professionalism would change the landscape of the game for ever. If some were slow to appreciate the enormity of what he had been offered, Andrew was never in any doubt. He boarded the first plane from Heathrow to Newcastle on the morning of Thursday, 21 September, and was installed, later that day, as the new rugby manager of Newcastle to a suitable fanfare at the soccer shrine of St. James' Park and made rugby headline news on Tyneside for the first time. It would not be the last, by a long shot.

Sir John, who might have had some difficulty recognising one end of a rugby ball from the other – never mind the difference between a ruck and a maul – was out in the middle of the football stadium exchanging passes with his new signing. They were a bit like two new frontiersmen embarking on a journey into the unknown, except neither quite knew where the new frontier was and, even if they did, what it would take to get there.

'None of us really knew where on earth we were heading,' Andrew says. 'There was no plan. The RFU certainly didn't have a plan. Nobody did. It was a case of make the rules up as you go along. We're probably still making them up.

'Those were very exciting times. At St. James's on that first day, it was a case of, "Well, I'm here. I've got a few ideas, and I'm going to try and develop those over the next few weeks. Let's see where we go under the new board – and hang on to your hats."

'The experience Sir John and Freddy had of running a football club as a business proved invaluable. They knew all about contracts and structures, and they were very astute in getting the academy for young players off the ground. They understood professional sport. They said, "Just get the team sorted out. Don't worry about anything else. Just get the players to get us out of the Second Division and establish playing credibility with the Premiership clubs. If we don't get there, this is a complete waste of time."

'We bought a team, and, at the other end of the scale, Paul McKinnon started work on the academy. We knew we couldn't keep on buying players. We had to buy a team to begin with, but in the long run we had to build one from within. It was a wonderfully exciting time.'

Before most of their rivals could grasp the full meaning of the new game, Andrew put Hall's chequebook to maximum effect, relieving his own club Wasps of Steve Bates, Nick Popplewell and Dean Ryan, persuading Doddie Weir and Gary Armstrong to take the high road out of the Scottish Borders and arranging for Tony Underwood to head north from Leicester. As the new recruits twiddled their thumbs as a result of the 120-day rule, Andrew's brave new club found itself stuck in the old losing rut.

Kingston Park had a grand total of 365 seats and sometimes not enough spectators to fill them. They lost to whoever they played against and wherever they went – to Wakefield, Bedford, Blackheath, Waterloo, London Scottish, London Irish, Moseley and, especially, Northampton, whose 52–9 win at Kingston Park came at the end of the same week that Wasps showed Andrew the door at their postage-stamp base in Sudbury, rather than continue to run the risk of finding more of their assets stripped and relocated to the Tyne.

Initially, Wasps had been willing to let Andrew and Dean Ryan – his prospective player-coach at Newcastle – continue playing for them, before they were eligible for their new club. It was a magnanimous gesture but one that illustrated their failure to grasp the wider ramifications of professionalism. Rugby's newest club owner had no such difficulty understanding the significance of Andrew's capture. 'We are going to do for rugby here what Kevin Keegan has done for football,' Hall proclaimed on that sunny autumn morning at St. James' Park. 'It's not going to happen overnight, and Rob's under no immediate pressure, but he will be soon enough. Newcastle United will see to that.'

Hall, the coal miner's son who became a Thatcherite multi-millionaire, had got it slightly wrong. Whereas Keegan failed to deliver the football Premiership, Andrew succeeded in winning the rugby version, the chairman having provided the financial clout for him to buy in a squad mean enough and good enough to win the title at the first attempt.

'During those first few months of professionalism,' Andrew said, 'there was a stunned disbelief as to what was going on. What does it mean? As more and more investors jumped in to take over other clubs, more top players were being signed up. We probably were first out of the blocks. As well as bringing players in we also stopped Richard Metcalfe and Richard Arnold from jumping ship to West Hartlepool.'

They survived that first season by the skin of their teeth, dragging themselves off the bottom and scrambling above Nottingham and Bedford only by virtue of a superior points difference. The expansion of the old Second Division meant that nobody went down, and before the end of the following season Andrew had recruited a team fit to be champions of England.

They cut a huge swathe through the Second Division in the 1996–97 season. Only Richmond, who were at that time in the same cheque-book league as Newcastle, could match them until their owner, the Monte Carlo-based Ashley Levett, pulled the plug with catastrophic consequences. Nobody else could live with Newcastle, least of all Rugby, who subsided to the tune of 156–5 at Kingston Park in October 1996 when two of the front row – prop George Graham and hooker Ross Nesdale – scored hat-tricks of tries.

They swept all before them the following season: not on the same massive scale, but at a level of consistency beyond the reach of their closest rivals, Saracens. Epic duels between the two clubs towards the end of the season – in particular, the one at Vicarage Road watched by almost 20,000 spectators – ensured that the race went to the last match of the season, and Newcastle, needing a win at Harlequins to clinch the first Premiership title, won at a gallop in a carnival atmosphere.

For all their international signings – topped off by Va'aiga Tuigamala from Wigan for a world-record union transfer fee of £750,000 – they found room, that season, to introduce an 18-year-old fly-half driven by an insatiable hunger and a work ethic that tended to make the average Trojan look like a slouch. Jonny Wilkinson forced his way into the team at inside centre for the last six matches of the campaign, leaving the stand-off in no doubt that his days were numbered.

In two seasons, Andrew had created a champion team in his own image. They won because flinty customers like Dean Ryan, Garath Archer and Nick Popplewell were every bit as hard-nosed as their player-manager. All those run-ins with the more Jurassic-like members of the Rugby Football Union, over a whole range of issues, had not been entirely in vain.

At last he had become a professional sportsman but not quite in the way he thought he might while growing up on the family farm in the Yorkshire Dales. The young Andrew made up his mind that if he was going to make a name for himself it would be as a county cricketer. It was no idle dream given his ability as an opening batsman who bowled off-breaks well enough to number among his scalps two Test openers of widely contrasting styles: Geoffrey Boycott and Desmond Haynes.

By the age of 22, Andrew had scored a maiden first-class century, captained a combined Cambridge–Oxford team against Allan Border's Australians and faced a varied number of mean fast bowlers, including Courtney Walsh, arguably the meanest of all. Andrew's unbeaten 101, for Cambridge against Nottinghamshire at Trent Bridge in July 1984, earned him a footnote in *Wisden Cricketer's Almanac*: 'Rob Andrew, an England Under-23 rugby player, showed himself to be a player of fine temperament who learned quickly in his first season.'

It also brought him the offer of a professional career with the East Midlands County where another international goal kicker, Dusty Hare, had been on the books a decade earlier. Andrew parried the offer, because he needed time to convince himself whether he would be good enough to realise his ambition of becoming a county cricketer.

After captaining Cambridge in the Varsity match the following year, he got down to some serious business with Yorkshire's second XI, playing alongside Ashley Metcalfe, who did go on to open for England, albeit briefly. 'Cricket then was my first love,' Andrew said. 'I'd had more success at school playing cricket than rugby. I had a deep passion for cricket, still do, and I would love to have been able to take it up as a career.'

His sporting future hung in the balance during the summer of 1985 when England, with David Gower in his pomp as captain, regained The Ashes. Not by the longest stretch of the most fertile imagination could Andrew claim to have played his part in softening up the Aussies for the Tests, but he did captain a one-day side against Allan Border's tourists, and, a few weeks later, he stood up to the 'grim ferocity' of the West Indian fast bowlers.

During those two summers at Cambridge, Andrew bagged the biggest scalp of all: Geoffrey Boycott. It happened during a match against a MCC XI at a time when the world's greatest living Yorkshireman needed the practice after returning from injury. The fixture also afforded Andrew the added opportunity of a consultation with Boycott at a time when he had still to decide whether he could make it in professional cricket.

'My cricket had improved dramatically in my final term at Cambridge, despite the personal disappointment of a poor showing in the Varsity match. The century against Nottinghamshire had attracted the interest of the club's cricket manager who had approached me about the possibility of joining the playing staff at Trent Bridge.

'I was going to start my first job in surveying with a firm in Nottingham in September, and my digs was conveniently situated next door to the ground. But I was a Yorkshireman born and bred, and if I was going to play county cricket anywhere it would be at Headingley.'

Earlier that season Cambridge had played the MCC: 'Boycott was recovering from injury and was using the game to get his eye in. He was doing very well, too, until I beat him all ends up, tempting him into an uncharacteristically rash shot to mid-on. I may not have taken many wickets in first-class cricket, but with Desmond Haynes and Geoff Boycott on my list of victims no one can argue about the quality.

'In the bar afterwards, Boycott came over for a chat. He knew that I had been offered a short-term contract, very much on a trial basis, to play for Yorkshire seconds. We talked about style and technique and the problems of making the grade at first-class level. In many ways my style was similar to Boycott's. I had a good defence and a number of scoring shots, without having a wide range of strokes. Despite the fact that I had scored a half century against the MCC, Boycott had spotted a number of technical failings. He also made the point that whilst my technical flaws might escape punishment on the slow wicket at Fenners they would be exposed on the faster tracks around the country.

'The most menacing bowler I ever faced was the West Indian Patrick Patterson. Yorkshire seconds were playing their Lancashire equivalents on a dank day at Doncaster, and, despite the presence of [Michael] Atherton, [Neil] Fairbrother and Patterson in the opposition, Yorkshire were on top. Patterson, in his frustration and fury, began to work up to Test-match pace. Nothing in my experience had been quite so terrifying.

'A few weeks previously against Sussex, I had been introduced to the real world of pace bowling, by the 6 ft 8 in. South African Garth le Roux. I had the temerity to pull a short-pitched delivery from him for four through the mid-wicket. The next ball was also pitched short of a length, but this time it came down five times faster. I was rooted to the spot, and my bat had scarcely moved from the crease when the ball smashed into my helmet, ripping out the bolt that secured the visor. There is, I suppose, an element of bravery required to stop a mighty second-row forward in full flight, but it takes a different sort of courage to withstand the sustained onslaught of fast bowling.

'I learnt a lot during that season in the Yorkshire second XI. Although I did all right, there were others like Richard Blakey, David Byas and Ashley Metcalfe, who I felt were a lot better than I was. And they couldn't get into the first team. I realised that it wasn't really going to be possible. I just didn't think I was good enough.'

By then, his rugby career had taken off. His international debut, against Romania at Twickenham in January 1985, produced six goals and eighteen points: an England record that catapulted him onto peak-time television as a guest of Terry Wogan. He broke the record twelve months later in a way that won him further national acclaim: six penalties and a late drop goal nudging England home against Wales, whose new scrum-half Robert Jones would be playing in harness with the opposition fly-half soon enough in the name of the Lions.

For all his initial success, Andrew rapidly found himself caught up in the controversy swirling around his duel with the other leading English stand-off of the time, Stuart Barnes. When 'The Barrel' declared himself unavailable to play for England in a fit of pique, Andrew established himself as an international of unflinching courage, and, although he would never claim to have been a running fly-half in the classical mould, his kicking – both off the ground and out of hand – dug his country out of many a hole.

The Lions had not picked an English number 10 for any Test match since Richard Sharp in South Africa during the early Sixties, and the chances of Andrew bridging the gap disappeared over the last weekend of the 1989 Five Nations. The title would have been England's had a nightmarish misunderstanding between Rory

Underwood and Jonathan Webb not allowed Mike Hall to claim the softest of winning tries for Wales at Cardiff Arms Park.

Whatever their reasons, the Lions selectors decided to leave Andrew at home and advised him to keep fit in case of any emergency. They had decided he was surplus to requirements: the third man in the fly-half pecking order behind Ireland's Paul Dean and the young Scot, Craig Chalmers. The selection of those two rivals left Andrew nursing a metaphorical kick in the crotch; not for the first time, nor the last.

He was playing cricket for Gerrards Cross against Thame when word reached him in the outfield that the Lions needed him after all: Paul Dean was injured. In times of despair, fate had intervened on his behalf often enough to create an impression of some superior force spiriting him to new heights. The 1989 Lions tour of Australia was a classic case in point: Dean's wretched luck in wrenching his knee during the first match against Western Australia in Perth paved the way for his English rival to play a pivotal role in turning a lost cause into a series victory.

'I was really upset about not being picked in the first place. Roger Uttley, then the England coach, was one of the coaches on the trip, and I remember having a round of golf with him at Harrow School a couple of days after the party had been selected. I was pretty gutted. He just said, "Well, you've just got to keep your head down, stick at it and you never know what might be round the corner."

'Fate has a funny way of intervening sometimes in life. Six weeks later Deano got injured, and I ended up in a 2–1 winning Test series having not been involved in the losing first Test. It was a quite extraordinary set of circumstances. Unbelievable, really.'

It was, as Andrew will acknowledge for the rest of his days, the 'biggest turning point' of his career. The tour was the making of him, not least because it gave him the belief that he could hold his own in the highest company. It was as if the early days had all been part of an occasionally painful apprenticeship, and now he had become the real McCoy.

'I came back thinking, "I can play this game. I know I'm pretty good." Most players find the Lions quite daunting. It takes quite a while for them to become comfortable in that rarefied international atmosphere, on and off the pitch. Each player needs an amount of time before he thinks, "Actually, I'm now beginning to understand the game."'

Andrew's contribution to two winning midweek matches was not enough to justify Chalmers being bumped from the Test team for the first of the three matches in Sydney on 1 July 1989. If Andrew had no real complaints beforehand, he certainly had none afterwards. The Wallabies' 30–12 win made it a good match to miss, not just for Andrew but also for Wade Dooley, Mike Teague and Jeremy Guscott, whose collective impact changed the course of the series.

Andrew struck up an immediate rapport with Jones, the Wales scrum-half, and on successive Saturdays the Lions pack beat the opposition up under the direction of three policemen from different constabularies: Dean Richards, Paul Ackford and Dooley. As befitted his image, 'Squeaky' stayed well out of trouble to play a part, however accidental, in the try with which the series was won and lost. With the Wallabies three points ahead, Andrew lined up a drop goal that drifted towards David Campese far out on his wing. Not for the first time, Campese made all the difference. To his eternal embarrassment, he threw a pass behind him into the in-goal area to where he thought full-back Greg Martin would be, and a gleeful Ieuan Evans fell on it.

History would probably have had a very different take on the 1989 Lions had David Young been sent off for kicking Australian lock Steve Cutler in the head during the second Test. The French referee René Hourquet failed to give the Welsh prop his marching orders, a major contributing factor to arguably the longest whinge in the history of Australian sport. It lasted so long that they were still whingeing when the Lions went back there 12 years later. The fallout never escalated to the point of jeopardising diplomatic relations between London and Canberra, but there were echoes of the 'Bodyline tour' by England's cricketers in the early '30s when the furore sparked by the number of Australian batsmen hit by short-pitched fast bowling reached government level. For a nation whose rugby players have never been slow to 'go the biff', the sound of the Wallabies moaning about foul play must have landed like a dull thud on the ears of those hard-as-nails Australian players like Steve Finnane.

On the 1989 tour, Australia could have done with a prop like Finnane, a lawyer notorious for dispensing his own brand of instant justice in the '70s. Finnane belonged to the old-fashioned school whose pupils did not believe in waiting for the referee to impose law and order. Graham Price, the legendary Welsh Lion, will vouch for that, having flown home from his country's painful tour of Australia in 1978 with a broken jaw as a reminder of an altercation with the walloping Wallaby. Whenever an opponent complained that he had not touched him, Finnane would give his victim the stock answer, 'Pass the message on to who did.'

After suffering defeat at the hands of the Lions in 1989, Bob Dwyer, the Wallabies' voluble coach, got his own back with a vengeance some 30 months later and at Twickenham, to boot. Australia beat England 12–6 in the 1991 World Cup final, thereby ensuring that the best team won the tournament. However, nobody will ever know to what extent England contributed to their own downfall by a radical shift in tactics away from forward power and Andrew's merciless boot to an expansive game that hardly came to them as second nature.

A permanent fixture at fly-half in the Grand Slam teams immediately before and after the World Cup – as well as during the tournament itself – Andrew reached Cardiff in February 1993 with England on track for a third successive Slam, a feat that had never been managed before. Had there been any kind of justice, their bid would not have survived the previous match – against France at Twickenham – when England pushed their luck to the outrageous extent that Ian Hunter scored their only try after a Jonathan Webb penalty had rebounded off an upright straight into his arms.

The only change England made for the Wales game was to drop the newly capped Martin Johnson and restore Wade Dooley, a late withdrawal from the French game. Wales rose to the challenge with demonic tackling from start to finish, and when Ieuan Evans caught Rory Underwood napping, after Emyr Lewis had chipped the ball into the space behind him, England realised they had given their luck a shove too far. As team manager, Geoff Cooke's reaction to the one-point defeat was to give his fly-half the biggest shove of all.

Andrew had been made the scapegoat and Barnes, back in favour after five years in the wilderness, made enough of a match-winning return against Scotland at Twickenham to ensure that he would go with the Lions to New Zealand that summer as their number one fly-half. Andrew also went and, typically, fought his way back into favour for all three Tests of a series memorable only for the rare mediocrity of the All Blacks, who still proved good enough to win the decisive match at a canter.

'It was a strange tour in many respects. Very different to the one before. The '89 Lions were run as a tight ship, a backs-to-the-wall action with everyone pulling together to get us out of trouble.

There was a real sense of togetherness throughout the whole squad, which wasn't there in '93. In '93 they weren't a very tight group. The midweek team lost the last four midweek games very badly. Morale was poor. The tour never had any great shape to it. Wellington in the second Test was a fantastic victory, but we got it wrong in the last Test, and it all drifted away from us.'

In ten years at the hub of England's operation, Andrew captained his country twice, a paltry return for a player of his influence. His first effort, against Romania beneath a scorching sun in Bucharest in May 1989, went so well that the injured Will Carling admitted to a 'crisis of confidence' that evening over whether he would ever get back into the team. Apart from Andrew's leadership, Jeremy Guscott had made the most of Carling's absence to score three tries on his debut.

The captain's anxiety having been seriously misplaced, Andrew had to wait six years for the privilege of leading England again and then only because Carling took a one-match breather during the pool games of the 1995 World Cup in South Africa. 'I never had any problem with Will being captain,' Andrew said. 'I had enough on my plate to ensure my position in the team. It wasn't really until the early '90s when I became much more secure.'

Throughout his record-breaking reign, Carling could not have asked for a more trustworthy lieutenant. 'Without the advice and support of Rob Andrew, I wouldn't have lasted two minutes in the job,' Carling said. 'He was my touchstone and his support and loyalty were remarkable, given that he was high on Geoff Cooke's list of choices to captain England himself. In the end, Geoff decided against Rob, because he felt he had not settled into his game with sufficient confidence and that to ask him to lead the side as well as dictate play was too much. If Rob was disappointed, he never showed it. Jealousy and resentment were not in his vocabulary.'

Andrew's unswerving loyalty to his captain went beyond the strategic issues of how to win matches and how to dig England out of a hole, and, on one celebrated occasion, he even helped Carling to push the RFU into a hole that they had dug for themselves by sacking their captain in May 1995, a few weeks before the team was to leave for the World Cup. The 'Old Farts' affair escalated into a cause célèbre when a reprimand from Twickenham and an apology from Carling ought to have unruffled the feathers of the 57-strong general committee.

The row centred on a throwaway remark that Carling made after a television interview with Greg Dyke. 'If the game is run properly as a professional game, you do not need fifty-seven old farts running rugby,' Carling said, in what he thought was an off-the-record comment made after the cameras had stopped. An immediate explanation would have saved a lot of heartache all round, but while Carling and his advisers failed to grasp the reality of a rapidly deteriorating situation, RFU president Dennis Easby, a Berkshire solicitor, former international referee and thoroughly decent man, chaired an emergency session of the Union's hierarchy at the East India Club. While they were assembling to sack their captain, Carling was playing golf and, therefore, incommunicado when I tried to advise him that his position was in some jeopardy.

Once the balloon went up, after an official RFU communiqué a couple of hours before that day's Pilkington Cup final, the England players closed ranks and stood four-square behind their shocked ex-captain. Not for the first time, the Union had underestimated the players' militancy. Andrew had told Carling, 'Take it from me, no one will accept the captaincy.'

True to his word, Andrew turned it down as did Dean Richards, before the two issued a statement on behalf of the squad asking Easby to reconsider. They were, in Carling's words, 'the key men' who 'played hardball with the RFU yet gave them a way out which allowed them to retain some dignity.'

'We all pre-empted that situation by sticking together,' Andrew said. 'It was a concerted effort on our part to say we were not interested in taking over the captaincy, only in Will's reinstatement.'

There were many other rucks with the RFU in the final years of 'shamateurism' before the dam burst. As more sponsorship money poured into the sport, the players felt increasingly exploited to the point where strike action was discussed more than once. They did not want to be paid for playing, but they did want to be able to cash in on their fame commercially. 'At the time, the issues were pretty serious, heavy-duty stuff. There were all these skirmishes which, with hindsight, we were probably never going to win. But it is crass for any ruling body to turn round and say, as the RFU effectively said to us, "If you lot don't want to play, we will pick another team."

'Apart from being totally disrespectful to the players, it showed a complete lack of understanding of the issues. If you [the RFU] have got to the point where the players are threatening to go on strike, it means you have mismanaged the situation in the first place. If your only response to your own role in that mismanagement is to say, "If

188

you don't play, we'll pick someone else," it's like a big kid saying, "It's my bat, and I'm taking it home." In the end we were banging our heads against a brick wall.

'The ultimate response was Dudley Wood's comment, "The rest of the world can go professional if they want, but we will stay amateur." How unbelievably naive and what a total lack of understanding of what his own players were trying to do. We were trying at that time to compete as amateurs – proper amateurs – against semi-professionals and really trying to do our best to close the gap between the hemispheres.'

The moment the RFU signed the first sponsorship deal, back in the early '70s, they had set the sport off on the road to professionalism. Incredibly, they were pretending it would never happen as late as 1994 when England's tour of South Africa confirmed that professionalism had already arrived.

'We went to a fund-raising dinner in the Orange Free State on that tour when the president of the Free State stood up and said, "I'd like to thank the England players for coming to this dinner. We are raising lots of money so we can pay our players and stop them going to Transvaal." Ian Beer was president of the RFU, and he was at the dinner! They could have created a centrally managed professional game if they had had the foresight to move quickly.'

In the final months before the administrators belatedly made the game honest by declaring it open in August 1995, Andrew was a key figure in the Kerry Packer-backed attempt to buy up a complete set of international teams to play rugby's version of a World Series. Rupert Murdoch had signed up the Unions of South Africa, New Zealand and Australia and they were still counting the money that had been promised – all £366 million of it over ten years – when it slowly dawned on them that the players were defecting to Murdoch's great rival, Kerry Packer.

As the chief recruiting officer for the new Packer-backed World Rugby Corporation, Ross Turnbull, a former Wallaby prop and Australian team manager, was doling contracts out all over the rugby world promising the players a signing-on fee of £50,000 and two years at £80,000 a year. There were fanciful plans for a European league and a southern-hemisphere provincial tournament. The global scheme lacked for nothing, except the money to get it off the ground.

Turnbull had put the cart before the horse. He could deliver the players but not the overall strategy and when Francois Pienaar, then

189

captain of South Africa, broke ranks and sided with his Union, the grandiose plan crumbled like a deck of cards. The players were the real winners, certainly in South Africa where Louis Luyt, the dictatorial Union president, made the extravagant gesture of matching the offers made by Turnbull, a panic gesture that would plunge the Springboks into financial crisis.

Far from seeing what was coming, the RFU was too busy squabbling with its clubs to notice that those players whom they had briefly put under lock and key were out of contract. The clubs signed them all instead, many on ridiculously inflated salaries, but if the owners had to fork out over the odds, it was a small enough price to pay for owning the most important pawns in the ensuing political power struggle.

Eventually, even Hall gave it up as a bad job, retreating to his villa in southern Spain, but not before he had done the decent thing by Newcastle and written off debts of some £9 million. The establishment saw him as a bogeyman, but there can be no degrading Hall's importance as a magnetic figure in the early days of professionalism whose dynamism gave Andrew the wherewithal to build a club of real substance.

'Sir John was a visionary. Where we are now as a sport in terms of crowds and investment, he thought we should have been there five years ago. He was so far ahead of everyone else's thinking that he could see where we should be. But he had all these fights going on with people trying to kill off the clubs that in the end he said, "I can't be bothered any more."

'We went through a nasty three or four months before Dave Thompson came forward to save the club from going out of business. Sir John handed the club to Dave for £1 with all the liabilities. He didn't get it for nothing, because it's cost him a fortune.'

Since then Andrew's crusade on Tyneside has generated £25 million worth of investment and enough support to justify the provision of a stadium with room for 10,000 fans. It was a good job he took Geoff Boycott's advice all those years ago.

13

DEANO

HIS FIRST ENGLAND CAPTAIN, NIGEL MELVILLE, REMEMBERS HIM WITH AFFECTIONATE candour as 'a big daft lad who never quite looked the part; someone who would be more at home riding his bike as a policeman than playing the rugby superstar'. His last England captain, Will Carling, admits that for years he 'just could not understand what made him tick'. A senior officer in the Leicestershire Constabulary described him as a 'prolific thief-taker' and a fellow Leicester player as 'a slow old carthorse', which did not say much for the speed with which the villains left the scene of their crimes.

Dean Richards straddled the chasm between the old game and the new like a colossus. He was one who never cared much for how he looked on the field and even less for the battalion of fitness experts with their iron-pumping regimes. Richards, socks rolled down to the ankles, shirt flapping outside his shorts, never allowed the dietitians to change his shape, which, if anything, developed from rotund to slightly more rotund as the years went by.

The more incongruous he appeared in the new streamlined, professional arena, the more the fans loved him, whether they were supporting Leicester, England or the Lions. They loved the rolling gait, the slightly dishevelled look, but, above all, they loved the heavy-duty authority he brought to their team through his mastery of the maul and control at the base of the scrum, which allowed him to manoeuvre his way to a flood of push-over tries.

191

Richards was more – much more – than a stick-it-up-your-jumper merchant. A sharp footballing brain explained why at times the ball seemed to follow him rather than the other way round. It was an awareness that, allied to an octopus-like monopoly of the ball, made him a truly formidable opponent. Once he had clamped those oversized mitts around the ball, he rarely let go. Scotland discovered this one year at Murrayfield when Jack Rowell, then under severe pressure as manager of a wobbling England team, brought Richards back into the side to help save the coach's job and the Leicester number 8 duly obliged with a masterful display. It was Scotland's misfortune to run into him at his commanding best. At the end of the match, they must have been sorely tempted to wonder whether the English had used some sort of magnetic device to put the ball into Richards' hands. It might have explained why the ball seemed rarely to be in anyone else's possession that day.

With so much natural ability and nous, why risk diluting it by over-doing it on the training field? In that respect, Richards belonged to a rare breed of international number 8s. Willie Duggan, the Irishman who had preceded him in the Lions back row against the All Blacks in 1983, was another who refused to change some old habits. Summoned from the dressing-room at Twickenham, Duggan took one last drag of his cigarette on the way out, blew the smoke along the tunnel and handed the smouldering remains of his fag to Allan Hosie, the Scottish referee who was waiting to follow both teams onto the field.

The old amateur ethos suited Duggan down to the ground. Arriving late for a club match at Lansdowne Road, the coach greeted him with a mild rebuke, 'You've missed the warm-up, Willie.'

'Ah now, I wouldn't agree with you on that,' said Duggan. 'Sure I had the heater on in the car. I'm warmed up rightly . . .'

Richards' aversion to training went right across the board, whether his next match was a midweek friendly for Leicester – in the days when they had such things – or a Grand Slam decider for England. As Carling soon found out for himself, the bulky Hinckley policeman had two favourite warm-up routines, both of which could have come straight out of the Duggan manual. 'One of his more celebrated warm-up routines in the dressing-room was to pat his stomach and see how long it would take for the wobbles to subside,' Carling said. 'While the rest of the team were stretching or jogging to loosen up, Dean would sit in the corner reading the match programme. There was nothing malevolent about him. He was simply a one-off, a survivor despite the fact that he broke all the rules. That's why he was so popular.'

Having floundered against the rock-like Richards in the England back row, Wales would not be amused to learn that they could have claimed him as one of their own, not that there would have been any realistic chance of his accepting their offer. His father Brian, who left his native Treorchy at an early age when the family joined the pre-war exodus from the Rhondda Valley to the English Midlands, set the ball rolling as a member of the 1st XV at Nuneaton.

Once his son, born in Nuneaton on 11 July 1963, had shot to early prominence as a schoolboy international while still at John Cleveland College in Hinckley – which was also the alma mater of Graham Rowntree, another Leicester Lion – Richards was always destined to go to Leicester. He made his first-team debut for the Tigers at the age of 18, for England at 22 and would have done so for the Lions the following year had the scheduled tour of South Africa not been abandoned as a protest at the apartheid regime.

His education, in rugby terms at any rate, extended to a season with Roanne and a Continental debut for Leicester that could have had fatal consequences. A Saturday night out with John Wells in the Alpine resort of Chambéry put the Tigers back-row pair in a tighter corner than any they would encounter on the rugby field for the rest of their days.

An Anglo-French tête-à-tête deteriorated rapidly enough for a gun to be pulled on Wells. Discretion being the better part of valour, they did what they had not done before or since and surrendered. 'We were walking down the street when Dean took some abuse from some blokes, and it got out of hand,' Wells said. 'This guy was holding a gun at my head and pointing at Dean. We put our hands up and backed away. I was trying to pacify things, but it wasn't one of those situations where language – any language – would be of much help. No shots were fired, but it was only when we sobered up the next morning that we thought, "Bloody hell!"'

Mercifully, Richards made it back home, and it would be only a matter of time before England asked him to end the merry-go-round of players selected at number 8. In two years from February 1984, they had tried no fewer than five players in that position: John Scott of Cardiff, Chris Butcher of Harlequins, Bob Hesford of Bristol, Gloucester's Mike Teague and Graham Robbins of Coventry, all in the space of 13 internationals. Against Ireland at

Twickenham on 1 March 1986 – a day so cold that they lit fires in the car parks to stop the brandy freezing – Richards performed as though he had been playing for his country all his life, scoring both tries in a 25–20 home win. It was a feat that no England player had achieved on his debut for more than half a century.

It was still being talked of 20 years later by another Lion of some standing. Fran Cotton considered it the greatest Five Nations Championship performance he had ever seen. 'Dean waddled on to the pitch behind the rest of the team, socks rolled down looking like he'd just come off the beat. His style of play, too, was unique. He was like a rock. Once he got hold of the ball, it was impossible to get it off him.'

The Deano legend was up and running. He went to the World Cup the following year, of course, but a quarter-final exit against Wales in Sydney confirmed the conviction that the inaugural tournament fell at least a year before England – under Geoff Cooke's managerial direction – got their act together. It also, somewhat belatedly, gave credence to the fear often expressed in the '80s by former Wales coach Clive Rowlands: 'Heaven help the rest of us if England ever get organised.'

Before the end of the following season, Richards had written his name into the folklore of the game by leaving an ugly mark on the Calcutta Cup or, to be more accurate, so many ugly marks that the famous old trophy, made from melted-down silver rupees, required lengthy restoration. His late Saturday night antics in tandem with the great Scot John Jeffrey ensured that an instantly forgettable match at Murrayfield – won 9–6 by England – would be remembered for what happened long after the 60,000 or so spectators had gone home.

Just as nobody ever accused Richards of over-training, so nobody could accuse him of ever losing his sense of fun. Nor did an increasingly serious business dilute his thirst as Jeffrey has not been slow to corroborate. The 'White Shark' has never been in any doubt as to his English sparring partner's greatest strength: 'His ability still to be drinking at the end of the night . . .'

Joel Stransky, the Springbok who patented the winning, extra-time drop goal in a World Cup final, eight years before you-know-who followed suit, marvelled at the Richards drinking capacity, which he saw at first hand during his spell at Leicester. 'He could drink the whole team under the table,' Stransky said, at the height of his English sojourn. 'And he could probably do it every night of the week. He's the man you cannot keep up with at the bar.'

Another ex-Leicester international, Will Greenwood, once claimed that 'players took it in half-hour shifts with Richards at the bar. You didn't want to be stuck with him for too long, because otherwise you wouldn't remember much about it.'

Now there are two world authorities on the subject of kicking the Calcutta Cup about the cobbled streets of central Edinburgh and one of them, Jeffrey, did take the lid off the dinner which preceded an event fuelled by whisky galore. With the stuff readily available, both behind the bar and on every table, the after-match dinner was always going to be more uproarious than the game itself – a dire affair that had been won and lost without a try in sight.

'There were two fights between England and Scotland players at the dinner that night,' he said. 'It degenerated into an unholy scrap. In fact four players didn't see it to the dinner; they were in their beds. Unfortunately, I had a stronger constitution. An impromptu decision was made to fill the Cup with fire water and pour it over Brian Moore [the English hooker]. Then he started chasing us so we just ran. Once the doors opened, it was out into the street, so we jumped into a taxi with the Calcutta Cup and went to two or three pubs.'

When the reckless episode became public knowledge, in the cold light of day the following Monday, the two protagonists were asked for their version of events only to be given widely contrasting punishments by their respective Unions. The SRU referred to it, in their quaint way, as 'a sorry interlude' and then proceeded to banish one of their most popular players to a longer and sorrier interlude than anyone could have imagined: they banned Jeffrey for six months. It was a draconian measure compared to the RFU's lenience, which has left Jeffrey as baffled now as he was then. Richards escaped with a seven-day ban, which, compared to his partner's fate, added a touch of almost 'Pythonesque' absurdity to an episode that provided a classic example of two Unions going to opposite extremes in their treatment of the same case. Clearly, Twickenham judged the 'sorry interlude' to be a lot less sorry than the Scots – a storm in a Calcutta Cup, as it were – although Richards did get a wigging from his chief constable.

The following year, none the worse for the experience, both went on the Lions tour of Australia, and while Jeffrey had to be content with a place in the midweek team, Richards played a leading role in turning the losing start in the first Test match into a series victory.

That the Aussies whinged about it then and were still whingeing about it when the Lions returned 12 years later was probably a fair indication of how well Finlay Calder's team had done their job in winning a series that saw a fair amount of spilt blood and busted guts. Bob Dwyer, who would win the World Cup for the Wallabies a little over two years later, paid the Lions the most enormous of back-handed compliments by calling them the dirtiest bunch he had ever seen.

Richards, he argued, was the only non-Australian victim. 'When the front rows of the scrum collapsed, the Lions second-rowers kicked their opponents in the head,' Dwyer said. 'This did not happen occasionally but nearly every time the scrum folded. On one such occasion, as a second-rower swung back his boot he smashed his own number 8, Dean Richards, in the face with his heel and broke a tooth. Suspecting that the second-rower had intended to kick an Australian, we found it hard to feel sorry for Richards.' And to think the Wallabies went into the series thinking that the Lions were a soft touch.

The view in the Australian camp, that the tourists lacked organisation, fitness and, worst of all, any ferocity, appeared to have been confirmed during the opening Test, the first at the Sydney Football Stadium adjacent to the city's famous cricket ground. The Wallabies scored four tries without reply as the Lions were counted out to the tune of 30–12.

The Lions dropped the Wales lock Bob Norster, Scotland flanker Derek White, Wales centre Mike Hall and Scotland fly-half Craig Chalmers for the second Test. Wade Dooley, Mike Teague, Jeremy Guscott and Rob Andrew replaced them, and the English quartet helped the Lions to square the series in Brisbane before going on to win it one week later.

As some of his teammates worked themselves into a raging fury before the critical second Test, Richards excused himself from the head-banging routine, preferring to sit in the corridor outside and conserve his energy 'for the pitch'. It was a ploy that prompted Andrew to describe him as 'a product of the silent, contemplative school of self-motivation'.

Finlay Calder's Lions flew home with some sweet music ringing in their ears: the sound of the macho Aussies gnashing their teeth and crying into their Tooheys at losing the physical battle. The forward duel being based on intimidation by its very definition, the Lions out-muscled and out-fought the opposition. They achieved their superiority by hook or by crook, devising a plan aimed at exploiting Nick Farr-Jones's fragile temperament: they instructed his opposite number, Robert Jones, to stand on Farr-Jones's foot at the first scrum. It worked a treat, provoking an immediate brawl. 'Next thing I knew,' said Farr-Jones, 'Calder came off the scrum and belted me.'

It set the tone for what followed, and while the more hard-headed Wallaby technocrats made a mental note to correct their skipper's tendency to be flustered under pressure for the forthcoming World Cup, their administrators were busy firing off a formal protest to the International Rugby Board. They enclosed a video to illustrate their complaints that ended up – as anything controversial usually did in those days – swept under a mountainous carpet. 'A year or two later, one of the Lions players on that tour cast a revealing light on the affair while speaking to an Australian administrator,' Dwyer said. 'Asked about the foul play his team had engaged in, he said, "It wasn't all of us. It was the English coppers."'

Dooley, Richards and the formidable Paul Ackford were the rocks against which the Wallabies floundered, and the three will forever be convinced that they would have scored a more famous victory against the same opposition two years later at Twickenham in the World Cup final had England not made a tactical change, forsaking the strength of their pack for a 15-man game, that was not exactly up their street.

Ackford, the best front-jumper of his generation who raised the art to new heights, began his working life teaching English literature before the Metropolitan Police put him on the fast track to the top. Before he could get there, the Harlequin, whom a previous RFU president had called Paul Ackroyd when presenting him with his cap, had proved himself a man apart. Here was a rugby player who actually took the trouble to write his own column, rather than leave it to the imagination of his ghost. It was the first step towards a full-time career in journalism as the *Sunday Telegraph*'s trenchant rugby correspondent.

Having retired immediately after the World Cup final, Ackford had made a big enough impression on at least one Australian. David Campese was forced to include one Englishman in the world's best non-Australian XV. 'This guy was tough and durable, a real workhorse in the pack,' Campese said. 'It's just a shame he was a Pom and not an Aussie. It is even more disappointing to reflect on his finest moment against us – the 1989 Lions series. I get a bit sick looking back on that particular three-match part of Australian rugby history. Still, "Ackers" is worth the painful revisit. He was one of the flint-hard Englishmen in that Lions pack, and they physically destroyed us up front. Like Wade Dooley and Mike Teague, in particular, two other Poms from that pack, he was very determined and extremely aggressive.'

Jeffrey watched it all in his role as an enthusiastic member of the supporting cast, none the worse for his six-month ban for the Calcutta Cup episode. Squeezed out of the Test team – initially by his compatriot White, then by the tough-as-teak Teague from Gloucester – the White Shark got a little of his own back on Richards with the only try of a draw against England in 1989. However, when Scotland famously ambushed the Sassenachs' Grand Slam at Murrayfield on St Patrick's Day, 1990, his sparring partner from the opposition back row was nowhere to be seen.

Richards missed the entire Five Nations Championship that season because of injury, returning the following season for the first England Grand Slam under Carling. However, Richards soon received a sobering reminder that such a bauble did not count for much in Australia. The Wallabies' 40–15 rout in Sydney a few months before the 1991 World Cup sent England home with their ambling number 8 carrying the can for more than one Wallaby try: it was the kind of excess baggage that he didn't want.

The idea that Richards was not indispensable after all had been fermenting for some months. It came to a head in Paris before the 1991 World Cup quarter-final at the Parc des Princes when Geoff Cooke as team manager, in consultation with Roger Uttley as coach and Carling as captain, took the decision to drop him. They moved Mike Teague from blindside to number 8 and picked Mick 'The Munch' Skinner, a Geordie from Wallsend via Harlequins, who had made the final 30 on the strength of what he had done in Deano's absence the previous year. When it came to doing the captain's bit and telling Richards, Carling admitted he 'flunked it'. He had found him 'difficult to handle'. Carling said in his autobiography, *My Autobiography*:

> I didn't understand Deano to begin with. Without doing anything, he had this quality where people just waited to see which way he would jump. Players looked to him for a lead. Brian [Moore] demanded attention because he was verbose and pro-active, whereas Dean just slumped along at the back

of the team meetings or at the back of the bus. He would rarely take the initiative or voice an opinion, although he had clear ideas on the game he thought England should play.

I never appreciated what a hell of a guy he was until my last two or three years. I just didn't understand what made him tick early on. I should have talked to him more, but I was scared of him, I suppose. I felt that the immense respect he had within the team was potentially threatening to me, not that he would deliberately undermine anyone.

That week in Paris, the respect the more senior members of the pack felt for Richards manifested itself in an almost contemptuous reaction to the news that he had been dropped. Moore called it 'suicide', which must have sounded odd to those who witnessed his dust-up with Richards in training after the surplus-to-requirements copper had belted the Pit Bull with a tackle bag.

Carling noted there and then that the 'shock' of Richards' omission had sent 'a tremor through the squad' but that it imbued them with the ruthless streak to knock France out in their citadel. Moore, despite what had happened pre-match, preserved his paid-up membership of the Dean Richards' fan club. 'Dean was never particularly dynamic on the ball, but he created platforms which the opposition could never dismantle,' he said. 'I was always anxious if he wasn't there. I would never have willingly gone into a game without him.' Wade Dooley, the giant Grasshopper from Preston, dismissed Richards' omission in two words: 'Absolute rubbish.'

Carling, to his credit, has not shied away from admitting that he could not bring himself to tell Richards man-to-man. 'Geoff had already passed on the news, and when it came to my turn for a heart-to-heart, I couldn't face him,' Carling said. 'I can cope with ranting and raving, but it was the silence which threw me. Dean's passive acceptance made me squirm. I blurted a few platitudes and left. It was a pretty undistinguished performance.'

England, with Skinner 'larging it', kept the same back row for the rest of the competition. The World Cup over, they attempted to persist without Richards, promoting Tim Rodber of Northampton for the first match of the 1992 Five Nations – against Scotland at Twickenham – only to bring his predecessor off the bench to dig them out of trouble, after they realised that the newcomer had been rushed in a trifle prematurely.

Richards, none the worse for the World Cup controversy, had

been re-installed for the return to Paris, resuming normal service amid the bedlam of a double French sending-off. He then guided England to a second successive Grand Slam against Wales, whose relief at losing 'only' 24–0 indicated how far their game had gone down the plughole.

Despite everything, Richards' sense of humour survived. During the week leading up to Carling's 50th international – against Romania at Twickenham in November 1994 – the responsibility of marking the occasion with a little something on behalf of the troops fell to Richards. He organised a team photograph in which Jeff Probyn featured prominently, despite the fact that the legendary tight-head prop had retired the previous year. Now Probyn was about as close to Carling as the Reverend Ian Paisley to the Pope and perhaps not as close as Sir Alex Ferguson and Arsène Wenger. Richards duly presented Carling with a photograph entitled 'Will and his friends', which showed the captain at the centre of the team surrounded by 21 players all of whom had Probyn's head superimposed on their bodies.

When the RFU stripped Carling of the captaincy at the end of that season over the notorious 'old farts' row, Richards played a leading role in the Union's swift about turn. He and Rob Andrew let it be known that neither would take the captaincy under any circumstance and asked the RFU to reconsider their decision, which they duly did.

Their announcement the following day reduced the Bath v. Wasps Pilkington Cup final to an insignificant side show. Barely a week before they were to leave for South Africa and the 1995 World Cup, England had fired their captain only to reinstate him three days later in time for the flight to Johannesburg for which Richards equipped himself with a Gorbachev mask to bring some levity to the proceedings.

England were never going to succeed where they had failed four years earlier, in what would be their old Tiger's last tilt at the biggest trophy. At least he had the satisfaction of prising it from Australia's grasp, driving the late maul from a lineout deep enough into Wallaby territory, in the quarter-final at Newlands, for Andrew to land his colossal goal.

Put to the sword by the All Blacks in the semi-final and beaten by France four days later in a desperate match for third place, Richards came home with his international career all but over. The same might have been said of his long association with Leicester. It looked like he was gradually being phased out by the regime run by Bob Dwyer, one of his old foes, whom the Tigers had hired to see them through the immediate post-professional era.

The St Valentine's Day weekend of 1998 would change all that. Richards had resigned himself to leaving when the club summoned him to an emergency board meeting that Sunday night. He had been helping his wife Nicola put their twin boys in their cot, before pouring himself a large glass of red wine ready to put his feet up for the evening, when the call came.

Figuratively speaking, he appeared to be on his last legs as a Leicester player: 'They were old and knackered. The game was overtaking me, so I could understand it if there were no plans for me to stay. I'd heard through the grapevine that Bob didn't want me at the club, and I'd made plans to go elsewhere at the end of the season.'

The night of the long knives ended with Dwyer's exit: as acrimonious a split as it was abrupt. Rather than risk losing their iconic number 8, Leicester put Richards in charge as their new director of rugby: an appointment that was to produce the most spectacular success in the club's history. He concentrated on managing and picking the team, leaving the coaching to his trusted old friend John Wells and putting the club's Australian centre Pat Howard in charge of the backs.

Dwyer's sudden demise followed a home defeat by London Irish and a training ground row with Austin Healey, a player who called him 'The Führer'. As a result of the spat, which took place on Friday, 13 February 1998, Healey did not play the next day. Dwyer, who had tried to sign the Argentinian scrum-half Augustin Pichot, then with Richmond, said that Healey had a thigh strain. The player countered that by saying he had never been fitter. The Australian, whose acerbic brand of man-management had inspired some of the World Cup-winning Wallabies to re-christen him 'Barbed Wire', was not going to waste any time humouring a player whose habit of talking as fast a game as he played earned him the dubious nickname of 'Mr Gobby'.

Five days after their verbal punch-up, Dwyer was looking for a new job. He did not go quietly, accusing Leicester of hiring him to do their dirty work and, more pointedly, of being 'gutless'. As Peter Tom, the club's multi-millionaire chairman, put it, 'Look at our waist lines. Most of us would like to have fewer guts . . .'

The board, almost entirely made up of ex-players like Tom, faced a stark choice – to keep Dwyer and risk losing Richards or keep Richards and lose Dwyer. 'We had to decide whether we were going to take up the option on Bob's contract or give Dean the job a year early,' Tom said.

Bristol welcomed Dwyer with open arms as their new director of rugby, and Sod's law decreed that Leicester would clinch the Premiership title in May 2000 from the last match of the season at where else but the Memorial Ground against their old coach's new team. Another heated exchange between Dwyer and Healey reopened the old wounds before the healing process could run its course: 'We were clapping Bristol off the field, and they were congratulating us when Bob came onto the pitch,' Healey said. 'I went to shake his hand, and he told me to get stuffed. I was trying to bury the hatchet. I went up with the sincere intention of saying to him, "Thanks very much, and good luck for next season." Instead, he threw it back in my face. He lost his temper and was going a bit mad.'

That Healey should want to thank Dwyer for anything seemed odd in view of what he thought of his coaching: 'I think I lost a season of my rugby life under Bob. He forced me into my shell by applying too much pressure. I didn't agree with the way he was trying to coach me. If he had stayed on, I would have left. He didn't want me there, and I didn't want to be coached by him. It had reached boiling point. I admit that I did have an attitude, but I am not a troublemaker.'

Twelve months later, Richards' switch of Healey from wing to fly-half, for the last quarter of the epic European Cup final against Stade Français in Paris, helped the Tigers to complete their first Double as champions of England and Europe. By then, Deano's name had been mentioned in the dispatches for the vacancy of England forwards' coach, left by John Mitchell's decision to return to his native New Zealand. The recommendation came from Jack Rowell, Clive Woodward's predecessor in charge of England. 'I would have no hesitation going for Dean,' Rowell said. 'He has the rugby brain; the management and technical skills. He has a huge presence and a record of achievement. Dean can give that extra to people which glues a team together. At Leicester, he has given them heart and soul. It all adds up to the rounded candidate. There are other people, but I'd like him to make himself available.'

Richards, never a man to use ten words when one will do, responded with typical candour. 'I am not interested,' he said. 'I'm quite happy doing what I'm doing.' While it would have been reasonable to assume that England would have asked him directly had they wanted him badly enough, he sought the media spotlight with about as much relish as the reclusive American aviator, Howard Hughes.

After a great deal of coaxing and just a little cajoling, I once achieved the mighty breakthrough of persuading him to talk about himself, his rugby and his job as part of the *Daily Mail*'s supplement for the 1991 World Cup. Early on the morning of its publication, I took a phone call. On answering, I heard a voice say, 'Mr Jackson?'

'Yes,' I replied.

'This is the Leicestershire constabulary.' My heart began to sink. 'It's about the article in today's paper on Dean Richards.'

'Yes . . .'

'Well, this is the public relations department, and we would like to reproduce it for our in-house magazine, if we have your permission.'

'No problem, but why don't you have a word with him?' I asked.

'Oh, he never talks to us . . .'

Actions usually spoke louder than words with Richards, as one uncapped member of the England squad discovered to his discomfort in the dead of night during the week leading up to a Test against the All Blacks at Twickenham in November 1993. At that time, England players doubled up two to a room and Kyran Bracken, the unsuspecting victim, found himself sharing with Richards.

That was the second mistake, even if it was not of his doing. The first, at the Memorial Ground earlier that year, most certainly was: Bracken scored a long-range solo try. It turned out to be decisive, giving Bristol a precious 15–10 win over Leicester and Richards, needless to say, had not forgotten it. Deano, the story goes, was not best pleased with the rooming arrangements. According to Bracken, he 'skipped the team meeting and spent most of the night in the pub with Jason Leonard. He still hadn't got back when I drifted off to sleep around midnight, but I do know exactly when he did return . . . It was twenty past two in the morning when Deano and Jase stormed into the room, stripped back my bedding and lifted me up in my boxer shorts, giving me the wedgie to end all wedgies.'

There were times when Leicester gave the impression of doing the same – in a strictly figurative sense, of course – to the rest of the Premiership. They won it four times in a row, and successive

European Heineken Cup victories over Stade Français and Munster brought them the double Double as champions of England and the Continent. Yet within two years, the supposedly fire-proof Richards had been fired.

When Leicester's board gave him the job, chief executive Peter Wheeler referred to his old teammate as 'a safe pair of hands'. The priceless quantity of silverware that subsequently passed through them made his sudden demise all the more difficult to understand, especially in view of some extenuating circumstances. The most pronounced of these was the fact that the Tigers had kept winning despite making the largest single contribution to England, supplying players at all age levels on such a scale that it would inevitably take a heavy toll.

With seven-eighths of their pack otherwise engaged helping England win the 2003 World Cup, even Leicester found the handicap too much. After the end of the successful competition, the seven hurled themselves straight back into the cause. For all their effort, they were unable to arrest the club's slide into the bottom four or stifle the rumblings of discontent emanating from the boardroom and, according to Richards' allies, from one or two disaffected individuals in the dressing-room.

The rumours of his sacking had been flying around for weeks before Stade Français sealed his fate. The Parisians' win at Welford Road on 30 January 2004, eliminating the Tigers from the last eight of the Heineken Cup, brought the long Richards era to an anticlimactic end. He had rejected the board's plan for a lesser role in a new management structure. They felt there had been a 'steady decline in the team's performances for the past two seasons'. Chairman Tom said, 'The board felt this decline could only be checked by significant changes within the playing structure. Dean did not find these changes acceptable.'

A victim of his own success, Richards headed for France and a season at Grenoble in charge of a fairly ordinary group of players. Leicester, under his old pal Wells, somehow scrambled back into Europe on the strength of nine straight wins, but the fallout from the abrupt and acrimonious demise of his predecessor was still evident months after the event.

Richards reclaimed every piece of personal memorabilia from Welford Road, removing virtually every trace of his monumental association with the club. The list of items withdrawn at their owner's request included a set of six international caps, among them those marking his three World Cup campaigns of 1987, 1991 and 1995. Framed jerseys, including the the 1991 Grand Slam winning shirt that had been given pride of place, no longer adorned the walls of the Tigers' inner sanctum, and a members' lounge bar, opened at the stadium in recognition of his legendary status, ceased to exist in his name. Deano's Bar disappeared, and all the signs pointing to its location were taken down.

That he did not wish his name to be associated overtly with the club provided a wounding insight into the depth of ill-feeling about his sacking. It said everything about the pain and hurt over what friends called his 'back-stabbing'. 'I am upset that it finished the way it did,' he said, months later. 'Leaving Leicester in the manner I did has been very disappointing. It would be fair to say, there would be some people there who I would not be speaking to very much in the future.'

The Ambling Alp licked his wounds and relocated his family to the Alpine village of Vizille, famous as the cradle of the French Revolution. As a Francophile who had bought a house some years earlier in the historic Pyrenean city of Carcassonne, the move gave him time to take stock far away from the intrigue of his old stamping ground in the East Midlands before returning to take charge of Harlequins following their relegation from the Premiership. 'I had great times at Leicester, and I still have a real fondness for the fans,' he said, 'but you can't go on forever, can you?'

14

JERRY THE PACEMAKER

TO BEGIN AT THE BEGINNING IN THE STORY OF JEREMY CLAYTON GUSCOTT, IT IS necessary to go back some four years before his birth and relate the tale, perfectly true of course, of how his mother fell off her bike.

Susan Taylor, a 17 year old whose family had moved to Bath from her native Winchester, was cycling down Lansdown Hill from her home in the Roman city, with her head down on the low-slung handlebars when she looked up and saw a not unfamiliar figure standing in front of her a few yards away. As a variation of the ancient boy-meets-girl theme, Henry Guscott's method of introducing himself was unusual to say the least.

'He lived quite nearby, and I'd seen him around. You know how it is – you eye each other up. On that particular day, he thought it would be a laugh to walk out in front of me. I fell off my bike. I didn't know whether to laugh or cry. I'm lying there really hurt and he said, "Would you like to come out for a drink with me?"

'I think I told him where to go. And then I said, "All right, tomorrow." I know how steep the hill is. When you see someone at the last minute, it was quite scary. I was so annoyed that he didn't ask me how I was, just would I come out for a drink.'

On such strange meetings are Lions tours won and lost. What if Susan had seen Henry in ample time and given him the big swerve without so much as a backward glance? The Lions might never have won their 1989 series against Australia nor the one in South Africa eight years later, or if they did the probability is that the family name would have had nothing to do with it.

Henry Guscott emigrated to England from his native Jamaica in 1960 at the age of 21. A carpenter-cum-furniture maker by trade, he left his home village in Portland and settled in Bath, hoping to combine work with studying architecture. Of his introduction to the future Mrs Guscott, he said, 'All I can remember is saying, "Hello." There was definitely a bicycle involved somewhere.'

The head over heels bit was not confined to Sue coming off her bike. They were married two years later and Jeremy arrived two years after that, in July 1965. The cycling accident paved the way for the birth of a Rolls-Royce of a centre, and if England often chose to keep it in second gear, as a result of the narrow focus of their game pre-Woodward, that had nothing to do with his parents.

They thought at one stage that if their elder son was going to make a name for himself it would be as a cricketer. Peter Wight, the West Indian batsman who scored almost 20,000 runs for Somerset prior to becoming a first-class umpire, coached the young fellow before rugby and soccer took over. It was inspiration from his boyhood idol, the incomparable Pelé, that fuelled his early love of football: 'I wish I'd been born a few years earlier, so I could have appreciated him at the peak of his powers,' Guscott said. 'For me, he had everything: grace, style, supreme skill and the killer instinct. I was always Pelé when I was kicking the ball against the wall at School Lane.'

The Guscotts encouraged both their sons, Jeremy and Gary, to take an interest in sport and music. Each had the same early introduction to rugby in its mini form at Lambridge, the Bath Rugby Club's training base, which was even more unpretentious then than it is today. Their mother's family had played rugby, and, for a while, it looked as though they had produced not one exceptional talent but two. 'At one stage, some of the rugby gurus reckoned Gary was a better rugby player than Jeremy,' Henry said. 'Gary played when he wanted to, whereas Jeremy played as often as he could. He was just such a natural rugby player.'

The nearest he came to being diverted down the round-ball route was an invitation to train with the juniors at Bristol City, but Guscott never had any ambition to become a soccer professional. Given his precocious ability, arguably the most surprising aspect of his first-class rugby career is that Bath kept him waiting until the ripe old age of 19 to give him his debut, by which time he had tried his hand at bus driving and bricklaying – though not simultaneously.

His debut, on Saturday, 5 January 1985, came two years before the advent of the Courage League, a time when every match was supposedly a friendly. Bath's professional attitude under Jack Rowell had changed the whole approach of the team fully ten years before the game itself went open and the rest began to catch up. Merseyside being something less than a rugby hotbed, the young Guscott was never going to have his introduction delayed by crowd congestion when he made his bow against Waterloo at Blundellsands.

Typically, the new boy was less than thrilled at spending the first weekend of the New Year making a long coach haul north, even if he had been called up to stand in for John Palmer, a Bath legend, whose miserable total of three England caps hardened the view in Rowell's boot-room that they were better judges of players than the national selectors at a time when England were often nothing better than another second-rate international team.

'I didn't fancy that long trip north with blokes I barely knew, and I'd have rather been on the Friday night drink-up with the boys in Bath. That was what I kept telling myself. It was a front to cover my own pre-match nerves. I was nervous as hell that Saturday morning, intent only on getting through the game and not making a total ass of myself.'

Barry Trevaskis scored two tries, John Horton dropped a goal, the new teenager with the big Afro haircut kicked four penalties and Bath won 23–13. Curiously, the newcomer was never called upon again as the front-line goal kicker during the next 15 years, despite the fact that he had taken to it as naturally as every other aspect of the game.

Tries were Guscott's speciality and his first at senior level followed a few weeks later, against Exeter University at The Rec on 27 February. He ended that first season with a trip to Twickenham for Bath's Cup final against London Welsh. He went not as a fan but as one of the reserve cast. At the time, soccer had substitutes and rugby replacements, the distinction being that in rugby a player could not be substituted for tactical purposes but replaced only through injury. However, the naive theory that rugby teams would never bend the rules to feign injuries was difficult to support. Plenty did, which left the IRB no option but to amend the law to allow players to be replaced for tactical reasons.

Guscott, who arrived at Twickenham kitted out, like the rest of the team, in a new blazer for the occasion, finished up on the right wing in place of an injured Trevaskis. If he touched the ball once that was about it, but Bath's victory – secured by tries from players at opposite ends of the spectrum, the elegant David Trick and the inelegant Gareth Chilcott – gave their youngest player a taste of what was to come.

Bath's homecoming with the Cup the following day, Sunday, 28 April 1985, had been turned into a civic occasion that the local boy considered slightly over the top. His bemused reaction to the reception typified the irreverent side of his nature, provoking a response that suggested that he thought it was all a bit of a charade. 'The team went on an open-top bus tour round Bath,' he said. 'It might have been the done thing in soccer, but in rugby you felt a fool up on the top deck glugging champagne, as a few hundred diehards cheered us below. I find it almost sad that some people push themselves to the point of passing out.'

For all his tries, Guscott will always be remembered in a Lions context for the drop goal that won the Test series in South Africa in 1997. Nobody was more relieved to follow its soaring flight between the posts than John Bentley, an extrovert Yorkshireman who had returned to union from league during the hectic months in the aftermath of the International Rugby Board's historic decision, at a hotel on the Boulevard Haussmann in Paris, to declare the game open. An ex-policeman who had made two brief appearances for England in the late '80s, Bentley turned out to be an inspired selection by the Lions despite having been studiously ignored by his country throughout the preceding Five Nations series.

England under Jack Rowell may not have seen much in him, but the Lions selectors, under Fran Cotton's inspiring management, saw plenty. Bentley's wonder try to save the tourists against Transvaal at Ellis Park won him a place on the right wing for the second Test at King's Park in Durban, although there was a moment when history might have judged him as the man given the run around by the Springboks.

In scoring South Africa's third try during a twenty-minute stretch either side of half-time, Andre Joubert had brushed Bentley's attempted tackle aside with an imperious hand-off executed with the minimal fuss of someone swatting a mosquito. 'Bentos' got up in time for a perfect view of Joubert's studs as the stylish full-back flew in at the corner.

The '97 Lions had been driven by a private belief that they never knew when they were beaten, but that third try, stretching the Boks clear at 15–9 with the threat of more to come, had them wobbling on the precipice. While one more push would have landed them in a pit of despair, Bentley felt as though he was already in it. 'I looked for a shovel so I could dig a hole and bury myself,' Bentley said. 'I felt shocking about making such a foolish mistake. I'd only made it on the biggest stage in the world. We had this unshakeable belief in our ability to get back into the game. I needed to pull something out of the bag. I wasn't able to, but I knew somebody would.'

In the end, that somebody was Guscott. For the goals that ensured that the 1997 team would be embossed in the golden pantheon, the Lions relied on Neil Jenkins's mastery of his craft and Guscott's uncanny sense of destiny. Jenkins, the Welshman who kicked his first penalty as a small boy in the field next to what was then the family's scrap metal business in Church Village near Pontypridd, brought the Lions level at 15–15 with six minutes to go in the match. Guscott's towering drop goal three minutes later secured the famous victory. In her excitement, Sue Guscott waved the Union Jack so wildly above her head that it slipped from her grasp and landed on the head of a Springbok supporter sitting some rows in front. Sensing that he was not at all amused, Denise Healey – Austin's mother – saved the day with a gleeful apology: 'Ever so sorry, but that flag belongs to Jeremy Guscott's mum.'

When the final whistle brought confirmation of a series victory, the Lions were out on their feet. When it came to self-control in the face of a ferocity far beyond anything any of them had experienced in the Five Nations, the chosen few were in a league of their own. That they had conceded only one penalty throughout the second half was an astounding example of their collective discipline in trying circumstances.

Of all the colossal performances, most notably from the Ulster lock Jeremy Davidson and Lawrence Dallaglio, nobody made a greater impact than Scott Gibbs. The Lions would never have survived had the Welshman not gone to work that evening with a sledgehammer in one hand and a scythe in the other. His tackles exploded into the South African solar plexus with devastating effect, and when Os du Randt, the strongest Springbok of all, crumpled in a heap after one Gibbs onslaught, the psychological impact could be felt all over the stadium. They did not call him 'The Exocet' for nothing.

Some idea of what the Lions meant to Gibbs could be gauged from what the Welshman had to say on the subject when he and Guscott were reunited at the House of Commons in December 2004 to receive a medal of honour from the All-Party Parliamentary Rugby Union Group chaired by Derek Wyatt, the former England wing. 'When I wore the Lions jersey, it was like pulling on a body armour,' Gibbs told guests at the black-tie dinner in the Members' Dining Room. 'I felt invincible.'

Du Randt will vouch for that. Keith Wood finished in a 'pulverised' state, so much so that he needed Jason Leonard to prop him up for the lap of honour. That 'Uncle Fester' was still out there at the finish was a tribute to his courage and limitless energy. His final contribution, a demonic chip-and-chase down the Springbok right flank, forced the World Cup holders to concede enough territory for the Lions to make their final push and allow Guscott to land the killer blow.

How the Lions recovered from a losing position to win an epic struggle will live forever as the stuff of legend. A night that began with a Zulu war dance ended in a tribal celebration of a different sort, one not seen since Willie John McBride's team had won there 23 years earlier. For one night, the indomitable Lions had reclaimed Durban, the so-called 'last outpost of the British Empire', although they could not have done it without some expert Irish assistance from both sides of the border.

They did it because the World Cup holders contrived to miss all six shots at goal worth fifteen points. Most of all, they did it by sheer blood, guts and unflinching self-discipline. When it came to heroics, Wood took some beating in more senses than one. He epitomised the spirit of a Lions team that never knew when it was beaten, except in the last, anti-climactic Test when, with the series in the bag, the result was of little more than academic interest.

A team of lesser character would have seen the Springboks score three tries without reply during a twenty-minute stretch either side of half-time and taken the hint. The *Britse Leeus* (to give them their Afrikaans title) held their nerve and proceeded to trump the three tries with six goals, a neat role reversal of the first Lions Test against New Zealand in 1959 when the tourists scored four tries without reply only to be bludgeoned by six All Black penalties from the prodigious Don Clarke.

Ever the cool dude, Guscott made the winning drop goal look easy. That it flew high between the posts was no more than everyone expected, given that he always created the impression of being cocksure in everything he did on the rugby field. As he occupied the vacant fly-half position at King's Park that night, a split second's anxiety flitted across his mind about what he was about to attempt. 'You look up at the posts, and a little doubt creeps into your mind,' he told me, minutes later. 'You think, "What will they say if I miss?" Then you tell yourself, "You've got to do it. It's got to go over." When Matt [Dawson] fired the ball out, the decision to go for goal was made easier for me because Austin Healey was outside me. There was no way he was going to get the ball. But, to be perfectly honest, it just happened. I've always been an instinctive player.'

A team composed of seven Englishmen (Jeremy Guscott, Matt Dawson, John Bentley, Martin Johnson, Lawrence Dallaglio, Tim Rodber and Neil Back), three from Ireland (Keith Wood, Paul Wallace and Jeremy Davidson), three Scots (Gregor Townsend, Alan Tait and Tom Smith) and two Welshmen (Gibbs and Jenkins) had won a rubber in South Africa for only the second time. That they did so despite being outscored 10–3 on tries over the three matches said a lot about the Springboks' tactical naivety under an inexperienced coach, Carel du Plessis, but it said a lot more about the Lions' will to win.

Matt Dawson's three Lions tours had one common denominator. He went on all three ostensibly to play second fiddle to Welshmen: Rob Howley twice, then Dwayne Peel. However, he did play an unforgettable part in the beating of the Springboks. Promoted to the Test team after Howley dislocated a shoulder the previous week, Dawson made a blindside break into folklore seven minutes from the end of normal time with the Lions in dire need of inspiration to avoid another hard-luck story.

Nobody can ever have sold a dummy to so many South Africans at the same time. That Dawson, holding the ball aloft one-handed like a discus thrower approaching the point of release, had the nerve to do it and that the Springboks had the naivety to fall for it took a lot of believing. The tactical ploy that changed the course of Lions history had been discussed on the hoof between the scrum-half and his fellow Northampton back row forward Tim Rodber.

As a scrum formed some 30 yards from the Springbok line, they agreed that Dawson should try his luck. He veered beyond the telescopic clutches of Ruben Kruger, guarding the blindside of the scrum, off towards the touchline. Then, when he threw the dummy that Springbok skipper Gary Teichmann and a few more bought so completely, he was left with a free run to the line.

Like all the greats in any sport, Guscott always gave the impression of having all the time in the world: that with his ability nothing was really too big a sweat. There was a swagger about him, particularly during the early years. It left nobody in any doubt that in the unlikely event of the young man failing it would not be for any lack of self-belief.

There were times when it was not difficult to imagine that he had an attitude problem. Fortunately, David Trick, one of his friends within the Bath dressing-room, took Guscott aside to tell him his fortune. Asked for an objective view as to what the rest of the crew thought, Trick gave him both barrels: 'They think you're a big-headed prat.' The message hit home. Guscott acknowledged that he had been a 'complete prat' – as opposed to merely a big-headed one – and that he had to do something to change his reputation as 'an arrogant upstart'.

It didn't stop him provoking Richard Hill, the England scrum-half, who responded by knocking the upstart out cold during a New Year training camp in Lanzarote. Hill's tormentor could do nothing more than rise to his feet and put it down to experience. He ought to have known better. At round about that time, in March 1987, Hill fired England up for one of their tastier matches against Wales in Cardiff only to achieve the notoriety of being the first captain to be disciplined by the Rugby Football Union, who, in effect, declared that he had over-wound his team. Hill was given a one-match ban along with his Bath colleagues Graham Dawe and Gareth Chilcott, and Wade Dooley also received a ban for good measure.

The Welsh Rugby Union, by contrast, took no action against any of their players. Their lack of action rather exposed their English counterparts to accusations of over-reaction, which might not have been so bad had they won the match. They lost it 19–12, and while the England officials were to be congratulated for taking a stand against violent conduct, that they felt it necessary to take action on such a scale was a condemnation of Ray Megson's failure to deal with the culprits in his role as the referee.

Incredibly for a player of his calibre, Guscott's entry into the England team was delayed until May 1989, by which time he had almost reached the ripe old age of 24. As if anxious to make up for lost time, he opened his account against Romania in Bucharest with a hat-trick of tries. It was the first hat-trick by an Englishman on debut since Dan Lambert ran in five against France at Richmond in 1907.

Chris Oti got four on that baking May day in Bucharest but clearly felt short-changed, to Guscott's chagrin. There were not exactly bosom pals. 'I never quite hit it off with Oti. He was his own man and it showed. He told me that I could have passed more often to him. I thought his comment was out of order, but, for once, I let it pass.'

When they clashed again on the training field, a few weeks later during the Lions' tour of Australia, Guscott could not resist giving the wing a piece of his mind. Their inability to get along had deteriorated. 'Chris got up my nose. In an early match against Queensland President's XV in Cairns, Chris messed up a pre-planned move by coming in when he shouldn't have done, and I gave him a mild – very mild – bollocking.

'After the game, Roger [coach Roger Uttley] took me to one side and asked me what had happened between myself and Chris Oti. He said that Chris wasn't very happy with my comments. I couldn't believe that an on-field remark, quite right in its context, had been turned against me by Oti. He was injured shortly afterwards and went home.'

Guscott's family had gone to Bucharest en masse to witness his debut, but clearly not everybody was absolutely sure as to the identity of the new centre. According to the new cap, Uttley 'spent 20 minutes at the post-match reception telling my brother Gary what a good game he thought he'd had'.

It was some way to celebrate his selection as a Lion, which had been announced earlier that week. The news had been relayed by tour manager Clive Rowlands in a phone call to Guscott's parents' home. Will Carling had been ruled out because of a shin injury and that had led the Lions selection committee to the obvious conclusion that they did not have to look beyond England's champion club for his replacement.

Ever sensitive to being the victim of a wind-up, Guscott's instinctive reaction was to assume that the call was a hoax played on him by one of Bath's more convincing mimics, second-row forward John Morrison. 'John did a passable imitation of several voices and had caught me out before. This one purported to be Clive Rowlands, manager of the British Lions party that was leaving very shortly to tour Australia.

'Good effort, John. A very plausible Welsh accent and it sounded sincere too. I knew, of course, that the squad had been picked a few weeks before, but "Will Carling was pulling out with a shin injury", said the voice. Not a bad line. Decent wind-up, this. I let him drone on for a bit. And for a bit longer. Just as well really. I would never have found out which plane we were catching otherwise.'

For one with a relatively low boredom threshold, who could never understand why anyone would become obsessive about playing a game, Guscott could take everything in his stride and shrug it off with a so what? The Lions captured his imagination in a way no other team did, and if Carling could never quite understand what all the fuss was about, his Bath partner could have told him.

The pair who played together in the centre for England on a record number of occasions could not have had more contrasting views on what the Lions meant to them. Carling, who declared himself not 'overly concerned' at missing the 1989 tour, never professed to have any real enthusiasm for the most renowned of all touring teams: 'I have always placed England above the Lions in my personal pecking order.'

The fact that he managed just the one Test appearance – one more than the vast majority but a miniscule return for one who captained his country a record 59 times – might explain his apparent disdain. Guscott's passion for the Lions, on the other hand, knew no bounds as a player, and nothing has changed since his graduation to pundit: 'For a rugby player, there's no better feeling, no greater status to be had, than to be selected for the Lions. It took a while for it to really sink in. At that time in my young life, I was more bowled over by all the free kit handed out than the historical significance of the Lions. It felt good, but I didn't appreciate what it really meant. I was intent just on doing it rather than analysing it. I'd gone from Bath and England to the Lions within the space of a weekend. If you'd pinched me, I wouldn't have woken up. It felt too good.

'The more I had to do with the Lions, the more I got swept up by all that it entailed – the historic battles, the glorious victories, the valiant defeats. Think of the great names of British and Irish rugby – names such as Gareth Edwards, Willie John McBride, Ollie Campbell, Gavin Hastings, Tony O'Reilly, Barry John – and you immediately think of them in a Lions context. The Lions is different: a chance to prove yourself in a unique way.'

Guscott did not take long on that maiden tour of Australia to sense the 'unique challenge'. His came with promotion to the Test team after the Wallabies had routed the Lions in the first game of the series. When the chips were down, he created one of the best tries scored on any tour, and one that also squared the rubber, because he had the nerve and the talent to engineer something different.

It was a try that no other English player of the time could have attempted, let alone scored. A delicate chip under the noses of the defensive line would have been useless without the extra gear to go into overdrive. Guscott had that, and he even arranged for the ball to bounce obediently into his hands. Class at the highest level can rarely have been demonstrated to such perfection.

'I don't know precisely why I did what I did,' he said. 'I had actually tried a similar little stunt in the ACT game, but it hadn't come off, and no one had noticed. It looked like a doomed ploy and that, apparently, was what went through Finlay's [Lions captain Finlay Calder] mind as he looked up from yet another bruising maul, having secured hard-won possession for us, to see me shape to kick.

'I was on cruise-control. Nothing could touch me. The Australian back line closed on me. Closer. Closer. There it went – a little stabbing kick behind them, a dab on the accelerator, a whiz past them. The ball bounced up. Thank you very much, a try under the posts. I rarely show emotion on a rugby field, but I showed it that day all right. I could have kept running and running. It was a mega moment.'

He would never have to worry about laying another brick in his life. No player has yet managed to appear in three winning series for the Lions but none went closer than Guscott. He won his first in Australia and his last in South Africa and was an automatic choice for the tour in between when the Lions failed to take full advantage of the worst New Zealand team of the last 20 years.

The All Blacks who confronted the Lions during the mild winter of 1993 were a shadow of the World Cup-winning untouchables of 1987. Grant Fox, one of only two back-line survivors from six years earlier (John Kirwan being the other), stole the first Test in Christchurch with a controversial penalty late on in the game that left the Lions feeling like victims of daylight robbery.

In Wellington for the second Test a fortnight later, the English representation at Gavin Hastings's disposal had been increased from nine to a record-breaking eleven although one of them, Dewi Morris, was a bona fide Welshman from Crickhowell, who had just happened to be brought up in the English system – first with

Liverpool St Helens, then Sale. Despite Carling being replaced by Gibbs, the English contingent beat the previous highest from one country, a record that up until that point was held by Wales, who provided ten players for the first Test against Australia in 1950.

At the old Athletic Park, in conditions unusually pleasant by Wellington standards, the All Blacks made a laughably obvious attempt, towards the end of the first half of the second Test, to circumvent the injury-only substitution law by sending skipper Sean Fitzpatrick a scribbled note calling for the withdrawal of Mark Cooksley. The Lions won so convincingly that the winning margin of 20–7 scarcely did them justice. A pack consisting of seven Englishmen and one Irishman, Nick Popplewell, laid the foundations of a victory secured by Rory Underwood's sprinting try. Inevitably, Guscott created it, drawing Kirwan, the last defender, until the last split-second and then releasing an exquisitely timed pass to ensure Underwood a clear run to the line for a score that put the All Blacks up the proverbial creek without a paddle. They were not so much beaten as outplayed, especially in the lineout.

With all the momentum behind them, the Lions reached Eden Park for the decisive Test, the following Saturday, confident that having left their opponents spread-eagled on the ropes they would put them out of their misery, thereby emulating the historic achievement of John Dawes' team in 1971 by winning a series against the All Blacks. Instead, they had overestimated their ability to finish the job and, more seriously, underestimated New Zealand's to find a strategic way out of a tight corner.

Andy Haden was summoned to work out a means of preventing the sky-scraping Martin Bayfield cleaning up in the middle of the lineout and the new boy, Martin Johnson, from doing the same at the front. When the Lions jumped into a ten-point lead, it seemed as though nothing would stop Ian McGeechan from being the first coach to win successive series in the Antipodes.

Instead, the All Blacks pulled themselves back from the abyss, obliterating the deficit with a devastating comeback built on three tries and six goals, the latter all scored by Fox, the most dependable kicker of his time. The Lions had been outwitted because they allowed themselves to believe, not unreasonably, that what had worked one week would work the next. More disturbingly, they lost because they never had the courage to make the most of a vastly superior three-quarter line in Ieuan Evans, Gibbs, Guscott and Underwood.

Guscott could always put it down to experience, but he knew the chance of a lifetime had gone. 'Modern rugby is unforgiving,' he said. 'You have to keep on the move and try new things, because the opposition spends as much time studying you as they do working on their own game. We'd forsaken our open game in the early stages of the tour, because we didn't have the nerve to take it to the Kiwis. I think we played into their hands.'

Had they not done so, Guscott's legendary Lions career would have assumed a still greater dimension. In three World Cups for England, he never quite matched what he achieved in three tours with the Lions. Three England Grand Slams during the first half of the '90s were very nice, but the Lions gave him a broader canvas, and, like a real artist appreciating the bigger picture, he decorated it in a way that brushed his name into history.

The bare figures of his England career – 30 tries in 65 Tests – tell nothing of the frustration of his earlier seasons when their narrow, forward-dominated game meant that he was never in danger of being overused. The no-risk policy, which stunted their growth before Clive Woodward appeared in the role of the liberator, meant they had a Rolls-Royce of a centre who was rarely allowed to get into overdrive.

Ironically, England's 11th-hour switch of tactics for the World Cup final against Australia at Twickenham in November 1991 could well have cost them the trophy, not that anybody, of course, has any way of knowing. The shift from the ten-man game to one involving all fifteen overlooked a fundamental flaw: namely that teams not used to attacking on the widest possible front are pushing their luck if they expect to become proficient in that style overnight. At that World Cup in 1991, Carling's team did what they did best from the start of the tournament and for every game up to the final. The most notable of these was the one that got them to that final, a war of attrition with Scotland at Murrayfield when all the points came from penalties, and Gavin Hastings missed the next best thing to a sitter, if any kick in a World Cup semi-final can fit the description.

When David Campese, the Wallaby wing and number one anti-English rabble-rouser, chided the hosts for being boring and dull, Guscott would have concurred. 'If anyone had just watched our game against Scotland, then they would have agreed,' he said. 'We'd never have forgiven ourselves if we had lost, but we offered nothing in that match. We played the percentages, and the percentages almost kicked us in the teeth.'

By the time the next World Cup came round, in South Africa in May 1995, England were under the command of Jack Rowell, whom *The Sun* once dubbed 'Jittery Jack'. Unfortunately, the tournament coincided with the Guscott Rolls jammed in second gear. Rowell, who kept saying he wanted to play the 15-man game – which may have been one reason why he kept picking Guscott – never got round to it. His loyalty to a player who had been with him over the years at Bath reached baffling proportions when he refused to drop him for the meaningless third-place play-off against France in Pretoria, an event rendered all the more mundane by New Zealand's steamrollering of the English at the semi-final in Cape Town a few days earlier.

If they were unsure of their second-class status, the flight to Johannesburg the next day removed any doubts in graphic fashion. Their All Black superiors were already strapped into their luxurious leather seats in business class when the vanquished filed past on their way to the cheap seats in economy. Nobody can have felt more dissatisfied with his lot than the player whose form, shown in the limited opportunities granted him, screamed out for recognition. Phil de Glanville, Guscott's fellow Bath centre who had been understandably miffed at being denied a place in the semi-final team, hit the roof at finding out that he had been excluded to the bitter end, including the third/fourth place play-off v. France in Pretoria. He had given Rowell 'both barrels' earlier in the campaign, during a drunken celebration of the quarter-final win over Australia, accusing him of being 'a chicken' who hadn't the bottle to drop Guscott.

Oddly enough, the same accusation was being levelled at Rowell the following year with Guscott the victim. De Glanville's appointment as captain in November 1996, following Carling's decision to return to the ranks, meant that one centre position had been spoken for and that the other one was a straight choice between the former skipper and Guscott. The general assumption was that England needed Guscott's creativity more than Carling's redoubtable defensive power and that the man who had become rugby's longest-serving captain, before relinquishing the title, would be the one to go.

Even Carling admitted that Guscott's 'should have been the first name on the team sheet'. In deciding otherwise, Rowell backed himself into a corner, and the most creative centre in the country managed two appearances as a substitute throughout the last pre-

Woodward Five Nations. France won the Grand Slam that year, which was due reward for their performance in coming from behind to win at Twickenham earlier in the championship.

The man who would clinch the Lions series in South Africa a little later that year was permitted three minutes as Carling's substitute against Ireland and forty for right wing Jon Sleightholme during the last international at Cardiff Arms Park. By the end of the season, the decision not to play Guscott made no more sense than at the start, other than to strengthen the suspicion that Rowell, ever the pragmatist, had taken the softer option in dropping Guscott rather than Carling.

Those who subscribed to that view included, not surprisingly, the victim himself. 'In celebrity terms, the dropping of Carling would have been a huge story, if only for a short time,' Guscott said. 'Jack might not have fancied all that, and he wouldn't have wanted all the stick if it had gone horribly wrong. The feeling was that he went for the safer option.'

The England reserve who promptly became an automatic choice for the Lions Test XV duly resumed normal business for his country. The drop-goal conqueror of the Springboks had one last opportunity to perform on the global stage, at the 1999 World Cup. England finished as far away from winning it as ever, reduced to a shambles against the Springboks in the quarter-final, by which time Guscott's glittering career had already ended in unusually anti-climactic circumstances.

In retrospect, the writing had been on the wall since the Centenary Test in Sydney that summer when an English defeat provided disturbing evidence that their centre had lost his purr. A chronic groin condition kept his selection in the final 30 for the World Cup in doubt until the 11th hour, and once the All Blacks had exposed Guscott's defensive frailty during the critical pool match at Twickenham, the end was never going to be far away.

That would probably have been the end had de Glanville not been forced to drop out of the next match, against Tonga, because of bruised ribs. Guscott, dropped some 24 hours earlier, won an unexpected reprieve and showed that, whatever else he might have lost, his sense of occasion was as keen as ever.

Just about everyone else in the side had got their name on the score sheet by the time his elegant stroll took him over under the posts. It wasn't any old try but one that gave Paul Grayson the formality of a conversion to bring up England's century, which counted for absolutely nothing when the Springboks picked them off nine days later.

The crowd, sensing that Guscott was leaving Twickenham for good, gave him a standing ovation until he had disappeared down the tunnel. Once in the home dressing-room, he told Clive Woodward that it was all over. He had given up the struggle for full fitness.

Soon he would be confronted by the so-called 'road rage' case that had been hanging over him since the previous March. In what became a cause célèbre, Guscott pleaded not guilty at Bristol Crown Court to a charge of causing actual bodily harm to Ken Jones, an antiques dealer, in Bath on 24 March 1999. After listening to four days' evidence, the jury was out for almost two and a half hours before returning a not guilty verdict, at which point the defendant and his family shed tears of sheer relief. He, and they, had been through some experiences in their time but never anything like that. It did nothing to diminish Guscott's standing as one of the most electrifying players of his generation. His enduring appeal as a Lion par excellence has only been strengthened by the failure of subsequent tours since his retirement at the age of 34 after 73 Tests for England and the Lions.

15

CAPTAIN COLOSSUS

MARTIN JOHNSON'S FIRST SPORTING AMBITION WAS TO WIN THE GOLDEN WONDER CUP, an annual soccer tournament named after a local potato crisp factory and competed for by the primary schools of Leicestershire. A budding centre-back with an advanced tactical appreciation not usually found in ten year olds, he applied a highly developed competitive instinct to his game. The winning of the 2003 Rugby World Cup, therefore, can be traced back to the soccer pitch at Ridgeway Primary School in the twelfth-century market town of Market Harborough.

Johnson remembers himself, with searing honesty, as 'an obnoxious little brat' who cut clean through the usual baloney that the game was there to be enjoyed and played for fun. From the very beginning, he played to win, an attitude not entirely shared by his contemporaries, the vast majority of whom approached the weekly kick-about as light relief from the classroom.

He could never quite understand why the teacher in charge of the team, Mr Richards, did not share his single-minded approach to winning the Cup and finishing top dogs among the Under-11 primary schools in the county. 'I took the school football team seriously,' he said towards the end of his farewell season, recalling a happy childhood. 'I had a natural understanding of tactics, and even then, as a little kid, I wanted to be successful. Nearly everyone else would be running after the ball, but I'd be playing the offside trap and getting the full-backs to push up so we didn't get caught out. The teacher in charge had a different attitude: that it was about everyone getting a game and enjoying themselves. I can see his point of view now, but I didn't at the time.

'That's what I was like as a little kid. I only wanted to do it as well as we possibly could, and we weren't going to be successful when we kept picking guys just because it was their turn. I liked sport, but, most of all, I liked playing it properly. There are those who are dead keen and others who are not that bothered. I was always one of those who was bothered about it. I had a point but I was never going to win it at the age of ten.'

The policy of giving everyone a game meant that the Golden Wonder Cup went for a Burton, as far as Ridgeway and its competitive centre-back was concerned. Growing up in the '70s, football tended to assume more importance for him than the other traditional pastimes for the more energetic boys of his generation: cops and robbers inspired by *Kojak* or war games against Germany, the perennial opposition.

When his favourite footballer, Kevin Keegan, moved from England to Germany to play for Hamburg, Johnson described it as 'one of the worst days' of his childhood – not because it shifted the goalposts for his war games with the neighbouring kids but because he followed the game as a Liverpool fan: 'He was the biggest name in English football at that time, the first guy I had any recognition of as a seven year old. He was a god. When Mum and Dad said they were signing Kenny Dalglish, I'd never heard of him. You just knew it was never going to be the same, which it wasn't but not in the way I thought.'

He went back to his Action Man collection. 'You spent most of your spare time fighting a war which had been finished thirty years,' he said. 'We had a huge collection of plastic weapons. Bizarre when you think about it. I had a letter recently from a guy I went to school with, and he said the same thing. It's very different nowadays. My daughter Molly got an invitation to a pirate party with a note which said, "Please do not bring any swords". I'd have gone armed to the teeth . . .'

Johnson's father David had taken his three sons to the occasional football match at Aston Villa and Nottingham Forest before taking them to see their grandfather's old rugby club Orrell play in Coventry, then a real force in English rugby. The future captain of England thought of rugby players as 'fat blokes in tatty kit', an observation based on an early exposure to Solihull RFC: 'There'd be six games on at the same time on various pitches, all these blokes running round in faded shirts and odd socks. You'd think, "What's this about?" It wasn't the rugby I'd watch on television.'

A couple of years later, the Johnsons broadened their horizons to take in Twickenham and the violent England v. Wales match of March 1980, which Dusty Hare won with a late penalty. 'That was the first big game I went to,' he said. 'I had no idea what was going on, and I don't remember anything about it apart from Dusty's kick and the crowd going mad. I was a football fan, and what I do remember was reading the programme and seeing all these guys who were playing for Leicester – Clive Woodward, Paul Dodge, Peter Wheeler, Dusty.

'When you're ten, Leicester is a long way from Market Harborough, but it put the Tigers on my radar. Friends from school went to watch them, and I knew I was going to start playing rugby at high school the next year, and, in those days, the Tigers gave schoolboys free season tickets to watch. One of the dads would take us, and the first game I watched at Welford Road was Tigers against London Welsh in September 1981. I was playing for the school, and I was getting more and more serious about it.'

Serious enough to start making a name for himself in junior circles, starting at Wigston. The club's president, John Tipper, described him as 'the finest young forward' he had seen in almost half a century of watching rugby in Leicestershire, an observation which included 'dear old Dean Richards'.

Acknowledgement of Tipper's recognition of a new star in the making came with Johnson's selection for the England Under-18 schools' tour of Australia in May 1988, a journey that would have a profound effect on his rugby future and make him the player he ultimately became. The tour alerted New Zealand to his potential or, to be more specific, it alerted a Kiwi from King Country, who would soon reap the rewards for his enterprise.

John Albert followed England's progress in winning a triangular tournament against the Wallabies and baby All Blacks from his home in Tihoi (pronounced Tee-hoy). Shortly after returning home, a letter from Albert reached Johnson in Market Harborough, inviting him to further his rugby education in New Zealand. It made an immediate impression. Johnson, grasping the significance of what he was being offered, wasted no time replying:

Dear John,

Thank you for your invitation. It came as a great shock and pleasure to receive an offer to play in New Zealand. Obviously, I am very interested in coming over as it would obviously be a great experience to play and live in New Zealand for a season.

Please could you write back giving more details such as when the season starts and how long it is and when you would want me to fly over, etc. etc. Your offer of employment and accommodation sounds great and I am willing to pay towards air fare but I'm sure you will be more specific in your return letter.

I am currently playing for the England Under-19 side along with Damian Hopley, Phil Maynard and Steve Ojomoh. My club side is the Leicester Tigers who were 1988 First Division champions. I look forward to receiving your reply.

Yours sincerely,

Martin Johnson

Once the correspondence had been swiftly concluded before the end of April 1989, the teenage Johnson was on his way. Albert, who had written to every one of Johnson's contemporaries and received replies from eight – including Damian Hopley, another future international – only ever encountered one problem with the English newcomer. It revolved around Johnson's arrival at the local airport and the vehicle that had been sent to ferry him to Taupo.

'My sister went to collect him in her little midget car,' Albert said. 'None of us had realised how big Martin was. We had never seen anyone that big, and it took quite an effort on his part to squash himself into the car. After being used to those multi-lane highways in the UK, he found our country lanes pretty frightening.'

Despite his size, the locals assumed that he was just another piece of English brawn to be bashed about. 'A lot of people in King Country rubbished him for being a soft Pom,' Albert said. 'In New Zealand, if you are different or you are good, people will try you out. Martin took a few knocks, but, after a while, he began to dish it back. After a while, we were all convinced he would be the first All Black from Tihoi way, out in the bush.'

His admirers included King Country's most famous son, Colin Meads. In next to no time, the 'skinny English kid', as Johnson described himself with characteristic self-deprecation, forced his way into the trials for the New Zealand Colts, and before the end of his second season, he won selection for the Junior All Blacks against Australia's Under-21s. He took his place at the Sydney Football Stadium on 30 June 1990 surrounded by embryonic All Black superstars like Va'aiga Tuigamala, Craig Innes, John Timu and Craig Dowd, who remembered the new lock as 'a tall, lanky Kiwi with an English accent'.

Johnson played his part in a 24–21 New Zealand win, despite jumping in direct opposition to John Eales, another second row who would go on to lift the World Cup. The All Black management went home congratulating themselves on unearthing a rough diamond with a big New Zealand future, and if he did happen to come from the other side of the world, so what?

'We picked him on the basis that he was going to stay in New Zealand,' said John Hart, who coached the Colts before going on to run the national team. 'We would like to have had him. He didn't have a lot of skill in the early days, but he certainly had a big heart. He was always going to make it big.'

Meads, the legendary 'Pine Tree' whose mauling strength was supposedly gained by running up the hills of his farm with a sheep under each arm, has always regretted that Johnson ended up in a white jersey rather than a black one. His understanding had been that the young Englishman intended staying, especially after meeting Kay Gredig, the farmer's daughter who would become Mrs Johnson.

'The selectors contacted me to say they were interested in picking Martin,' Meads said. 'They said, "Is the boy going to stay in New Zealand or is he going back to England?" I had talked with Martin, and I told the selectors that, as far as I knew, he planned to spend the rest of his rugby career in New Zealand.

'I told him to tell the selectors that he was staying and that's what he did otherwise they wouldn't have picked him for the Colts. Martin was a young beanpole in those days, slightly ungainly, but he had all the courage in the world. As a 19 year old, we often thought he lacked a bit of aggression. While he has certainly proved us wrong in that respect, I recall him as a great competitor who developed into a rugged, no nonsense type of lock.'

Despite New Zealand's referees traditionally turning a blind eye to a bit of Old Testament-style justice, Johnson's readiness to box his own corner landed him in a spot of bother during a club match. A run-in with a local Maori lad called Dale McIntosh, who would go on to become a folk hero in Pontypridd and play for Wales, resulted in Johnson being sent off, miraculously for the only time in his long career.

Moving rapidly into the King Country team, his opening matches in the National Provincial Championship included one against Auckland, then unquestionably the best non-Test team in the world. Almost 20 years later, a star-struck Johnson could still reel off the names in a reverential tone: 'Front row: Steve McDowell, Sean Fitzpatrick, Olo Brown. Second row: Gary Whetton, Marty Brooke. Back row: Alan Whetton, Zinzan Brooke, Michael Jones. Half-backs: Ant Strachan, Grant Fox. Three-quarters: Va'aiga Tuigamala, Joe Stanley, Bernie McCahill, John Kirwan. Full-back: Terry Wright.'

Reminiscing years later about Johnson's loss, Meads ascribed it to a 'twist of fate'. The twist of fate in question rested on a shoulder injury and an inaccurate diagnosis. After 18 months in Taupo – with a Kiwi girlfriend, a job in the local bank and both feet on the stairway to New Zealand's team for the 1995 World Cup – Johnson had ample reason to stay, and he fully intended to be back early in the following year, 1991, for a third season in King Country.

'It was all to do with my shoulder,' he said. 'They thought it was a ligament problem, but it kept dislocating, and it wasn't until the following April that I had it diagnosed properly. If I'd had the surgery done in the first place, I'd have spent the English season recovering and then been fit to start again in New Zealand. As it was, the belated operation wiped out the possibility of going back. It was one of those things.'

Eighteen months in the best finishing school of all had made Johnson tougher, smarter and technically more proficient. Leicester might not have initially had a troubled conscience at losing him to a club none of their supporters had heard of, but they certainly ought to have had. Mr Albert had poached a future All Black from under their noses, and Johnson's newly acquired reputation prodded the Tigers into urgent action once he had rejoined the club for the start of the 1990–91 season.

Of all the turning points during his formative years, the most crucial took place on Saturday, 24 November 1990 in a paddy field of a pitch at Bath where Leicester won a Pilkington Cup tie 12–0. Two significant happenings conspired to give Johnson a leg up onto the bottom rungs of the England ladder and, because of the state of his shoulder, prevent him from going back to New Zealand.

He had played a full part in Bath's knock-out despite having to 'clunk' his left shoulder back into place on three occasions. 'It kept popping out, and the club thought it was some sort of tendon problem,' Johnson said. 'If I'd had the surgery done there and then, I'd have been fit to have gone back to Taupo near the end of our season in April.'

The operation eventually took place that very month, which, as luck would have it, left the patient no option but to spend the summer recuperating and report back for pre-season training at Welford Road. Some 18 months later, he was making his debut for England, standing in for an injured Wade Dooley against France at Twickenham, and leaving his friends in Taupo to wonder what might have been.

There is no doubt that he would have been the third Englishman to play Test rugby for the All Blacks, emulating Jamie Salmon in 1981 and John Gallagher six years later. When Johnson raised the World Cup to the skies on that wondrous Saturday night in Sydney, Meads would have been forgiven for thinking that the King Country old boy could have been doing exactly the same for New Zealand.

'It's funny to think of what might have been,' Meads said, discussing the issue the night before a Johnson-less England went down the tubes at Eden Park in June 2004. 'There was never the slightest problem with Martin going back because the circumstances were unforeseen. It was just a twist of fate that prevented him from becoming an All Black. We have great memories of Martin. He's had a tremendous career from humble beginnings.'

In retrospect, it is surprising that the budding colossus had to wait until he was almost 23 before winning his first England cap. Even then he only won it because the old warhorse Dooley had gone temporarily lame at the start of the 1993 Five Nations. Johnson stepped in and promptly back out again, once the 'Blackpool Tower' had been put back in full working order. In contrast, John Eales, his gigantic contemporary, had by then become a fixture in the World Cup-winning Wallabies.

More surprisingly, Johnson failed to make the Lions squad to New Zealand at the end of that 1993 season. He went to Canada instead, for two non-cap matches with a team of young hopefuls some of whom were scarcely heard of again. When the call came from the Lions, Johnson was appearing before the tour court, and 'his honour' Judge Chris Oti, on a trumped-up charge and, therefore, had no way of knowing that he was required in New

Zealand, following the emergency of Dooley's departure due to his father's sudden death.

If he had, he was not in the best state to comprehend. 'Every time I got gobby, Chris Oti made me drink more as the punishment. I was in a horrible state. Somebody grabbed me in the court and said, "Hey, you might be playing for the Lions on Tuesday."

'I said, "Don't be ridiculous. It's Sunday in Canada, so it's already Monday in New Zealand." I was still comatose when I got on the plane for London. I slept all the way back, went home to wash my smalls, called in at Twickenham to grab my kit and jumped on the plane.'

Never one to blow his own trumpet, Johnson used his self-deprecating humour as a defence mechanism against his soaring status. He described himself as a Midlands Neanderthal, grumpy, unfriendly and monosyllabic and, at various stages of his career, he proved himself right on every count. But he could just as easily have described himself as the most successful rugby player of all time.

Apart from possessing the essential tools needed for an often violent trade, Johnson succeeded because of his attitude. None of the captaincy appointments of his career were ever treated as a cause for even the most modest celebration: 'What's the point when you have a job to do and you haven't shown anyone that you can do it?'

There was no outpouring of emotion, no cartwheeling around the lounge. When Fran Cotton rang him one Sunday evening, in his role as team manager, to offer him the captaincy of the 1997 Lions tour to South Africa, Johnson responded not with a roar of acceptance but with a routine 'thank you, very much'.

Four years later, when Cotton's successor Donal Lenihan rang with the same offer, Johnson was in the midst of filling in his census form. At being invited to do something that nobody had ever been invited to do before – namely captain successive tours – he issued another routine 'thank you, very much', went back to join his wife Kay poring over the form and reputedly said, 'Now, where were we?' Classic Johnson.

An old-school rugby type, he played the game for the game's sake, and if someone belted him or he gave an opponent a bloody nose, so what? Dispensing that kind of summary justice at Wigston was one thing, doing it live on television as captain of Leicester and England was another matter entirely.

He certainly did not play the game for fame or fortune and when both descended upon him in vast quantities after the 2003 World

Cup, the combined effect, apart from making him a wealthy man, was to increase his aversion to the limelight. Of all the awards, honours and guest appearances on television programmes – ranging from the 40th anniversary *Match of the Day* to *The Frank Skinner Show* – Johnson never failed to deflect the praise to the other 14 players. 'Great teams make good captains,' he is fond of saying. 'Not the other way round.'

As a sort of Sir Edmund Hillary, Tenzing Norgay and Sir Chris Bonington rolled into one ugly, big lock forward, Johnson had his share of setbacks on the way to his Everest. On one day in 1993, for instance, he missed the bus taking the Leicester team from Welford Road to the Pilkington Cup final against Harlequins. For whatever reason, the only fact not in dispute was that the Tigers drove off without him.

'We were leaving at 9.15 in the morning,' he said. 'I dropped Dad and Kay off at the Post House Hotel, and I was driving to the ground with all the time in the world when I saw the team bus drive away in the opposite direction down the one-way system. In those days, a few players would be picked up at various points along the way, so it wasn't that unusual to leave without a full squad.

'Remember, there were no mobile phones at the time. I was told the bus was heading for the M40. I shot down the M69, got on the M40 and couldn't see a trace of them. Then I notice that the petrol gauge is going down so, with no services on the motorway, I pull off into rural Oxfordshire, fill up at this country garage and then find I can't get back on the M40 going south. No option but to go into Oxford, so I'm trying to find my way back out with an atlas on my lap. Eventually I get on the M40 wondering where the bus is and at this time I am bursting to get to the toilet.

'I'm relieved in more ways than one, I can tell you, by the time I got to Twickenham. I found out later that every time the team bus passed a supporters' bus, they're going, "Where's Johnno?"

'Tudor Thomas, the team secretary, said in that lovely Welsh way of his, "Oh, Johnno, I'm so sorry." They said I was late, I said I wasn't. That's the dispute.'

Finding his way to New Zealand to join the Lions without a hitch some weeks later, Johnson applied the same old-fashioned logic to his new environment. 'It's only natural to think, "Am I good enough to do this?" I'd seen Peter Winterbottom play for England when I was a boy of 12 and, all of a sudden, there I was playing in the same pack. Dean Richards took me aside and said, "Look, some of these guys in the front five are not up to it. You've got a real chance."

'You just hope you can justify your place. You don't even know yourself whether you're worth it. I'd played one international, and there I was with the Lions. You try to put yourself in their shoes and they're thinking, "Is this a guy we can rely upon? Is he going to stand up in a crisis?" I got my head down, and I got on with it.'

He also got straight into the Test team and stayed, despite catching a haymaker against Otago at Dunedin's fabled 'House of Pain'. Regrettably, Johnson's was inflicted by his second-row partner, Martin Bayfield. 'I forgot to duck and didn't come round until the second half,' he said. 'Overall, I took far more on the rugby field than I gave, believe you me.'

Twelve years would elapse before the Lions played another Test without him, at Christchurch in June 2005, and then only because he chose to stay retired as a Test player rather than make himself available for a fourth tour. Had he played, it would have been something that no Lion had done apart from the Ulster endurance men, Mike Gibson and Willie John McBride.

When the Lions began planning their first professional tour, to South Africa in 1997, captaincy became an early issue. Phil de Glanville, Will Carling's successor as skipper of England, had been declared a non-runner by failing to make the long list of tour contenders drawn up halfway through that season. It was an omission that enhanced the claims of the two national captains who were good enough to warrant automatic Test selection: Ieuan Evans and Keith Wood.

Johnson's experience of the job had been limited to standing in for Leicester's long-term captain Dean Richards, whose rugby twilight had been all but plunged into early darkness under Bob Dwyer's stewardship of the Tigers. As manager, Cotton knew what he was looking for: someone big enough and nasty enough to send out the right message and Martin 'if you think I'm ugly now, you should have seen me when I was a baby' Johnson fitted the profile perfectly.

'As the season progressed, it dawned on me that there might be a chance I'd be asked. Then Fran phoned me at home one Sunday night and said, "We'd like you to be captain of the British Lions." I said, "Fine. Thank you very much." It was an intimidating thought. I've always said there was no honour in doing the job if you did it badly.'

Johnson, nursing a groin problem at the end of a gruelling domestic season, had hardly played when the tour showed early signs of careering off the rails. Jim Telfer, the forwards' coach working in tandem with Ian McGeechan, put it back on track with a scrummaging session that deserves a special place in Lions' folklore for its savage intensity.

'Jim gave us all a dressing down after the Northern Transvaal game along the lines of, "Toughen up or we are going to lose. You guys have to jump." He beasted the midweek team in a way which was painful to watch. It made grown men cry. At the end they were dragging themselves around the field, and you could say that wasn't the thing to do two days before the next game, but they produced a really gritty performance to beat Transvaal, and we didn't lose again until the end, after the series had been won.

'I thought Jim was great. You knew that when he was doing a session, there would never be an inch of slackness. In terms of discipline, he was outstanding. Very few guys have that real edge about them. "Geech" was a great coach and motivator who spoke softly but carried a Jim Telfer round with him. Whenever I see Jim now there is always a glint in his eye about South Africa in '97. It was great for him. He got to be on a winning tour at last.'

In Australia four years later, Johnson's reappointment made him unique – the first Lion to captain more than one tour. In hindsight, he is critical of his captaincy and admits that Keith Wood's superior people skills would have made the extrovert Irishman a better choice: 'I don't think I did a very good job. It was very, very hard for everyone, and I found it as hard as anyone to keep going after a long season. It was a hard school physically. Mentally, I found it very draining, and I guess some of the guys were not prepared to make the sacrifice. There was a bit of them-and-us about the midweek team and the Test team.

'We could have done things better off the field, and if we had done, we might have got the result on the field, but it wasn't for any lack of effort. The '97 tour was organised brilliantly. Compared to that and how the team behaved and operated, the way some players responded to some things was very disappointing. I take personal responsibility for that. I should have been able to get them more together as a team, but we still had a better chance of winning the series than we did in '97.'

They could still have won the series from the last lineout of the last Test, but a price was going to have to be paid for the severity of the training regime. Johnson's agreement that it had 'definitely' been excessive raised the question why something was not done to make it less so. 'We said at the time, "We're doing too much. We're doing too much."'

'That tour wasn't a lot of fun at times, and you have to enjoy what you are doing. In '97, the communication between the senior players and the management was a lot better. In 2001, what we said wasn't listened to. We couldn't get our points across. All the coaches all wanted their time on the field. We certainly fell into the trap of every coach having to do his little bit, which they admitted, for a lot of the time, they were doing for themselves.

'There comes a time when more is less. You've got to be careful at the end of a very long season. With England, Clive was better at handling his coaches and telling them, "You've got this amount of time and no more."'

'There never seemed to be any time on that tour. We were either training, travelling or playing. I remember trying to have a meeting with the coaches in the departure lounge at an airport. I should have found the time to talk to the players, but we never seemed to have a minute from day one. Possibly, Keith would have been a better choice as captain. The players were mentally overloaded when they got on the plane at Heathrow.'

When Clive Woodward, following the tour as a television pundit, pronounced that he would have sent Dawson home for publishing negative comments about the Lions management in a newspaper, Johnson took a stand that, had push come to shove, would have provoked a crisis without precedent in Lions' history. When the player told his captain about his fears of such a fate, the skipper backed him to the hilt: 'Mate, if you're sent home, we're all going home.'

Johnson was not one for making idle threats. 'I would have done it,' he said, some four years later, the experience still fresh in his mind. 'Matt was stupid and he knew that, but what he was saying was, "The tour shouldn't be like this. It should be better."'

'The players didn't have a problem with him. A lot of them agreed with him. I agreed with some of his points as well. It gave the management a hard time, but it didn't really affect the squad. I thought they might have been upset enough to send him home, but once I'd spoken to them about it, I knew it wasn't going to happen. What did they make him do? Say sorry to the boys, which was hilarious . . .'

The tour ended with two Charlie Chaplin-esque episodes swirling around the deciding Test. Austin Healey's ghost-written attack on the Australian lock Justin Harrison as 'a plank' understandably took the clowning too far for an incensed Graham Henry and a grateful Australian press. While all that was going on, Healey's back trouble left the Lions so short of scrum-half cover that Scotland's retired captain Andy Nicol, who had been following the Lions as a tour guide, suddenly found himself one of the team.

He never said so at the time but there was another tradition about captaining the Lions that Johnson loathed: running out with a stuffed lion, not to be confused with a team stuffed full of them. 'I hated having to carry out the stuffed toy. I remember getting off the bus at grounds in South Africa, and it was always, "Johnno, don't forget the lion." I felt like saying, "Go away with your stuffed toy." I didn't like it because it was crap.

'Someone gives it to you before you run out, but you shouldn't be running out for a Test match with a stuffed toy. I think that's wrong. I'd boot it onto the side of the field. They say it's traditional on Lions tours but then so is losing, mainly. The Springboks don't walk out holding a cuddly springbok.'

Losing the series was Johnson's one big regret. 'We'd certainly do things differently. The second half of the second Test in Melbourne was one of those where you say, "What the hell happened there?" We went from dominating a side to letting them right back into it. That made it tough in Sydney. We should have had a scrum-half replacement as soon as Rob got injured. You shouldn't have been playing a deciding Lions Test match with a tour guide as your reserve scrum-half. It didn't come to that, but that was more luck than judgement.'

Two years later, Johnson's England outclassed Australia in Melbourne, where, throughout the first half, they reached a level of technical excellence that was as close to perfection as any team could get. Within six months they had won the World Cup against the same opposition, glittering confirmation of their captain's status as one of the all-time greats. The long journey had taken him to a summit that had not existed in the pre-World Cup days when he joined Wigston.

'You don't start playing rugby because people watch you. The first time I played, nobody watched. I didn't do it to be a professional, because there wasn't even a League when I started. I just played the game. I enjoyed it because it was hard and difficult which made it good. I enjoyed the camaraderie and the team thing of winning. Sometimes you watch yourself on TV when you get upset with the ref. You think, "What are you doing there?" and, "don't do that". You get involved in a bit of drama, but it's just what happens when you're trying to do what you're trying to do.

'At times, there was a massive over-reaction as though nobody ever got punched on a rugby field before. In one of my last matches for Leicester, against Sale, I got punched in the face by their prop Andy Sheridan right in front of the referee, and he didn't do anything except give a penalty to Leicester. You've got to get your head down and take it. We have better punches than that in training sessions.'

Johnson's sheer cussedness and ruthless will to win drove him ever upwards to scale peaks that no rugby player is ever likely to scale again. Having been sent off during his Kiwi apprenticeship – playing for College Old Boys Marist against Taupo United – for a late tackle on McIntosh, the fact that he was never sent off again is probably the eighth wonder of the world.

When taking the law into his own hands – for example, the time he left Duncan McRae with cracked ribs during a Leicester v. Saracens match, violent even by the pugilistic standards of the fixture in recent years – Johnson never wasted any breath uttering hypocritical apologies for the sake of political correctness. His attitude was that the obstructive McRae had to be taught a lesson whatever the cost – in that case a five-week ban.

Johnson had been on the receiving end of enough blows during his career to raise concern over his future many times. Johan le Roux, a prop who could punch his weight, put the Englishman out of the 1994 Test series in South Africa with one blow. It was no consolation to his victim that le Roux might have been warming up for a still more outrageous shot at notoriety – biting Sean Fitzpatrick's ear during a Test match against the All Blacks.

'I had to have a brain scan after that tour. I had a lot of problems with concussion at that point. It was a vicious circle. Basically, you've just got to rest and try to avoid being knocked out for a while – difficult because it's a violent thing which we do. Having to run full pelt into someone to tackle them is violent. We have a working environment where violence and foul language is encouraged. It's good fun.'

A losing farewell to the Tigers in their Premiership Grand Final beating by Wasps in May 2005 was not exactly a fun way of bringing the curtain down on a monumental career. Just as he got it absolutely right about retiring from international rugby with England on top of the world, so Johnson needed no second thoughts about bowing out at the age of 35, some 16 years after his debut.

'I've been here since I was 17 – more than half my adult life,' he said, sitting on a splintered old wooden bench at the Tigers' training base at Oval Park, in front of a fir tree planted in memory of his heroic mother Hilary, a noted long-distance runner, who died in 2002 at the age of 58. 'I almost felt sometimes I'd been here too long, that I should have gone two years ago.

'With the same guys you can get a little stale, and that's probably what happened to us after we did the Double in 2002. Change is a healthy thing. Look at teams who have carried on being successful by changing their players: Liverpool Football Club, Wigan Rugby League Football Club, the San Francisco 49ers.'

His was not the only towering playing career to end in the summer of 2005. Within weeks of Johnson taking his final bow at Twickenham, Neil Back had made his in New Zealand. Ignored by successive England regimes during the first half of the '90s because of a reluctance to pick a back-row forward shorter than seven feet tall, Back had been used to fighting against the odds, before finally convincing those who mattered that size didn't. True to form, he fought his way back to become the oldest post-war Test Lion of all at the age of 36 and leave Sir Clive Woodward no option but to admit that he discarded him too soon after winning the World Cup.

Woodward refused to concede the point during the series of heavy defeats in New Zealand and Australia in June 2004, which turned out to be his last in charge of England, but he has since admitted that he did Back a disservice by dropping him for the start of that season's Six Nations. 'Neil had the right to be angry and he was,' Woodward said. 'I let him go too early.'

Back took the hint when Ireland took Twickenham by storm in February 2004. The Irish ended England's five-year-old, 22-match home winning run, while their most senior professional witnessed the shambles from the bench without being required. As a redundant substitute, Back promptly worked out that if he wasn't needed to sort out that mess, then he really had come to the end of the road. The old Tiger thought he could have 'changed the course of that game'. England clearly thought he could not, and, after 66 caps, Back decided 'enough was enough'. He said, 'Clive had explained his selection policy – that they would look at their options for the first two games: Italy and Scotland. I fully accepted that.

'I made myself available to help the guys through the transitional period of the Six Nations and the tour that summer, which was always going to be a massive task. The easiest thing to have done would have been to say I'd won everything, and I'll let you get on with it.

'After the Irish game, I thought. "What am I doing here?" The club were going through a really tough time, I'd taken on the captaincy and a coaching role, and I was going away sitting on the England bench and not being used. Perhaps I should have made the call to retire before what turned out to be my last game, but I wanted to do the right thing and help out as best I could.

'I phoned Clive to say I was no longer available for family and club reasons. He said, "Look, I'll pick you against Wales in a week's time." I said I'd made my decision, and there was no going back on it. There was no ill-feeling on my part whatsoever, and I thanked him for seven fantastic years.'

After the long weeks of celebrations on a nationwide scale, Woodward realised how much England had missed Back's streetwise craft. 'In hindsight, I should have kept the whole World Cup team in place – every single one of them, regardless of form, with the exception of those who were injured or retired,' Woodward said. 'I tried to move the team on too quickly. That was an error, and I don't mind admitting it.

'It was my fault. I was in charge and if I had my time again, I would have picked him [Back] for that first game and picked him throughout the Six Nations. My whole mantra is preparation, and we didn't get together until the week of the first game [against Italy in Rome]. The one time you really need top preparation, because you are bringing in new players, you haven't got it.'

He paid Back the compliment of restoring him to the most demanding stage of all, some eighteen months later, when he picked him for the Lions. Back became the oldest figure in Woodward's flawed attempt to turn the clock back in the hope that the Lions would do to the All Blacks what England had done to the world in Sydney in 2003. The world had moved on. Back was one of those who paid the price for the night in Christchurch when it all came apart at the seams, but to have been there in the first place, at the end of his 18th season, took some doing.

Richard Hill, part of the same England and the Lions back row as

Neil Back, since his debut against Scotland in February 1997, had fought all season long to recover from one serious knee injury only to suffer another barely 20 minutes into that same match. His brutal elimination halfway through the previous Lions' expedition – the victim of a stiff-arm tackle by Australian centre Nathan Grey that broke his cheekbone – was a major factor in the loss of that series.

Johnson, of course, never got where he was by worrying unduly about contravening the old biblical dictum about turning the other cheek, at least not on the field. No player, not even Jonny Wilkinson, has been singled out globally for so many honours and with every acceptance speech, Johnson always talks about the team, never about himself. Trying to cajole him into doing so is generally not a good idea. He was in a largely monosyllabic mode for a reporter from a Sunday broadsheet who called to talk to him just before the France match in February 2003. At the end, an irritable Johnson asked an official, 'What was all that about?'

The official replied, 'Ten years with England, Martin.'

Johnson, genuinely at pains to understand why anyone would be interested, replied, 'Who gives a s***?'

Yet his devotion to the sport is as colossal as his achievements. Over breakfast early one Monday morning last summer at the Belfry, he wished the hackers on his golf day well and apologised for having to shoot off for pre-season training. With the World Cup under lock and key, he could have asked for the morning off. 'Yes, I could,' he said. 'But what sort of example would that have been for the rest?'

The 'Mr Grumpy' bit is no more than he deserves – and no doubt cherishes, being a private individual who never sought the limelight – but it masks a dry humour and sharp wit as revealed by the following magazine question-and-answer:

> Q: Who would you most like to be stuck with in a lift?
> A: A lift technician.
> Q: Who would you least like to be stuck with in a lift?
> A: Someone who knows nothing about lifts.
> Q: What were your first impressions of Neil Back, your fellow marathon man?
> A: He's short. We played in an England schools trial, and he had a tooth damaged which he spat out. I thought, 'He's hard.' Then I found out it was a false one. And he is short.
> Q: Have you been lucky?
> A: I should say so. So many things have been lucky. My

parents moving from Birmingham to Market Harborough. Would I have been inspired to be a rugby player by Leicester Tigers being up the road? Probably not.

Johnson would be the last person to draw up a list and tick off all the boxes – Lions tours, Grand Slams, World Cups, European Cups, Premiership titles. He won the lot but any list would serve only as a permanent reminder of the trophy that got away, the most elusive one of all, the Golden Wonder Cup. Overrated, that Johnson. Couldn't cope with the pressure . . .

16

THE CRAFTY COCKNEY

PICTURE THE SCENE: IT IS FRIDAY, 19 JUNE 1994 AND JASON LEONARD IS SITTING IN THE England team room at their hotel in downtown Pretoria, listening to a giraffe of a man dispense his peculiar brand of acerbic motivation. England are playing the Springboks the next day on the parched grass of Loftus Versveldt, and Jack Rowell prowls around the room, picking out a random selection of individual targets for his provocative one-liners. He works his way round to Leonard and looks down on the squat figure from altitude, which takes some doing in a city 5,000 feet above sea level.

Rowell, a captain of industry who has not got where he is by being nice to all the people all the time, gets straight to the point. 'Jase,' he said, 'you've got to prove to me that you aren't just a crafty cockney collecting caps. Or are you?' A more volatile character might have leapt to his feet in moral indignation and given the manager a piece of his mind. Leonard lets the rhetorical question hang in the air and 'keeps schtum', deflecting the jibe with a shrug of his barn-door shoulders.

At the comparatively tender age of 25, there could be no denying that, in cap terms, he already had quite a collection. Even back then, the pundits reckoned that if he stayed in one piece, it would only be a matter of time before he reached three figures. Maybe Rowell, the master of the verbal dig in the ribs, had that in mind and was implying that Leonard thought he had become part of the front-row furniture.

The next day, the 'Crafty Cockney' had won cap number 36 in record-breaking circumstances. England had roused themselves from a losing start to their tour of South Africa, against Natal in Durban, to beat the Boks as never before. Tim Rodber, another Lion-in-the-making, enjoyed his finest hour that day, and Rob Andrew capped a prodigious afternoon's work with a rare try, doubling his points tally in the process.

'The night before, Jack went round the team winding everyone up, saying, "You're playing rubbish. So are you. And you and you, and I thought Rob Andrew was meant to be the world's best fly-half."

'Then he got to me and fired out that crafty cockney bit. It went straight over my head, didn't bother me at all – water off a duck's back. It had no bearing on how I was going to perform the next day. It wasn't going to wind me up. I think that's what he was trying to do: instigate some sort of backlash.

'Jack wanted to make a point, but when you're about to play in front of 60,000 people and millions more are watching on TV, you don't need it. You're not playing for yourself – you're playing for your family, your friends, everyone who has helped you along the way. It's not about egos but the respect of your peers.'

A win of historic proportions, over a team that the late Kitch Christie would convert into World Cup winners down the road in Johannesburg 12 months later, justified a hearty amount of self-congratulation and back slapping. Rowell's was the back being slapped more than anyone else's by the senior officers of the Rugby Football Union travelling with the party, even though only the tallest amongst them were able to do so literally.

As the happy throng milled about the foyer of the hotel, before boarding their bus to the airport for the flight to Cape Town and the return match, Rowell broke away from those acclaiming his motivational powers for a word with Leonard, within earshot of his beaming admirers from Twickenham.

Rowell said, 'So, Jase, what did you think about what I said to you on Friday night?'

'What was that, Jack?' he replied.

'About you being a crafty cockney collecting caps.'

'Nothing, actually.'

'Nothing?' asked Rowell.

'Didn't have any bearing on how I played – none whatsoever. Now that you mention it, there was one thing which struck me about it.'

'What was that?'

'Well, if you try to say it quickly three times, it's a bit of a tongue-twister – crafty cockney collecting caps, crafty cockney collecting caps, crafty cockney collecting caps. You try it, Jack.' The subject was never raised again during the next three years of Rowell's reign.

'Everyone was a little the worse for wear in the hotel lobby that Sunday. I remember Don Rutherford [the RFU's technical director] being there and a few others from the RFU, and Jack was obviously lording it, as such, that his team-talk had spurred us on to greater things.

'I'm not so sure about that. The reality was that we'd played poorly on tour, but we were coming together as a team, and we really clicked for the first Test. Jack was Jack, very different, and I had great fun when he was manager. Even though he said that, there was never any animosity.'

Rowell could always try and claim that his jolting jibe made some small contribution to Leonard's longevity, not that he ever needed anyone to remind him about taking anything for granted once his old mentor, the Solomon-like Jeff Probyn, had taught him the virtue of treating every international as if it were his last.

Apart from a technical inaccuracy about the strict definition of a cockney – someone born within the sound of Bow bells – Rowell proved to be spot-on, though not quite as he meant during that long-gone South African tour. Leonard certainly did collect caps, quite unlike any other player since William Webb Ellis first grabbed the football and ran with it.

Despite early mutterings to the contrary which Rowell's sensitive antennae had picked up, the notion that anyone could coast along by doing just enough to survive would have been an affront to England's professionalism and Leonard's pride in giving nothing but all he had, all the time. As for being crafty, he could not possibly have survived in such an unforgiving place as the front row for as long as he did without being equipped with a certain amount of cunning, albeit disguised as front-row technical nuance.

When he won his first cap, on a steamy night in Buenos Aires in July 1990, the new prop from Saracens was a 21-year-old carpenter. A book published the following year offered a prophecy as to what the then England front row would be up to three World Cups down the track, in 2003. In Leonard's case, it turned out to be uncannily true: 'It's a spooky thing this, but I've always remembered reading the chapter in that book on the front row. They said Jeff Probyn would be retired and indulging his hobby of sailing by travelling round the world in a boat. They said Brian Moore would be cutting a high-flying path through the legal world and that Jason Leonard would be telling his son how he got to win more caps than anyone in the world. I've always remembered that, thinking how ridiculous it was at the time and laughing my head off. Not in a million years.'

By the time he retired fourteen years later, he had played one hundred and nineteen Tests, including three Lions series and two World Cup finals. He won one of those finals, along with four Grand Slams, and made a host of friends the world over, all of whom loved him for his decency as an all-round good bloke. Unlike a few of his colleagues, he never needed to change the size of his cap.

As a boy, he never did the tourist bit of posing in front of Buckingham Palace for a photograph, preferring to await the summons from Her Majesty. It came twice in the space of three years: first to receive the MBE for services to rugby as Britain's first centurion, then to be awarded the OBE as the senior member of the World Cup-winning contingent: 'At one point, I was such a regular up there, I think all the guards knew me by my first name. You'd never have sat there as an 11-year-old kid at Warren Comprehensive School in Chadwell Heath thinking, "One day I'm going to be at Buckingham Palace."'

It was a bit of a miracle that he ever stayed alive long enough to get there. When Leonard talks, as he always does, about how lucky he has been, he acknowledges that his luckiest breaks were in escaping largely unscathed from a series of road accidents, all of which were entirely of his own making. During his formative years, he learnt from first-hand experience what it was like to be thrown over a car and trapped underneath a van but nothing about a thing called the Highway Code.

'Six times I was knocked over by cars,' he says, matter-of-factly, before stating the obvious by way of explanation. 'I had no road sense whatever. I was always doing things on an impulse. If I saw someone I knew on the other side of the road, I'd run across without bothering to look. I got knocked over twice doing that and once on a bike with a mate on the cross-bar when the brakes broke going down the hill, at Chadwell Heath railway station. There were two nuns in the way, and they stood there with their fingers in their ears because of my foul language shouting at them to get out of the way. I ended up crashing into the incoming traffic and got hit.

'Luckily, it was never worse than bumps and bruises. I was thrown over the top of one car right outside my house. At that age you think you are invincible. Then there was the day I was sitting on the kerb. I must have been about eight and my mate had a magnifying glass, and we were burning cigarette ends and whatever crawled into our path.

'Unfortunately, we were sitting behind a transit van which was parked up. The driver didn't see us, and he reversed over us. We were stuck under the bottom, but, luckily, it was on a grass verge. The spare wheel went over my head and pushed my head into the grass, which made my nose bleed. When the driver realised we were underneath, he shot forward by accident, and we both got dragged along for about ten metres.

'After it got to accident number six, my uncle said to me, "I'm not trying to be funny Jason, but that's six times, right? I've had enough of this. Do it once more and that could be the one that kills you. You've got to learn to look after yourself on the roads, because the next one could be the end of you."'

Thankfully, his uncle's deathly warning did not come to pass, but the young Leonard did survive another mishap, long before he ever got round to playing his first match in the First Division of the old Courage League with Saracens. This one happened on a Saturday night after one of Barking's under-age teams had played at Ilford.

'We always used to have a saying, "Last one out of the taxi pays the fare." So I jumped out of the taxi with the Barking boys onto the road and got hit by this car. There's me laughing saying, "I'm not paying for the taxi." Then, wallop! I hit the car and bounced over the roof, but, luckily for me, I was quite well lubricated. I was absolutely fine. The woman driving it was absolutely terrified. I said, "Don't worry, love. I'm absolutely fine." I walked straight into the curry house and had my curry. Later I found out that I'd wrenched my right knee, and the doctor had to put it back in place. I was very, very lucky.'

Rugby and the young Leonard were always going to find each other, irrespective of how long it would take. Growing up in a working-class community where only football mattered – and, more particularly, the football played by West Ham United – meant it took him a little longer. Again, a stroke of luck helped him on his way when his school broadened its sporting curriculum to include rugby. At the time, the fat boy had been playing his own version of it on the soccer field: 'My earliest memories are of chasing a ball at break time in junior school. It was supposed to be soccer, but it was as close to rugby as you could get. No referee, no touch judges – just 30 kids following the ball around. You'd chop people down, tackle them without the ball and get your knees grazed on the tarmac. There were no rules. Anything went, and whoever was left standing at the end had the ball all to himself.'

He did not overly concern himself with the rules or the niceties of the game: 'In the more organised games, I was the left back. I was there for one purpose and that was to chop people down. There was no finesse to my game whatsoever. If anyone got past the other nine players, I would chop him down and save the goalie the bother.

'Shortly after I got to Warren, a couple of rugby teachers turned up and organised a team. The beauty about that was that rugby could take kids of all shapes and sizes: little kids who ran like the wind were on the wing; the passing and kicking boys were at half-back; the nut-cases who ran all day long were your flankers; the gangly kids were in the second row and the short, fat kids were in the front row. I never got taller just fatter, so nobody ever moved me from the front row.

'Being told by a teacher that you could go out and play this game and knock lumps out the opposition without breaking the rules was unbelievable. I thought it was the best thing since sliced bread. For a kid like me to be told that you could hit people with tackles, and you could hit rucks and mauls, was a Godsend. What a great game!'

As their boy began taking his first steps down the road to becoming the most-capped international of all time, Frank and Maria Leonard went out onto the touchline to give him their moral support. What happened within a few minutes of the first game starting threatened to cause a matrimonial ruck far more serious than anything on the pitch. It was a fraught moment triggered by a mother's concern for the safety of her 14-year-old son.

'I was at the bottom of a ruck. I'm stuck under a pile of 12 kids. My mum's thinking, "He's broken and battered, and he can't breathe." She was actually going to run onto the pitch and start peeling people off me.

'My dad said to her, "If you dare walk onto the pitch and embarrass that lad, I will go ballistic." She walked away and didn't watch me for a number of years after that.'

Leonard could look after himself so expertly that at 15 he was in the Barking Under-19 team and in the 1st XV at 17. Although the RFU were beginning to spread the gospel of rugby as an egalitarian game, his climb up the England ladder would have started sooner had he gone to a recognised rugby-playing school in Essex like Campion. Nobody was looking for props at a school like Warren, then associated with producing England footballers of a different kind, like Tony Cottee, and Leonard suffered accordingly.

'I wasn't from the right school. I played in a couple of schools trials where I absolutely annihilated the opposing prop but never seemed to get any recognition. I missed out on the England schools teams all the way through, but it didn't bother me.

'I never lifted a weight in a gym until I was 18. I didn't do any proper training because I was doing so much during the week – football, boxing and rugby – so I was as fit as a butcher's dog anyway. I have kids now at 13 asking me, "What weights should I be doing?" I tell them, "You don't need to do that until you're a bit older. Just enjoy your rugby. Have fun."'

'The Fun Bus', as former England and Lions lock Martin Bayfield famously dubbed him, was up and running, even if the schools selectors failed to notice. At the age of 18, Leonard had worked his way up through the ranks of Essex, Eastern Counties, the London representative team and into the England Under-19s. He got there despite having been sent off for kicking the then England Under-19 captain, Howard Lamb: 'I was sent off for kicking him in the head, which I did, no mistake about it. Howard was far too good a player, and he was starting to get right on my tits so we had a bit of a fracas, and I ended up lumping him. Luckily, I got into the England squad despite that, and I ended up in contention at loose-head with a Bristol lad who went on to play for Scotland – Alan Sharp.'

Leonard got the nod, and when he arrived at Saracens during the summer of 1988, they gave him a questionnaire. How he filled it in revealed a great deal about the teenager who would become the world's most-capped player. Asked to list his strengths, Leonard wrote, 'Scrummaging and tackling'. Working his way through the questions, he arrived at the one asking him to list his weaknesses. Leonard thought for a moment, crossed a line through it with his biro and wrote, 'Not applicable'.

Four and a bit years later, on 2 November 1991, he was trotting out at Twickenham for England against Australia in the World Cup final. Harlequins supplied enough personnel that day to know that whatever the result, at least one of their players would leave with a winner's medal in his pocket. As it turned out, it was Troy Coker of Australia.

His seven fellow Quins on the other side – Leonard, Will Carling, Paul Ackford, Brian Moore, Peter Winterbottom, Mickey Skinner and Simon Halliday – departed wondering not what might have been but what should have been. Leonard's video of that match has been gathering dust ever since: 'I've never watched a tape of it. We were the better team that day, and I didn't need to put the video in the machine to realise that. At the time it was hard and then I promised myself I would watch it one day but never got round to it. I didn't need to watch it to know that we should have won the game.

'All the forwards made the same point, "We are absolutely killing them here." I think the thought process behind the decision to change tactics was valid. We'd lost by 40-odd to Australia in Sydney that summer, and for the first time our forwards were not able to stifle them the way we stifled everyone else.

'Geoff Cooke, Roger Uttley and Will Carling got together and reckoned that if we threw the ball wide, we would catch the Aussies by surprise. The concept was sound enough. What was wrong with it was the ability to change tactics on the pitch, and that was a criticism which had been levelled at England for a number of years. As a macho forward you thought, "We'll stuff 'em up front. Don't worry."

'We couldn't dominate them in Sydney, but in the first 40 minutes of that final we tore their forwards asunder. In the huddle at half-time, we all made the point, "Look, we're killing them. We've got to go back to playing it through the forwards." It wasn't Will on his own, despite what certain England forwards have said. It was a group thing with senior players like Rob and Rory saying, "No, we will win doing it as we planned."

'The forwards were vocal about it with people like Brian Moore and Peter Winterbottom saying, "Absolute rubbish. We've got to take them on up front."

'If you think of what might have been if we had changed tactics, you'd only torture yourself for the rest of your life. I look back on that match with regret, and I always will. We got to the final and lost. Nobody will remember that we were the better team, only that Australia won the World Cup 12–6. I lost a World Cup final. To get the chance of winning one 12 years later makes me the luckiest person in the world.'

That he was still able to play rugby beyond the 1992 Five Nations Championship was a bit of a miracle in itself. A one-sided home win over Wales, securing a second successive Grand Slam – a small consolation for losing the World Cup final – ended with Leonard barely able to raise his left arm to bind himself into the scrum. Repairing the damage to his neck required a delicate bone-graft operation that meant drilling a hole through his throat to remove a piece of bone from the cervical spine and replacing it with bone from his pelvis.

'I know of people who didn't come back from that same problem,' he said. 'I'll never forget the surgeon, Jonathan Johnson, telling me, "If you follow my instructions to the letter, you will be back. If you deviate from them, you won't." Thanks to Mr Johnson, a great physio in Don Gatherer and my fitness adviser Dave Crotty, I did.'

Against all the odds, Leonard was putting his neck on the line for Harlequins again at the start of the following season and resuming normal business with England as if he had never been away, which, of course, he hadn't. Twickenham's reconstruction meant a switch to Wembley for the first match of that season, against Canada in October 1992. Leonard was there, as good as new, to experience the novelty of trotting out in front of the twin towers, blissfully unaware of the indignation that his comeback had aroused among one member of the medical profession. The stories heralding his comeback included one in the *Mail on Sunday* by John Taylor. 'After I retired, John sent me a letter which the editor had received from an orthopaedic surgeon back in 1992,' Leonard said. 'This chap lambasted me saying, "This is an absolute disgrace. How dare Jason Leonard go back and play rugby. Nobody has ever made a recovery from this injury. It's pure nonsense that he is even attempting a comeback. He will cripple himself, and that means he will have to be funded by the welfare state as a cripple." One day I will write to the surgeon and just ask him, "What was all that about?"'

Later that season, Leonard's not inconsiderable backside proved to be one of the foundation stones of a glittering career for the new cap packing down behind him in the second row, Martin Johnson.

During his childhood, the Barking boy would spend hours on end sifting through a treasure trove of old boxing magazines that his father kept in a suitcase. This could explain how a World Heavyweight Champion from a period long before Leonard was born came to be one of his heroes. Rocky Marciano was famous for using a bludgeoning power and huge heart to punch above his weight – being one of the smallest heavyweights of any era – and retired as the unbeaten world champion.

'As a boxer, I was like him, but being my size, it was easier for me,' Leonard said. 'I never thought about him in the ring, because if you stand there pretending to be someone else, you'll end up getting your teeth rattled.'

He immediately identified Johnson as a Marciano-type figure: 'With Martin there was never any holding back. No coasting. No taking it easy. He never once looked for the easy option, just like Marciano.'

Leonard's pugilistic ability has been put to the test from time to time during his career, perhaps most notably during the classic Grand Slam decider against France at Twickenham in March 1991 when he tangled with the opera-singing Pascal Ondarts. What happened in the first minute helped give the French prop top billing, along with the All Black Olo Brown, as the Englishman's toughest opponent. 'I got an uppercut from Pascal in the first scrum, and in the second, I smacked him back,' Leonard said. 'We didn't have any problems after that. It was like we understood each other . . .'

At the end of that first season with his reinforced neck, Leonard made the first of his three Lions tours, ousting the Scottish tight-head Paul Burnell after the first Test against New Zealand and playing in the next two.

As one of precious few qualified to play at the highest level on either side of the scrum, Leonard went on the next Lions tour with a double shot at a Test place. For many, including the management, the question was not if he played but where. However, the Lions won that series in South Africa in 1997 without him. For just about the only time in his career Leonard found himself playing second fiddle, as did the other fancied English prop, the Leicester loose-head Graham Rowntree. Both were overtaken by Celtic rivals: Rowntree by the whispering Scot, Tom Smith; Leonard by the Irish tight-head, Paul Wallace.

The Fun Bus had failed its MOT.

'I played in the match when we lost to Northern Transvaal and, as a pack, we were poor,' he said. 'Had I played well that day, I would have been in the Test team. Missing out was a right old kick up the backside that I had to play better. Paul and Tom took their chances so well that I'd have had to play an absolute blinder to replace either of them.'

He won his 50th cap for England that year and his 100th six years later, against France at Twickenham in February 2003 at the start of England's blazing run to the World Cup. He still had enough energy for three more run-ins with the French that year, as a second-half substitute for the back-to-back friendlies in Marseilles and at Twickenham and for the last two minutes of the semi-final in Sydney.

All told, he appeared 18 times against France with none more uproarious than the game at the Parc des Princes in February 1992 when two-thirds of the French front row – Vincent Moscato and Philippe Gimbert – were sent off by referee Stephen Hilditch, the headmaster of a school in Belfast. Leonard never fails to chuckle at the mention of that match, not because of the front-row aggro but scrum-half Dewi Morris's screaming appeals to the ref to give penalties against the French for infringing at the ruck: 'Dewi would be shouting, "Monsieur, monsieur. Le ballon, le ballon. Monsieur, monsieur."

'Then the ref would tell him, "It's all right, Dewi, I understand. I do speak English." Ben Clarke played that day, and he and I just cracked up. It took a real effort to stop laughing.'

By the time he eventually got round to calling it quits, shortly after appearing for the last quarter of an hour against Italy in Rome in February 2004, Leonard, in his thirty-sixth year, had raised Philippe Sella's world cap record by three to one hundred and fourteen. An international career spanning 15 seasons – equalling those played by Colin Meads and David Campese – was one more than Sella and Willie John McBride managed and one less than Mike Gibson. Yet bare statistics, however impressive, do Leonard less than full justice. They cannot tell the story of how he kept reinventing himself as a prop, of how the species changed shape from the pot-bellied grunt merchants of the amateur days, who pushed in the scrum and blocked in the lineout, to the streamlined professionals, who needed on-field mobility on top of all the basics merely to survive. Leonard managed this transition without ever creating the impression that he was hanging on, even if many of his late caps were won off the bench.

When he came on in the World Cup final – his penultimate appearance for England – in place of Phil Vickery four minutes from the end of normal time, his presence had a soothing effect on England's night of nights.

With the wisest and oldest head restoring calm to a front row distressed at being penalised quite so often by the South African referee Andre Watson, England eventually ensured that justice was done and that Leonard would not be required to drop a goal as part of the shoot-out.

'Most of us had been together for seven or eight years. Some fell by the wayside, and there were some who should have been in the World Cup squad but didn't make it.

'So you come to understand your comrades, and in the end we only won the World Cup by one kick at goal with 30 seconds left. It could quite easily have gone the other way.'

Over the period of his career, England capped sixteen other props: five loose-heads (Paul Rendall, Graham Rowntree, Kevin Yates, Trevor Woodman and David Flatman) and eleven tight-heads (Jeff Probyn, Gary Pearce, Victor Ubogu, John Mallett, Robin Hardwick, Darren Garforth, Will Green, Phil Vickery, Julian White, Robbie Morris and Mike Worsley).

As Leonard always used to remind himself in the early days, a 30-cap career was exceptional. It took an equally exceptional player, therefore, to withstand the vicissitudes of selection long enough to win 50 caps. Peter Winterbottom, an international from the age of twenty-one against Australia at Twickenham in January 1982, achieved the distinction of being the first English forward to play fifty times for his country in a match against Ireland ten years later when Leonard was still a novice.

The 'Straw Man', a *nom de guerre* inspired more by his fair hair than his first job on a farm in the Yorkshire Dales, moved from Headingley to Harlequins and from baling hay to trading on the money markets in the City. He also developed into the leading European contender to the openside throne occupied by Michael Jones for the ten years after his advent as an All Black in 1987. Winterbottom, hailed by Will Carling as the 'hardest man' he had seen on a rugby field, is the only Lion to start and finish as an ever-present in Test series in New Zealand ten years apart.

Even better at the age of 33 in 1993 than he had been in 1983, the selfless Yorkshireman bowed out with the clamour from the then England coach Dick Best, and others, ringing in his ears. Little did Leonard know that he would not only surpass his fellow Harlequin's 58 caps but virtually double the tally into world record proportions before retiring after a grand total of 119 Tests for England and the Lions.

'Did I ever think then that I'd have one hundred and fourteen caps for England, five for the British Lions? Fourteen years at Harlequins, two at Saracens? Of course not. Am I grateful for every second of my life in rugby? Too right I am, because I know how much of a knife-edge my career was on. It could have gone either way, but I've been able to enjoy every second of it.

'You need luck along the way, and, touch wood, I've had it all the way through, but I've also made my own luck to some extent. I have never once taken playing rugby for granted. I am not a person who ever has regrets. Everything that has happened in my life has happened for a reason and made me a stronger person.'

He had the best of both worlds, the last seven and a half years of the amateur era, the first seven and a half of the new professional one. 'People ask which was the best career. Each as good as the other, in my book. Very different but I wouldn't swap one for the other, which surprises some. They say, "Yeah, but you'd rather have had 14 years as a professional, wouldn't you?"

'No, I wouldn't, because I believe I am richer in another sense for having played in the amateur era. If somebody offered me money to play harder, I'd say, "Mate, I can't play any harder than I am."

'You give so much that sometimes you think your heart is going to explode. I'm honoured that I had a chance to play in both. Nowadays I have to remind some of the younger players that we used to play the game for nothing. The fun is still there, but it's a different kind of fun.'

Typically, he has given away most of his jerseys, and Barking RFC proudly display some of them in their clubhouse as a shrine to their most famous player. His father, Frank, has the one from the first World Cup final. The more recent one is being kept for his children – Harry, Jack and Francesca.

'I don't hoard stuff or hide it away at the bottom of a drawer. What's the point? It's nice if you can help others in some small way by giving it to charity so they can raise some money for a worthy cause.'

In his time, Leonard tangled with some of the roughest, toughest props the game has seen, among them the French quartet of Pascal Ondarts, Laurent Seigne, Christian Califano and Franck Tournaire and the All Black trio Richard Loe, Craig Dowd and Olo Brown. 'You respect them, but you can't wait to get into that first scrum, to get into a ruck and knock them back in the tackle, which fires you up all the more. But that's the way I've been brought up. I've always been the local lad, always aware that I was representing Barking and the surrounding area.'

While success may have left one or two of his more impressionable colleagues in danger over their own inflated egos, Leonard's cap size has never changed. 'I do believe that at the end of the day we only play rugby. It is only a game no matter how serious people get about it. When you feel your heart's going to explode, you are playing for your club and your country, you carry on. If I'm so shattered I'd have to crawl round the pitch, I'd do that.

'Going to the Palace was a huge honour, but you feel a little embarrassed. You have people there who have done fantastic work for charities and what have you done? They are far more deserving than me. People say to me, "Ah, but you've given us 16 years of pleasure watching you play rugby." It's still just a game. A great one but a game none the less.

'I can't get big-headed about it. My feet are firmly on the ground. You do what you can, and if you can do a little more to help a charity, you do it gladly.

'Over the years, I've seen a couple of people getting a bit too caught up in themselves. I'm a big believer in what goes around, comes around. Certainly, a few players have got a little too big for their boots. Instead of "we" and "the team", it's me, me, me. They think they're the bee's knees. All of a sudden they're not playing so well because they're being distracted by off the field stuff and they get dropped. That brings them down to earth with a bump.'

His father, a keen darts player, never has any trouble on that score. Frank Leonard has been known to pull his son's leg about the pressure of drinking 15 pints and still hitting a double 20: 'Son, you've done great, but always remember this – there's only one athlete in this house . . .'

17

TRIUMPH AND TRAGEDY

WHEN VINCENZO DALLAGLIO ARRIVED IN LONDON FROM HIS NATIVE TURIN IN APRIL 1958 at the age of 23, he couldn't speak a word of English. Making light of the linguistic handicap, he worked his way up from being a humble waiter to the position of general manager of one of the West End's largest hotels.

Eileen Marriott, one of an Anglo-Irish family of ten from the opposite end of the capital, was driven by the same work ethic. After resigning her job as an airline stewardess, the newly-wed Mrs Dallaglio used her redundancy money to buy a newsagent's in her native Stepney and turn it into a mini-supermarket. She would often juggle the demands of rearing a family with other jobs: for example, as a dental nurse and, briefly, as a chauffeuse with the Bowater corporation.

Eileen worked for thirty-two years to help her husband give their two children every chance to follow their dreams, ensuring them a better start to life than they had growing up during the Second World War. Vincenzo had almost been crushed to death beneath the wheels of a lorry, while trying to escape an aerial bombardment near his home in Parma as a nine-year-old boy in 1943. 'I was in hospital for six months between life and death,' he said, more than half a century later. 'Fortunately, it was not my turn . . .'

His future wife survived the war despite the best efforts of the *Luftwaffe* to blow Stepney, and the rest of the East End, to kingdom

254

come. The air-raid sirens had almost become a part of daily life, forcing Eileen, along with her six brothers and three sisters, to seek refuge underground and hope she still had a home to go to once the bombers had flown back to Germany. After one apocalyptic night, the family woke to find a neighbouring house obliterated by the dreaded Doodlebug long-distance bomb. 'My mother told me it was the last one to be dropped on London. We lived at number eleven Havering Street, and it obliterated the four houses beside us,' she said.

Some 30 years later they were able to give their children the opportunities they had been denied. They put their daughter Francesca through the Royal College of Ballet and provided their soccer-mad son with the privilege of a £10,000-a-year education at one of England's leading public schools: Ampleforth College in North Yorkshire. It was there, far from the footballing streets of west London, that he was introduced to rugby. It changed his life and set him on the way to becoming one of those rare rugby legends who transcended the game itself: an iconic figure across the sporting spectrum. Despite his huge success, he never forgot where he came from and how much he owed to those who had sent him on his way. 'I can never thank my parents enough, although it certainly isn't for the want of trying. They gave me a very loving, caring start in life. There were always a lot of outward displays of emotion and affection, which wasn't the typically English attitude.

'For instance, every time my parents picked me up from primary school, I'd run to my dad and kiss him on both cheeks, like the Italians always do. The other kids at the school found that odd. My parents would do anything for me. You don't always appreciate the huge sacrifices they make on your behalf, until you are older and have children of your own.

'My parents put their children before themselves. My mum held down four or five jobs to put me through school, working non-stop like my dad. I know the sacrifices they made to give me a real opportunity to make something of my life – the same with Francesca.

'My sister would have been a dance star, and to have her taken away from me and the family was terrible. Like me, she had been given the chance to do something she loved doing. My parents know how greatly I appreciate what they have done for me. I will never, ever forget it.'

Few international sporting figures can have had to cope with quite as many traumas: the tragedy of Francesca's death in the *Marchioness* disaster, when her not-so-little brother was at the highly impressionable age of sixteen, and the scandal eight years later of drug allegations made by the *News of the World* after he had fallen victim to their entrapment. A crushing knee injury was, by comparison, relatively routine. All it did was threaten to finish him. 'I have seen this boy come back from so many pitfalls,' his mother says, with understandable pride. 'Francesca's death was a terrible tragedy.'

It had a devastating effect on the family, not least on the youngest member. 'Coming from a close-knit family, it blew us apart. We went in different directions for a period of time. For a couple of years, I was all over the place: on a different planet, so to speak. My sister was an incredibly hard worker who had achieved an enormous amount in her very short life. After her death, I found it very hard to cope.

'I was kind of wandering around, not lost exactly but not knowing what I wanted to do: whether to go to university or get a job. My mother was determined that I made something of myself. She'd come upstairs and wake me up at 7.30 in the morning. There was never any hanging around or lazing about. Her attitude was always, "Come on, time to go out and get a job. If you want anything in life, you have to go out and work for it." If you were up and out of bed, then at least you had some sort of chance.'

Francesca's younger brother had intended to go to the same fateful party on the Thames pleasure boat that Saturday night in the summer of 1989 but felt unwell and decided, at the last minute, to give it a miss. 'Lawrence didn't play rugby for two years after that,' Eileen said. 'When we finally persuaded him to start again, it took him only seven matches to go from obscurity to a place in the England schools squad. After they picked the team, he said to me, "Mum, I'm on the bench. That is unacceptable to me. I will never, ever fail another England test."'

His father demonstrated his support for his son's progress, in a brand of football bewilderingly different to the one he first followed from the steps of the old Stadio Comunale watching his beloved Juventus, by not letting the laws of the new game defeat him. Vincenzo bought himself a book entitled *The Laws of Rugby Football* and slowly grasped the difference between a ruck and a maul. Privately, Lawrence was thrilled that his dad had gone to such trouble, but it didn't stop him pulling his leg about it: 'Dad, in rugby there are so many laws that nobody knows them all, not even the referees . . .'

Perhaps it was just as well for Vincenzo that he remained blissfully unaware of the often brutal physical toll that the new professional game would exact, especially on its back-row practitioners. Years later, as an established international, injury could have ruined Dallaglio long before he reached the promised land of the Olympic Stadium in Sydney and the World Cup final on 22 November 2003. 'He had such a bad knee injury at one stage that it would have finished most people,' his mother said. 'Ten days after the operation, he was pumping iron thanks to the surgeon's skill and his own determination. He got back playing again and then there was the tabloid sting. That's when you find out who your real friends are. It is a mark of the man, and his family, that it didn't destroy him.'

Eileen championed his cause with the same passion that drove her on the crusade to win justice for the families of the victims of the *Marchioness* disaster. Nor was she backward at coming forward during the embryonic stages of her son's career, if she felt the dithering England management needed the benefit of some homespun advice. Jack Rowell, then a lofty captain of industry who ran England's 1995 World Cup operation as the last of the amateur managers-cum-coaches, had an idiosyncratic style that often baffled players, coaches and journalists alike. The young Dallaglio was finding his way through the 1994 tour of South Africa as the uncapped new boy when his mother bumped into Rowell at an after-match reception. 'You've said some nice things about Lawrence. Perhaps now you'll think about picking him.' Rowell could be an intimidating figure, but just in case he had missed the point, Mrs Dallaglio drove it home with her parting shot: 'Come on, Mr Rowell. Get him into the team . . .'

Whether that made any difference or not nobody will ever know, but for the last match of that tour – the second Test in Cape Town – Dallaglio was closer than he had ever been to getting his first cap as one of the replacements. He stayed on the bench and has always counted his blessings that he did, because it meant avoiding a beating from the Springboks bigger than the one England had given them in Pretoria the previous week.

It was a mightily close run thing. Ben Clarke, whose outstanding series for the Lions against the All Blacks the previous year had earned him the ultimate recognition of being one of New Zealand's five Players of the Year, appeared at one stage as though he would be forced to succumb to an injury. Dallaglio waited on the touchline to make his entry.

'I nearly got on, and who knows how differently it might all have been had I done so,' he said. 'My whole career could have been affected. South Africa gave us a right kicking that day, and if I'd been part of a losing team, people might have said, "He's not really up to it, that Dallaglio." Who knows? Things happen by chance. Ben got up and played on, and whenever I see him I always say, "That was probably the best thing you ever did for me, getting back on your feet that day in Cape Town . . ."'

It seems hard to understand now that England could return to South Africa the following year for the World Cup without Dallaglio. The last two back-row positions went to Steve Ojomoh and Neil Back. 'I was disappointed because I felt I had something to offer, but, again, not being involved maybe wasn't a bad thing,' Dallaglio said. 'If there was a choice to be made in those days between a player from Bath and one from Wasps, there was only one choice. Jack always went with who he knew. You couldn't blame him for that, I suppose.'

When South Africa played at Twickenham the following November as reigning world champions, Rowell recalled the long-absent Andy Robinson, another of his Bath stalwarts, to join Clarke and Tim Rodber in a back row that had a distinctly makeshift look about it. Dallaglio had to settle for a place on the bench alongside his 'mate' Graham Dawe, the hard-as-nails Devon farmer who had scrapped for years for the hooker's spot in unfriendly rivalry with Brian Moore.

'I'd roomed with Graham in South Africa and he said to me, "I've sat on the bench thirty-five times and got on four times. This is your first time. I bet you get on."'

He did, as a late replacement for Rodber, which was the cue for Mrs Dallaglio to give Mr Rowell more of the same, straight-from-the-shoulder advice at the reception in the Rose Room beneath the South Stand: 'You could have got him on a bit earlier, and you'll be needing to make some changes.'

Dallaglio, cringing within earshot, thought to himself, 'Mum, leave it be, pleeeeease . . .'

Moments later, Rowell headed his way: 'Met your mother, Lawrence. She is a formidable lady.'

'Yes, she is,' he replied.

There could be no holding him back any longer. When the

England team to play Western Samoa was announced a few days later, Dallaglio's name was amongst those chosen. However, he had not been selected in either of his favoured positions of number 8 or number 6 but at number 7. 'That conversation must have had the desired effect,' he said, chuckling. 'To this day, I still find it absolutely bizarre that I was picked at openside. I had never played a game there in my life, but if they pick you at prop, you're not going to turn it down.'

Shepherd's Bush – where he was born and bred – to Twickenham is not that far as the crow flies, but Stamford Bridge was closer in every respect. He was six and already a 'football fanatic' when his father first took him to watch Chelsea, a time long before the Abramovich era, when the team, struggling more often than not, was nothing much to shout about.

Two years later, after carrying a football under his arm to school on a daily basis, a friend took him to Staines RFC on a Sunday morning, thus giving the English game one of its biggest breaks. 'That was my earliest memory – mini-rugby at Staines,' he said. 'Football was what I wanted to play, but I looked on rugby as another string to my bow.'

It would probably never have been any more significant than that had his parents not scrimped and saved to send him to Ampleforth at the age of 13. 'My parents had spent so much money kitting me out they couldn't afford to drive me up there, so I went by train on my own. I'd been brought up in London, and suddenly to be going to a boarding school in the far north of Yorkshire was quite daunting. I stood out as the new kid like a sore thumb, but they were quite impressed that I'd made the journey on my own. I'd never seen snow before until I got to Ampleforth.'

There was something else he hadn't seen before: rugby pitches galore. He also had the culture shock of discovering that soccer at the school didn't exist. 'A football was not on the list of things required, which was a bit upsetting. It was an interesting school with wonderful facilities, like rugby pitches as far as the eye could see. There were twenty-seven in all, which was an awful lot, especially when you think that some schools struggle to make do with one. Once I looked out of my window, I had a pretty good idea which sport I would be playing.'

It was not quite love at first sight. 'In my first match, for the Under-13s, I played on the wing. It was a colder climate than I had been used to, and hardly ever seeing the ball made it feel colder still.

The ball rarely got to the wing, which I later found was a problem at all levels in English rugby at that time. I did not find it much fun.'

When Dallaglio reached the age of 15, one of the coaches, Frank Booth, had the smart idea of switching the loitering wing to number 8 and the fun began. 'Suddenly I realised that it was a totally different game, that they had a thing called the ball, and if you played number 8 you had a fairly good control over it. I started to enjoy it. Then one summer, I grew five inches, and, all of a sudden, I had a few more mates.'

Once he broke into the 1st XV, the fixture list took him into contact with another famous Roman Catholic public school across the Pennines called Stonyhurst, and a young fellow named Kyran Bracken, then a budding fly-half, who would be standing up there alongside him on the winners' rostrum in Sydney some 15 years later.

After his separation from the sport, during the confused and grievous aftermath of his sister's death, Dallaglio embraced rugby again with all his heart and soul. He saw it not as a career, but as something to be enjoyed for the game's sake, an old-fashioned Corinthian ideal that, to his eternal credit, he never lost sight of at any stage of a career perhaps more immense than any of his contemporaries', given the crippling obstacles he had to overcome. A natural extrovert, the sheer force of his personality and generosity of spirit set him as a man apart. Dallaglio, like his fellow Londoner Jason Leonard, would always try to find time to observe the rituals of the game. In an unforgiving professional arena, they, more than anyone else, would go out of their way to maintain some of the more endearing customs of the amateur era. For example, they would always make a point, wherever possible, of seeking out their opposite number for a post-match beer – not because they felt obliged to but because they wanted to.

The Italians, naturally enough, tried their best to claim Dallaglio as one of their own. The president of Amatori Milan led the charge after the brawny Londoner had played against their Under-19 team at Cambridge. The offer of a place at university in Italy and the chance of being fast tracked into the national team was tempting enough for the family to go to Milan. They declined the offer despite the encouragement of another famous rugby son of an Italian migrant, David Campese, then enjoying lucrative winters as Milan's star player.

'Campese said to Lawrence, "Get over here, man. This is where the money is,"' Eileen said. 'I thought that was very interesting, because back then I was still buying him boots at 60 quid a pair, money which I could ill afford.'

Nothing could divert Dallaglio from his goal: it would be England or bust. He enrolled on a course at Kingston University in urban estate management as a prospective surveyor, something which he tackled with less than bone-crunching enthusiasm. If nothing else, it gave him time to think about what he was going to do, without quite realising that rugby, the last great bastion of amateurism, was on the cusp of professionalism.

Urged by his rugby master at Ampleforth, the former England full-back John Willcox, to join a club in London, Dallaglio bought a newspaper one Saturday morning to find out where the capital's teams stood in what was then the Courage League. 'It just so happened that Wasps were on top. They were the best club so I went there and couldn't believe what I was joining.'

The only problem he ever encountered at Wasps was finding out whether they really existed and, if so, where they had hidden the ground. That first journey by tube from Hammersmith to Sudbury, the station nearest to the club's postage stamp of a ground, made him wonder whether he had made the right decision. 'I got off the train, out into the high street and asked the first person I saw for directions to the ground. Then I asked the next four people the same question, and they all gave me the same answer: "Wasps? Never heard of them mate."'

Non-plussed, Dallaglio ploughed on until someone pointed him in the vague direction of Repton Avenue, a few hundred yards away. 'You'd have thought the locals would have had some idea, especially when it was just up the road. I was a bit shocked by that and even more shocked when I got to the ground. It was stuck out on a limb in a community to which it didn't seem to belong. Yet I was struck by its warmth and friendliness and how the players came from miles around for training every Tuesday and Thursday night. Wasps gave my life a focal point, and I was just going out and having fun.'

Breaking into the 1st XV at 19, he did not have to wait long to be taught a few facts of rugby life that had escaped him at Ampleforth: that not everyone had the same sense of fun. A harder, infinitely less forgiving school awaited and his third match for Wasps, against Leicester, brought him a thumping welcome to the real world, as meted out by one Dean Richards: 'When you get a bang on the nose from someone like him you know all about it. That kind of thing didn't go on at school level, and so you have to learn very quickly. I was ball watching at a lineout when I felt my eyes water and some blood in my mouth. Dean Ryan was captain of Wasps and he said to me, "You've got to clock him one otherwise he's going to be on your case for the rest of the game."

'I was always used to doing what I was told but clock a legend like Dean Richards? That's what the captain said, so at the next lineout I threw a punch which probably didn't hurt Dean anywhere near as much as he had hurt me, that's for sure. In those days, that sort of thing was completely ignored by the referees, as if it hadn't happened. As a lad, playing against a back row of Richards, John Wells and Neil Back was interesting. Dean came up to me in the clubhouse afterwards, and he did buy me a pint. Interesting . . .'

He was off and running, helping England to win a World Cup at Murrayfield in 1993 as a member of Andrew Harriman's all-conquering seven-a-side squad that ran David Campese's Wallabies ragged in the final. With the overnight onset of professionalism, Wasps made Dallaglio captain in the hope that he could rescue them from the distress left by Rob Andrew, Dean Ryan, Nick Popplewell, Steve Bates and Graham Childs decamping to Newcastle.

The emergency call came from Rob Smith, then the club's first-team coach. 'I was in the library at university trying to do some work,' Dallaglio recalls. 'Well, to be perfectly honest, I wasn't doing any work but following Alice Corbett [his future partner], who happened to be there at the same time. Rob's call got me thinking rugby very quickly, and while I didn't think twice [about accepting his offer], it was an indication of the chaos we were in at that time.'

Under their new leader, and financially secure thanks to Chris Wright pouring several of his millions into the club to save it from the rocks, Wasps recovered to finish fourth in the league in the first year of professionalism. Within the next 15 months, Dallaglio had inspired them to smash the Bath–Leicester duopoly and been an ever-present force in the Lions' winning series in South Africa.

Before embarking on what would prove 'a life-changing experience', Dallaglio had immersed himself in the history of the Lions, absorbing every last scrap of information he could as a means of understanding the unique nature of the squad he was about to join. 'A friend of mine, Ray Cole, who owned a bookshop in Fulham, got in touch saying he had all these wonderful books about the Lions written by people like Carwyn James and would I be interested. I picked up a box load of them and read every one, then spoke to Roger Uttley at the club to get a real feeling as to what they were about.'

As luck would have it, the tour proved to be the happiest since the Lions had last won in South Africa, almost a quarter of a century earlier. Dallaglio loved every minute of it. 'Few people are ever lucky enough to play for their country, but even fewer get to play for the Lions. It is the pinnacle of anyone's career, a wonderful opportunity to break bread with the best players from the other home countries.

'The concept is unique. The players are drawn from very different cultural and economic backgrounds and, by some twist of fate, you end up in the same squad. You meet for a week, then fly out to take on a great rugby nation like South Africa. The shirt gives you powers that you didn't realise you had.

'You learn a lot about a player's character by what he does on the rugby field and by what he's prepared to do for his teammates. You cannot begin to compare rugby with war but, in a strictly sporting context, when you are thousands of miles from home and manning a rearguard action, the toughest Test matches are fairly close.

'You have to give everything, and I'd like to think I am one of those who has always given everything. That Lions tour was ahead of its time in the way it was run. Ian McGeechan, as coach, was first-class. Fran Cotton, the best team manager I have ever known, didn't take any crap from anyone. He must have been some player, because he could command a room full of Lions. When he spoke, people listened.

'We'd meet once a week in his hotel room with senior players representing the four countries, like Keith Wood, Scott Gibbs, Rob Wainwright and, of course, Martin Johnson. Fran would open a bottle of wine, and we'd chew the fat. Every issue would be discussed, and Fran made sure every issue was nipped in the bud. He must have been some player . . .'

The rooming list for the first week meant Dallaglio sharing with Wainwright, his rival for the number 8 position. 'You had no choice but to get on, even though you were fighting for the same Test spot. The battle lines were drawn down the middle of the room. We were very polite and very civil to each other, but we were both thinking, "It's you or me." In the end it was both of us, because Rob made it as well.'

The Lions under Cotton had chosen Johnson as their captain. A few months later, England, under Clive Woodward, chose Dallaglio to be theirs. Neither party had any idea of the storms that would quickly gather and all but engulf them, starting with the Machiavellian politics of the bitter power struggle between the elite clubs and the Rugby Football Union over control of the players.

'Clive had a vision, but we were, in his words, skiing uphill. He didn't have a clue what he was doing in many respects. We were making mistakes left, right and centre. Clive was trying to fight the system, until he realised that it was pointless trying to take everyone on and better to concentrate on coaching the team.

'He and I were never afraid then to stick our necks out to comment on the political state of affairs when we might have been better off taking a step back and saying, "We're just here to coach and to play." That England team made mistake after mistake but the wonderful thing was that Clive made sure we learnt from every one. That was a big factor in the ultimate achievement a few years down the line.'

Dallaglio had achieved so much so quickly and, with the sky the limit, there was always the danger that, like Icarus, he would fly too close to the sun. The fall came with the drug allegations made by the *News of the World*: allegations that would cost him far more than the lost Grand Slam against Wales at Wembley a few weeks earlier. He was left with no option but to resign the England captaincy in the frantic fight to clear his name. However, unlike Icarus, he lived to tell the tale. In fact, there was no shortage of people wishing to tell the tale on his behalf, and it seemed as though a whole rain forest in Brazil would be razed to provide enough paper to accommodate the newsprint published in the wake of the scandal.

He does not disagree that, until then, he had considered himself fireproof. 'Yes, I probably did. I'm quite headstrong. Some people look at me with some envy because I enjoy myself, and I've never been afraid to display that enjoyment. Whilst I have never meant to rub people up the wrong way, I may have done. Perhaps some have thought of me as being cocksure of himself.'

The *News of the World* exposé would have destroyed an individual made of lesser stuff. Two under-cover reporters had tricked him into believing they were executives from a multi-national company offering him a sponsorship deal worth £1 million. The RFU's two-month inquiry ended with the ex-captain being fined £15,000 and ordered to pay another £10,000 towards the costs of the hearing after pleading guilty to a charge of bringing the game into disrepute.

The inquiry had been headed by the late Sir John Kay, the distinguished High Court judge whose son, Ben, won a World Cup medal with England before becoming a Lion in his own right in New Zealand in 2005. Announcing the verdict at Twickenham in August 1999, Sir Oliver Popplewell, chairman of the independent tribunal, did not let Dallaglio off unscathed. 'That he should lie to the inquiry panel is also to his discredit and casts doubt over his judgement as England's captain,' Sir Oliver said. 'Mr Dallaglio was undoubtedly set up. He was incited to express his views, which otherwise would have remained private. To that end, a great deal of drink was supplied. He has already suffered a period of suspension voluntarily and given up the captaincy voluntarily. Given all the circumstances of this case, we do not think that it is an appropriate case for suspension.'

Dallaglio had engaged the late George Carman, QC, to defend him. 'Knowing you are innocent is one thing,' the player said at the time, 'proving it has been another. It has been a long and difficult battle, and I am content with the outcome.'

Now it is little more than a fading memory. 'I was disappointed with myself more than anything else and disappointed for the people around me. It was irresponsible of me to have put Alice and my parents in that position.

'It was created out of nothing. I don't think it would have happened in any other country. It was hugely regrettable, but, fortunately, it didn't cost me my place in the '99 World Cup. After a couple of difficult months, I was able to carry on as if it had never happened.'

A little older and an awful lot wiser, England's number 8 won immediate reinstatement, resuming a few weeks later against the American Eagles in the first of the friendlies before the '99 World Cup the following month. It was as if he had never been away, except that England now marched out behind Johnson, a captain driven by the same unflinching ambition, even though he was a very different character from a very different background than Dallaglio.

First impressions were not at all favourable, at least not from Dallaglio's perspective and what he remembered of 'a grumpy, miserable sod' from England's tour of South Africa in 1994. 'He'd been knocked out playing against Transvaal at the time, which probably explains a lot as to why he didn't speak to me back then,' Dallaglio said. 'When I first met Johnno I found him quite dour. We didn't know each other during those early England squad days. After a training session, he'd sit down with all the Leicester players. I couldn't really sit down with the Wasps players because there weren't any apart from me, so I sat with Jason Leonard.

'That kind of them-and-us thing existed for a while. Johnno was supportive of me as captain in 1997 but, in all honesty, we'd do the bare minimum for each other. Slowly, we realised that we had a lot of common ground, but it wasn't until after the tour of South Africa in 2000 that the whole harmony changed for the better. We went as rugby teammates but came back as real mates. That tour broke down all the barriers. Once I had the chance to get to know him and find out what made him tick, I realised that he was a lot funnier than I ever thought.'

There was nothing nice about either man when it came to the shuddering business of dominating an international. Without the ruthless quality that each brought to his game, England would never have won on the scale that made their World Cup triumph in 2003 appear to be pre-ordained. Only Dallaglio had been singled out by Woodward for public criticism during the tournament, a source of irritation that drove him to be the only English player to appear in every minute of all seven matches.

When Johnson quit after the final, Dallaglio reclaimed the prize he had lost four years earlier – a proven leader straight out of the same granite-like school. He had thought about joining Johnson in Test retirement but England needed him more than ever. Besides, there was some unfinished business to attend to, even though by then his relationship with Woodward was not what it had once been.

Of all the English players who have been accorded the privilege of taking a bow out in the middle at Twickenham before the start of their 50th international, only Dallaglio had to make his from the bench as a temporary substitute for Richard Hill against Australia in November 2002. While Woodward never got where he did by allowing sentiment to influence his decisions, the downgraded manner of reaching the 50-cap milestone still rankles with Dallaglio. He felt he deserved better treatment.

Having stood by him in his hour of desperate need, Woodward needed Dallaglio almost as desperately when he reappointed him in February 2004. England, holed amidships by retirements as well as long-term injuries, were always going to be in for the roughest of rides, post-World Cup. Dallaglio stood out like a rock in a weary team that found itself all at sea in Paris, Dunedin, Auckland and Brisbane. They lost all four, but no captain could have been more heroic in adversity than Dallaglio, and the mind boggles at how much more water England would have shipped without his magnificent defiance. There had to be a limit to how much even he could take, but his sudden retirement in September 2004, after 73 internationals, was still a surprise.

As England stumbled through their worst season for a generation without him, the ex-captain took his game to new heights. Wasps' rout of Leicester to clinch a third successive English Premiership title in May 2005 ruined Johnson's last match for the Tigers and convinced him – not that he needed any convincing – that his time had truly come and gone.

It also left no doubt about Dallaglio's return to the Test stage as a major figure in the Lions' strategy to defeat the All Blacks a few weeks later. The gods decreed otherwise, and a dislocated ankle 21 minutes into the opening tour match against Bay of Plenty in Rotorua destroyed his third Lions tour even more cruelly than the cruciate ligament damage to his knee had destroyed his second tour in Australia in 2001. Any realistic hope of the All Black series being a contest went with him.

His place among the greats had been assured long before the truncated end to his life as a Lion. Some players are judged by what they win and little else, whereas others are judged as much for how they played the game as by how many Premiership titles, European Cups, Grand Slams, World Cups and Lions tours they accumulated. Nobody is more impeccably qualified for entry to the latter category than the boy who used to kick a football around Shepherd's Bush.

There always had to be more to the game than winning for winning's sake. 'For all my loyalty to Wasps, I would never have stayed had I not thought they were capable of winning things,' he said. 'I've been very fortunate, but I'd like to think it's not been about what I have won. It's about the people I have played with, the places I have seen and, as much as anything, it's about the game itself . . .'

In that respect, he has enriched the game immeasurably across the globe. Rugby owes him a debt it can never repay.

18

BILLY WHIZZ

THEY CONDEMNED HIM AS A TRAITOR ON ONE SIDE OF RUGBY'S IRON CURTAIN AND A waste of money on the other, but within four years of crossing the Rubicon from league to union, Jason Robinson had conquered every rugby frontier: from winning the World Cup to leaving an indelible mark on the Lions and captaining his country.

How he made the journey from skippering the Hunslet Boys' Club Under-10s, as a 'knobbly-kneed' scrum-half, to leading England out at Twickenham is truly the stuff of legend. None of the chosen few who have had the privilege down the decades of captaining the mother country took a more improbable route to achieving the distinction than Robinson.

Back in the old days, when the English game was perceived to be the preserve of the public schools and Oxbridge, English captains tended to come from precisely the kind of social strata where rugby wasn't rugby but 'rugger'. They did not tend to come from the working classes, and they most definitely did not come from the humble background of a terraced house in Chapeltown, the inner-city suburb of Leeds, a city at the heart of rugby league and justifiably proud of it.

Union, for most of its existence, struck no chord with the working man in Britain beyond the rugby belt of South Wales and isolated pockets in the West Country, Cornwall and the Scottish Borders. That Robinson would one day emulate Lord Wakefield of

Kendal was somehow utterly in keeping with a career unique in the annals of the sport in its widest context, including both codes.

'Billy Whizz' had been defying the odds all his life: from the bad old days of 20 pints and a bottle of vodka a night, to the reformed, God-fearing character who chose to test himself in an alien game when the soft option would have been to stay put at Wigan. The son of a Scottish mother and a Jamaican father, whom he never met, Robinson made it to the top of his chosen profession despite a troubled upbringing in which he would help his hard-working mum Dorothy in her job as a cleaner so she could make ends meet and raise her three sons. Through it all, the youngest of them imbued himself with a moral courage, which was never more in evidence than when he decided to leave the code that had been his life from childhood for one about which he knew very little and infinitely less about the baffling complexity of its laws.

'I stepped out of the comfort zone of league into a non-comfort zone because I had the faith to do so,' he said. 'I was leaving a game I'd played since I was a child for a game I did not understand. I was offered more money to stay at Wigan than go to Sale, although everyone thought it was the other way round.'

Several individuals, most notably his wife Amanda and the All Black wing Va'aiga Tuigamala, rescued the immature Robinson from drowning in a flood of alcohol. Others played significant roles in his development on the rugby field, but nobody had as profound an effect on his professional life as Clive Woodward, whose ability to think laterally had been stimulated by his failure to go beyond the quarter-finals at the 1999 World Cup.

As part of his grand scheme for winning the trophy at the next attempt in Australia in 2003, Woodward presented his paymasters at the Rugby Football Union with a short-list of rugby league targets. It was a list of four names that also included those of Henry Paul, Andy Farrell and Kris Radlinski. Robinson topped the list, and it is a tribute to Woodward's powers of persuasion that he convinced his immediate superiors as well as the player.

With typical zeal, he had even thought about financing the five-year deal himself, which would have left him very little change out of £1 million. 'I thought about everything, even mortgaging the house,' Woodward said. 'You've got to take risks in business. Running my own business was the best pre-requisite for this job, because if you have your own business you re-mortgage your house more times than you care to think of. I was going to do it because

I had made commitments to Jason, and I wasn't going to let him down. I didn't think it was an especially bold move, just common sense.'

A transfer that ought to have been relatively straightforward, once Robinson had agreed to it, turned out to be nothing of the sort. Instead, the parties involved had to negotiate an obstacle the size of Beecher's Brook, because, once the word got out, the rest of the Premiership clubs ganged up on Sale and threatened to send them to Coventry. Because they were seen to be getting an unfair advantage by signing a player whose salary would be half paid by the RFU, Sale would be ostracised.

Such a boycott sounds laughable in retrospect, but nobody was laughing at the time. In their myopia, the other 11 clubs could not see that Robinson had the potential to do them all a favour at the box-office, that they would all benefit from his presence in their midst. Despite the dispiriting atmosphere the deal was done at a wine bar in Knutsford where Robinson and his agent met Brian Kennedy, the multi-millionaire owner of Sale, who refused to be sidetracked by what he called 'an unnecessary distraction'.

'I promised Jason I'd pay his wages, irrespective of what came from the RFU,' Kennedy said. 'They agreed to pay roughly 50 per cent, but the clubs threatened to boycott all matches with Sale if I took that payment. Bearing in mind the delicacy of the relationship between the Union and the clubs at that point, I agreed to underwrite Jason's deal. I didn't release the RFU from their commitment, but, to take the heat out of the situation, I told the clubs I would not press for payment from the RFU right away.'

The arrangement spared Woodward the bother of calling his local building society, if not the wrath of some who were unable, or unwilling, to see that the deal would be a snip at twice the price. Robinson's debut for Sale – a cup tie against Coventry on Sunday, 5 November 2000 – brought a stark reminder of what he had left behind at Wigan. If Guy Fawkes had been there at Heywood Road on the anniversary of his big day, he would have kept the Catherine wheel up his sleeve and walked out at half-time in protest at the damp squibs all around him.

In their attempt to make it an occasion, Sale offered free pies and cans of beer to those buying tickets in advance. For all the club's commendable enterprise, the attendance might have said as much about the pies as local enthusiasm for a Sunday afternoon fixture. Whatever the reason, a crowd of 2,547 – smallish even by Sale's modest standards – peered out into the gloom, scarcely lifted by the anaemic floodlighting at Heywood Road, for a glimpse of the new man.

As he waited and waited for the ball to come his way, it can be safely assumed that Robinson did not rub his hands in glee and make a mental note of the fact that he would be playing in a Test series for the Lions on the other side of the world at the end of the season. He would have been too busy wondering what on earth he had let himself in for.

Less than 60 seconds remained of the otherwise nondescript tie, when the new convert finally tired of waiting for someone to give him a pass. After spending the rest of the match watching his new Premiership colleagues make hard work of the Second Division's bottom team, Robinson followed his instincts across the pitch to sniff out a try from the last move of the game.

Scoring it required nothing more onerous than arriving in support of full-back Vaughn Going to cross unopposed from about ten yards out. His only touch of the entire second half at least rescued Sale's big day from being a complete non-event. The performance was even bad enough for the club to offer the newcomer an apology for their crass failure to put the ball in his hands more often.

It had, without doubt, been the strangest period of his life. His league career had finished the previous weekend, on 14 October 2000, in the Grand Final at Old Trafford, where defeat by St Helens meant no addition to his tally of sixteen winner's medals during nine years at Wigan. The roars of 60,000-plus at Manchester United's towering cathedral had barely stopped ringing in his ears than he was driving into Sale's postage stamp of a ground at Heywood Road where a capacity of 5,000 had been more than enough in the days when club matches, especially of the northern variety, attracted the proverbial two men and a dog.

Robinson's humility and innate sense of decency had a muting effect on the mutterings of disapproval from the bigoted diehards of both codes to his transfer. In the days before joining Sale, he had armed himself with a rugby law book and studied photographs of his new teammates, memorising their names so that he knew who was who before he met them.

The new signing in their midst was no mercenary, as some had suggested, but a man on a mission. A devoutly religious man who had seen the error of his earlier ways, Robinson felt moved by a superior force. Before deciding to cut the umbilical cord with league, he had spent a considerable amount of time on his knees. 'I prayed for about six months, because I knew that if I prayed, the Lord would look after me,' he said. 'The Bible is my guide to life. As a born-again Christian, all my decisions revolve around my faith. I prayed for guidance, and this is where the Lord led me. People think I came for the money, but they don't know the facts. If it was money, I'd have left Wigan a long time before when I was offered a fortune to go to Australia.

'Money can buy you nice things, but it doesn't necessarily make you happy. The decision to leave league was hard enough but harder still because Sale were not a glamorous club. It would have been easy to have stayed at Wigan, to have become the highest paid player in league and had a testimonial.

'I know a lot of people talk about needing a new challenge, but in my case it was absolutely true. It really was now or never. But just because I'd done it in league didn't mean that I would do it in union. I crossed over not as any sort of superstar but as someone willing to learn and work hard. International rugby was always the bigger picture. England and the British Lions were possibilities, but there were a lot of things I had to get to grips with.'

League's reinvention as an essentially summer sport had given Robinson the opportunity to flirt with union as a Bath player during the autumn of 1996 when he scored his first tries in a European Cup tie against Swansea. If he could make that sort of an impression without understanding, or even pretending to understand, the laws of the game, the mind boggled at what he might achieve if he actually knew what he was doing.

In that same season, shortly after their loan star had rejoined Wigan for the start of the inaugural Super League campaign, Woodward joined Bath as a part-time coach. At round about the same time, Robinson had taken the most important single decision of his life. He had seen the light in time to save his talent from being destroyed by alcohol, and the man who showed him the path to the straight and narrow was a New Zealander who had left the All Blacks in the final years of amateurism for Wigan: Va'aiga Tuigamala, alias 'Inga the Winger'.

The contentment that exuded from the smiling Samoan slowly made a deep impression on Robinson and made him realise that he was off the rails, careering towards oblivion. 'I thought, "How can anyone be happy when he doesn't drink and doesn't go to nightclubs chasing women?" Inga was not consumed with the materialistic side of life. I was drinking at the time and probably too full of myself to take any good advice before Inga came along. I just watched how he lived and slowly realised that I also wanted peace and a good family life, not to be chasing material things like flashier cars and bigger houses.'

In the wild days, Robinson's idea of a drink went far beyond a couple of pints. 'I used to go out after matches and have 20 pints or whatever,' he said. 'It wasn't just after matches. Often, it would be five nights a week. We didn't have a few pints. We had a few barrels, and, on some occasions, we could easily down a bottle of vodka each as well.

'Rugby and beer have always gone hand in hand, and it used to be no different for me. I don't know how I could drink that much and still play, but I knew I had a problem which very nearly ruined my life. Thankfully, my days of heavy drinking are long gone. I was too immature at the time to handle the situation I found myself in, but I'm glad to say I haven't had a hangover for years.' He has been the cause of quite a few, most famously among the more inebriated England supporters who have celebrated victories the world over, as well as a fair number from Ireland, Scotland and Wales rejoicing in the name of the Lions.

Before leaving Wigan, Robinson's devout faith prompted him to defy the popular image of the professional sportsman as a driven, one-dimensional individual, cocooned and cosseted in his own narrow existence. For a while, he rolled his sleeves up and went to work for the underprivileged in the more deprived areas of Manchester, driving a mobile café most Sunday evenings into the streets around Chinatown and Piccadilly on behalf of the homeless. On one occasion, he played for Wigan in the afternoon, drove straight home after the match and jumped into the van loaded with soup, sandwiches, burgers and flasks of tea.

'There were five of us in the beginning, and then, as others began to offer help, we branched out into providing blankets. A local company provided the van, and others helped us out with the food. In the morning, I'd get it all loaded up with food and park it at my house so I could drive off as soon as I got home after the match.

'Sometimes people would recognise me and ask why I was doing this work. I think a lot of them must have thought we were getting paid for it. It was only a small thing, and I didn't want to be seen as though I was doing it to be a goody-goody. We were never going to solve the homeless problem in a place like Manchester, but I've always thought it was the best thing I've ever done. It was also one of the hardest, particularly when it came to separating the genuinely needy from the not-so-needy.

'We got some stick from some of the people out on the streets who were not right, whether it was because they had a drink or a drug problem. We weren't going to let them spoil it for the rest. In a very small way, we just wanted to make a difference. Dedicated people do this kind of work all the time without getting any recognition for it.

'I did it for two years. The reason I finished was that, in the end, I was doing most things on my own: going out getting the food and making it. Amanda was pregnant, and there are times when the family has to come first. As for the future, I'll have to see where the Lord leads me, but I'd like to do voluntary work again when I finish my career, working with those who are not so fortunate. I'd really enjoy doing something like that.'

With the rugby goals clear in his mind, Robinson was never going to waste a moment in pursuing them, and while Woodward integrated him into the England training squad from the start, nobody can have imagined that he would achieve them at such breakneck speed, even allowing for the high velocity of his nickname. Ten matches for Sale was all it took whizzing Billy to win his England cap, as a second-half substitute against Italy at Twickenham on 17 February 2001. His appearance in place of Ben Cohen transformed a strange match – which England had been losing at one stage – but in a manner that almost defied belief. In the course of a truncated debut, Robinson spent thirty-five minutes on the field, during which time he received not a single pass and England scored six tries.

Every time they moved the ball his way, someone else stole through on the inside to poach the try; among those guilty of denying him a scoring debut were his fellow substitutes Mark Regan and Joe Worsley, a pair of forwards who until then had never scored an international try between them. On the one occasion he did get his hands on the ball, at a ruck in midfield, Twickenham got a sight of what was to come – a mesmerising dance through the *Azzurri* creating a try for Will Greenwood.

Robinson declared it 'an honour', and if the deceased bigots on both sides of the rugby divide were spinning in their graves, then that surely made it all the more of an honour. England allowed him less time against Scotland a fortnight later – 17 minutes – but it was long enough to win himself a place on the Lions tour of Australia at the end of that season. The postponement of Wales's match against Ireland because of the foot-and-mouth epidemic had allowed the Lions coach Graham Henry to be at Twickenham to see Robinson play. 'Jason had a priceless game-breaking ability,' Henry said. 'He was extremely quick, and he fairly fizzed about the field. He had a jagged step off either foot that could ruin a defender inside a stride. He was there one moment, away the next – like a Gerald Davies for the new millennium. He had a compact, powerful physique, played low to the ground and was expert at spinning out of the tackle. All this made it very difficult for a tackler to meet his targets in space and time when he was trying to mark Jason Robinson.'

Exactly how difficult was something the players representing the Queensland Country found out for themselves on a sultry night in Townsville during the run-up to the opening Test in Brisbane. Robinson ran in five tries during the space of thirty-three second-half minutes, and had the Wales centre Mark Taylor passed outside instead of inside to Ireland's Rob Henderson in the last minute, the Yorkshireman would have equalled the all-time Lions record of six in a match.

Henderson, a noted bon viveur who had changed his cavalier attitude to rugby and knuckled down to surprise everyone – probably himself included – by winning a Test place, had been Robinson's room-mate. It did not take him long to understand why the Irish centre answered to the nickname of 'The Snorer'. As Robinson observed, 'It was like sleeping in a room with a real lion – actually, more like a bat. He could sleep through the day, and then at night he'd come alive. At 1 a.m., he'd want to chat. You'd be half asleep, and he'd be ordering room-service pizza and chips. Really funny!'

In spite of the late night snacks and the snoring, Robinson made more history the following week, by gaining a place in the Test team, which meant he was starting an international for the Lions before he had started one for his country. This achievement put him alongside Dickie Jeeps in South Africa in 1955, Bill Patterson, the Sale centre, in New Zealand in 1959, Delme Thomas in New Zealand seven years later, and the Welsh pair Brynmor Williams and Elgan Rees in New Zealand in 1977.

Despite the warning he had given the Wallabies in tropical Townsville, Robinson put the heat on them in real style, standing up

Chris Latham in classic fashion when he appeared to be hemmed in tight to the left touchline with no room to go anywhere but inside. Instead, he left Australia's full-back rooted to the spot, shooting past on the outside to set the Lions off towards a landslide win.

Just as he scored the first try of the first Test, so he scored the first of the last, at the Olympic Stadium in Sydney a fortnight later. The series went down to the last lineout, when Justin Harrison stole Keith Wood's throw to Martin Johnson yards from the Wallaby try line and turned himself into an all-Australian hero overnight. The Lions had failed, but Robinson, one of the guiding lights of the tour who took his own guide from the bible he always packed into his suitcase, had nothing to reproach himself for. Besides, before too long he would be back in the same vast stadium to help England claim the greatest prize of all.

Weary beyond words, after more than two years on the rugby treadmill with barely a break, Robinson would have been too weary to think about winning the World Cup, as he retreated to the far north of Queensland for a holiday with Amanda and the family. The new season would come round all too soon, and, when it did, new challenges would be waiting in the next phase of his union education.

The first was to become England's new full-back, another example of Woodward's lateral thinking. All he had to do was accelerate the evolution of the twenty-first-century full-back away from the traditional British heavyweight personified by Gavin Hastings and J. P. R. Williams: commanding figures from a time when defence was the first principle of the job.

As the Lions' choice in all three Tests a few months earlier, Matt Perry could reasonably have expected to continue as England's full-back, all the more so since another English Grand Slam had turned to dust without him in Dublin, a few weeks before Robinson took the plunge at number 15 against Australia at Twickenham on 10 November 2001. For Woodward, a safe pair of hands was not enough, not if England were to fulfil his *raison d'être* and beat the world.

Two years before the World Cup, Woodward had a clear vision of what winning it would entail, and Robinson's redeployment was all part of the grand plan. Yet at the time, the architect found it necessary to defend some of the more iconoclastic decisions behind that creation, including the choice of his new full-back.

'I'm not pressing the panic button,' Woodward protested. 'What

I am doing is changing the mindset of players, coaches and public in terms of what we are trying to do, which is picking the most talented players and going for it.'

The All Black Christian Cullen had gone some way to breaking the mould but, at 5 ft 8 in. and barely 13 st., Robinson had to challenge the stereotype further, if he was to succeed. The fastest feet in the game would ensure that he broke enough first-up tackles to turn the old-fashioned last line of defence into a new-fangled first line of attack. Typically, he took it in his stride: 'It's all about judgement. You catch the ball, look up, make a decision and go for it. If you can't catch the ball, well, you're going to find it a struggle. And if you're a big bloke of 6 ft 2 in. and 15 st., there are some things you won't be able to do, like going through a small gap.'

England went through every gap in the next two years, winning 27 of their 29 matches culminating in the World Cup final when who else but Robinson pounced for their only try in rapid response to the one which Lote Tuqiri scored for Australia. 'We knew we had to get back at them quickly and that if we kept our nerve, the opportunities would come. "Lol" [Lawrence Dallaglio] did some good work before passing inside to Jonny, who had Ben Cohen to his right and me to his left.

'Realising that the cover would be coming across, he passed the ball to me, and I knew I had to dive just before the line to be sure of scoring. I deliberately used the momentum and the wet grass to skid over, rather than mess about and run the risk of being knocked into touch.'

The match will be talked about for as long as rugby is played: how England failed to turn their forward superiority into a comfortable win in normal time and ended up with their renowned will-to-win pushed to breaking point, before winning with a drop goal in the final minute of extra time.

'When the final whistle went, I jumped so high in the air that I wondered if I was ever going to come back down again. I shall remember that match for the rest of my life – every single moment of it from start to finish – but most of all I shall remember the scenes at the end: the absolute elation at realising that we had achieved our goal and the sheer pandemonium in the dressing-room afterwards with everyone singing and taking photographs.

'I had played in some big games over the years, but I have never experienced anything as emotional as that night in Sydney, and I know I shall never experience anything like it again. The best thing about the team was that every individual was able to do his job because everyone else had done theirs.'

The team that had set out on English rugby's greatest night would never play together again. Retirements and injuries had taken such a toll that when Australia turned up at Twickenham on the first anniversary of the final, who should be leading the World Cup holders out of their dressing-room but Robinson. In Jonny Wilkinson's unavoidable absence, head coach Andy Robinson had turned to his namesake who responded in predictable fashion.

'I went away and said a prayer. I have done so many things in my career that there have been times when I thought, "I can't possibly do any more." Then I get the captaincy of Sale and again I think, "There is nothing left to do." Just when I've convinced myself of that, I get the England captaincy and the opportunity to do something I never dreamt of.'

Lawrence Dallaglio's retirement from the Test arena at the start of that season had created the vacancy, and Wilkinson's injury pushed Robinson to the top of the short-list ahead of Mike Tindall. After an apprenticeship as rapid as one of his corkscrewing runs, he had become the first rugby league player to captain England's union team. What's more, he had done so on the strength of just eight matches in charge of Sale, thanks in no small part to the club's enlightened French coach, Philippe Saint-André.

Blissfully oblivious to the fact that nobody had captained England from full-back since Bob Hiller in the early '70s, Saint-André ignored the taboo that decries full-backs and wings as suitable captaincy material on the basis that they are too peripheral to call the shots. Never one to be hidebound by convention, he had done it himself from the wing at the highest level as captain of France on 34 occasions.

'It's not the position you play which really matters,' he said. 'It is the character of the person concerned. I made him captain of Sale because he understands the strategy of the game, because everyone respects him and everyone listens when he speaks. He does not need to shout.'

There were plenty of times when he would have been forgiven for doing so as captain of England. His appointment having come at a turbulent period during the post-World Cup slide, the captaincy was never going to be a bed of roses, not after so many of the principal 'Red Rose' figures had called it a day. A 70-point romp against Canada preceded a decisive home win over South Africa's Tri-

Nations champions, which not only stopped the rot of five defeats in the last six matches under Woodward but encouraged the naive belief that England would carry on winning as before.

At the start of the 2005 RBS Six Nations, Robinson had gone from being a complete novice to the senior survivor of the World Cup final in the space of four years, and England's novel decision to pitch their pre-tournament training camp with the Leeds Rhinos meant that his career had turned full circle. Appropriately, they rolled out the red carpet at Headingley to welcome the first England union captain to go to work with the champions of rugby league.

It made quite a change from the first time he had gone there on business in the summer of 1991, supposedly to sign for his home-town club as a budding scrum-half only to be shown the door and told he would never make it, or certainly not at Headingley. He had gone back there, on a raw Monday morning in mid-January, wondering what all the fuss was about. History was not one of his better subjects.

Growing up in Leeds, the young Robinson assumed that only one form of the game existed and, as he put it himself, 'it wasn't rugby union'. England's liaison with the Rhinos represented the first reunion of the codes since the 'Great Schism' of 1895 when 22 northern clubs seceded from the Rugby Football Union as a result of their refusal to allow broken-time payments as compensation for players giving up their Saturday morning shifts. At the height of the Industrial Revolution, and particularly in the booming cities of the north, the working man did a six-and-a-half-day week.

Robinson's personal schism with Leeds was no less shattering, forcing him to consider a different career and apply for an apprenticeship in bricklaying. Eric Hawley, the scout who would sign him for Wigan a few months later, recalled, 'Leeds told him on the Tuesday that they were going to sign him on the Thursday. For a young lad setting out in rugby league, it was the equivalent of joining Manchester United. Then he got a phone call from them on the Wednesday to say they weren't going to sign him. The kid was terribly upset.'

His local amateur league club, Hunslet Parkside, were left to pick up the pieces. Colin Cooper, club secretary and general dogsbody who had known 'the little lad' from the age of 13, remembers it well. 'He came heart-broken back to the club,' Cooper said. 'He'd had his hopes built up and then destroyed. He was very distraught coming away from Headingley.

'They'd told him he would never be good enough. The little lad was shattered by that, but the coaches at Parkside, Steve Kempton and Steve Hamill, did a grand job in picking him up. That experience will always stick with him. Every time he's played at Headingley, for Wigan and then Sale, he always seemed to score tries. It was as if he put in that little bit extra, because of what happened all those years ago. He's proved his point time and time again.

'The first night I saw him was when he came to us from the local boys' club as a little lad of 13. He just sat in the corner of the tearoom. Didn't move. Didn't say a word to anyone. Just sat there. To say he was quiet was an understatement.

'To be perfectly honest, if someone had said to me that night, "You see that lad in the corner? One day he will be a great player. And then he will go to union and win the World Cup and be captain of England," I'd have said, "Don't be daft."

'In the years after that, he started to develop physically and as a player. Jason became a real match-breaker. You could see that he had it. When he started doing his jinks, everyone knew it was there except, of course, the people at Headingley. Special people have special talent. Wigan brought it out of him. When he started to make it big, one person connected with Leeds commented to me, "Blimey, we didn't realise how good he was . . ."'

It would be wrong to conclude that Robinson's career has been one of endless success. The crushing sense of rejection he felt about his experience at Leeds, where he had been a ball-boy, affected him every bit as badly as Hawley and Cooper relate. 'It broke my heart when they told me I wouldn't make the grade,' Robinson said. 'To be told that at 16, just when I thought there was a career waiting for me, was very hard to take.'

At that confusing time of his life, he had never heard of Eric Hawley, who, coincidentally, had resigned from representing Leeds as a scout before the Robinson fiasco and had started working for Wigan instead. 'I had my contacts so I knew about this young fellow, and I went to watch Hunslet Parkside play at Featherstone,' Hawley said. 'The pitch was about 100 metres from the dressing-room so, when the team came out, I introduced myself to Jason and chatted to him as we walked over.

'He played quite well that day, then had a cracker the following week. The week after that, Wigan were playing at Wakefield Trinity, and I had a coffee with the directors on the coach in the car park before kick-off. I recommended they sign Jason the following Tuesday.

'He got a £15,000 signing-on fee, which was staggered over a certain period. I did not get a cent more than my salary and expenses. You've got to love the game. You don't do it for the money. I took Steve Kempton from Parkside to the signing because Jason's mum didn't want to come.

'While we were waiting to go into the boardroom, I took him into the gym. The players were all there pumping iron and Jason, who was still very shy, looked at me. "Eric," he said, "I won't be able to do that."

'I said, "Look, these fellows are professionals. In time, you will be just as good as they are." There was one exercise where you had to pull yourself up so your chin was above the bar. Eighteen months later, he was so good he broke every record.'

They kept in touch and when Hawley retired some years later from his job, as a sales representative for a safety equipment company, Robinson made it his business to attend the farewell bash and provide a suitable send-off for the man whose intervention rescued him from the imminent prospect of learning how to build brick walls, instead of dodging through them on the rugby field.

Despite his protégé making a name for himself on the other side of the Pennines, Hawley has called on Leeds to recognise the unique nature of Robinson's career. 'They ought to make him a freeman of the city, because he has been an absolute credit to the place,' he says. 'All I did was give him the opportunity to show what he could do.'

Robinson never did get to work with a trowel and spirit level on the building sites of his native city, but it sounded a close-run thing. The day he signed for Wigan, on his 17th birthday in July 1991, was the day before he had been due to start his apprenticeship. Instead of laying bricks, Robinson concentrated on the rather more rewarding business of building himself a legend in rugby league and union.

After captaining England in Jonny Wilkinson's absence for their first six internationals of the 2004–05 season, Robinson missed the last two matches in the Six Nations because of injury, before recovering to lead Sale to victory over Pau in the final of Europe's secondary tournament, the Challenge Cup. A second successive Lions tour followed, but New Zealand in 2005 proved to be a stark contrast to Australia in 2001.

Indispensable against the Wallabies, Billy Whizz suffered like the rest of the back line behind a badly beaten pack in Christchurch, reverted from full-back to right wing in Wellington and ended up losing his place to another Sale player, Mark Cueto, for the finale in Auckland.

19

THE ROAD TO PARADISE

JONNY WILKINSON HAD BEEN THROUGH THE SCENARIO A THOUSAND TIMES IN THE solitude of the training ground, imagining that the next kick was the one to win the World Cup.

He was driven by an obsessive conviction that one day he would be asked to do it for real and that, when that day came, he had better not fail. In the wake of their demoralising exit from the previous World Cup in the autumn of 1999, England put a plan in place designed to give their fly-half the chance of winning the next one by the drop-goal option.

On the long, lonely road to paradise, practising drop goals became an integral part of Wilkinson's routine at every practice session. He was prompted to do so following the most miserable match of his career: the Paris quarter-final against South Africa in October 1999 when Jannie de Beer fired his historic volley of five drop goals. Wilkinson watched in helpless isolation from the touchline, bewildered at having been dropped to the bench and bemused by what was happening right in front of him.

In the course of ignoring a few irresponsible calls for his dismissal, Clive Woodward learnt the lesson that would allow England to win the greatest World Cup final of all. The seeds of an unique achievement had been sown. With time fast ebbing away in the 2003 World Cup final, Martin Johnson manoeuvred his team into the perfect position, like a general marshalling his forces for the decisive strike.

Wilkinson knew the moment had finally arrived just as he had always told himself it would. He was never going to miss, even if it meant using his 'wrong' foot. His right had been supposedly weaker, until by sheer will power and iron discipline he had made it almost as lethal as his left. Johnson's critical intervention in setting up the final ruck drove the Australians deep enough into Wilkinson's 'red zone' to leave him no excuse for missing.

The minute the drop goal sailed over the bar, the ball went soaring ever higher into the English sporting echelons until it landed alongside the one Sir Geoff Hurst thudded against the underside of the bar and over the West German goal line during England's other World Cup final victory almost 30 years earlier. The journey from Farnham in Surrey to the World Cup final, and the incessant hours of practice at the local rugby club, involved many staging posts but none more significant than the Parc des Princes in Paris in October 1999.

'Probably the toughest debrief we had after any match was after that one,' Phil Larder, England's defence coach, said. 'That was a significant defeat in our development, and one of the things we added to our armoury as a result of that match was a drop-goal routine. Since then, before every Test, we have practised getting into position close enough to the sticks and giving the ball to "Wilko". Because we have worked so hard on that for so long, I felt that if we could get into their red-zone we would nail it.'

England, therefore, had planned for every eventuality, although neither Woodward nor Wilkinson could ever have imagined they would have to cut it quite so fine. The greatest drama in rugby history had held the world in suspense for more than two hours, and there were only twenty-nine seconds of extra time left when he cocked his right leg for the pressure kick to end all pressure kicks.

The sweetest of drop goals confirmed the theory that he had been born to win the World Cup. From the age of ten, when he first played at Twickenham in a curtain-raiser to the 1990 Pilkington Cup final, Wilkinson had been working towards the ultimate goal, pursuing it with such single-mindedness that he had spent the previous six weeks of the World Cup in between matches either on the training ground or closeted in his hotel room.

While some questioned the effect that might have on his sanity, it was Wilkinson's way of ensuring that he could carry the nation's hopes on his shoulders and still deliver: 'I have put my whole life into this. It's about putting yourself under pressure. Every time I kick on the training ground, I'm thinking to myself, "Right, this could be the kick to win the World Cup."'

Other motivational forces have long been at work, most notably the one put there by his clubmate at Newcastle, the former All Black wing, Va'aiga Tuigamala. 'He once told me that it would be a waste of time, if after you have hung up your boots, nobody ever mentions you again. I want to be seen as the best I can possibly be.'

England's man of destiny was always going to make a mark on the game, but not even he could have dreamt that it would be such an indelible one. It set the world ablaze, the fireworks exploding high into the night sky over the Sydney Harbour Bridge proclaiming the new world champions as they paraded the gold trophy.

Johnson even began a little jig of delight, to the amusement of the foot soldiers, before thinking better of it, perhaps reminding himself that goliaths do not dance. Will Greenwood, whose tournament had survived the scare of complications to his wife's pregnancy, sank to his knees in supplication. Mike Catt draped himself in the flag of St George, not bad for a South African who came to England on a holiday ten years earlier to look up his uncle in the West Country and never intended to stay for more than a month.

Dave Reddin, the fitness coach who ensured there would be enough in the tank for 'Dad's Army' to keep going when younger packs might have faded, cradled the trophy in his arms. Three weeks earlier, he feared that he might have been the victim of a gross injustice and would be chucked out of the tournament as a result of the 16th man affair against Samoa when he and England finished up before a disciplinary tribunal.

Ben Kay, gracious in victory, found time to comfort the inconsolable Wallaby lock Justin Harrison. Phil Vickery, in his hour of triumph, sought out his Wallaby counterpart, Ben Darwin. Vickery was relieved to be back on his feet, albeit in a neck brace after his frightening injury in the semi-final against New Zealand.

Above all, there was Wilkinson, inevitably the last English player to leave the pitch almost 45 minutes after applying the *coup de grâce*. In other circumstances, England would have strolled home by ten or fifteen points, and after missing a few drop goal attempts with his stronger foot, their number 10 would have flown home as a fly-half with a battered shoulder. Instead, the gods decreed otherwise. His team's failure to win it comfortably in normal time – partly explained by Kay's nightmarish try-line fumble, as well as the mistakes of others in the team – at least gave the world a final it would never forget.

At the precise moment when Elton Flatley dragged the Wallabies level at 14–14 with the penalty that ensured 20 minutes' extra time, Mrs Philippa Wilkinson was on the other side of the world, at the vegetable counter of a supermarket in Newcastle-upon-Tyne. As usual, nerves had got the better of her when it had come to sitting down in front of the television to watch the match. As Philippa passed Marie Haddon – a 40-year-old mother of two who was busy stacking shelves – the supermarket employee just so happened to hear from one of her workmates that Australia had taken the match into extra time. 'This lady turned to us and said, "I didn't really want to know that,"' Haddon said. 'I asked her if she was a big rugby fan and she said, "You could say that. I'm Jonny Wilkinson's mother."'

She was still in the supermarket when another employee broke the news: 'Mrs Wilkinson, your Jonny has just won it for England.' She received a text message on her mobile phone almost simultaneously with the news of England's victory. It was from her husband Phil, who had also taken some evasive action of his own at the Olympic Stadium in Sydney. As the tension mounted, he left his seat in the stand and paced about the concourse. 'I couldn't sit still,' he said. 'So I watched the last few minutes on a television downstairs on the concourse. I saw the drop goal and then caught the last 20 seconds back in the stadium. It was just a feeling that you are there but you can't do anything to change anything.'

On the pitch, England had done as they always did during that period when there was no other team in the world to touch them. They stayed calm, trusting in their knack of finding a way out of any tight spot and refusing to be the least bit panicked at a time when the credibility of the World Cup was lurching towards the lottery of a drop-goal shoot-out involving five players from each side.

On that night of nights, England's backroom staff had decorated the dressing-room with enough motivational banners to make it look like Twickenham. It was a pertinent reminder that England expected on the most momentous of days for English rugby since William Webb Ellis picked up the football and created a whole new ball game. The banners provided graphic reminders of the squad ethic and that special missions demand special people, all the more so when the mission was wrestling a world title from the Australians in their own paddock. 'Through these doors walk the nation's toughest competitors' said one. 'The pride and talent of England will not be entrusted to the timid or the weak' said another.

Woodward's renowned attention to detail ensured that England would turn the dressing-room into their very own Red Rose bunker, bedecked for the occasion by the flags of St George. The personal rose-embossed name-plates identifying each player's locker had been transferred from Twickenham along with the motivational slogans that had carried them through the storms of Test rugby. Now they were being asked to do something nobody had done before: beat Australia in a World Cup final.

Lest England were in any doubt that the whole of the host country were against them, the Sydney Opera House was bathed in Wallaby gold, the harbour ferries likewise and to ram home the point a jumbo roared over the stadium with three words daubed on its fuselage: 'Go Wallabies, Go'. Like the plane, it all sailed over Johnson's head.

Then, of course, there was the media campaign waged by the Australian papers as a sure sign that they were running scared. The *Daily Telegraph*, a Sydney tabloid newspaper, dreamt up a 'Stop Jonny Voodoo Doll' and urged readers to stick a pin in it, and a radio chat-show host urged listeners to create a noise outside the England team's hotel beside the seaside in Manly in a pathetic attempt to disrupt their sleep.

Insults flew thick and fast. Accusations had been hurled by the Australians throughout the tournament, with the Wallaby back-row forward Toutai Kefu leading the charge. 'The English have always been an arrogant race,' he said. 'Go back in history, look at the English army who go to war dressed up in red coats.'

Then there was the *Daily Telegraph* proclaiming a 'very important correction'. 'The *Telegraph* reported yesterday that the English rugby team was boring. This was incorrect. The entire country of England is boring. The *Telegraph* wishes to apologise for the error.'

They followed that up with another barrage on the same childish theme from their columnist Mike Gibson, who is not to be confused with the Irish Lion of that name:

> Anyone who doubts the English are boring has only to check what they watched on television over the years. *Coronation Street* – the sorry saga of a bunch of miserable Poms living in the dullest backwater on earth is the most successful programme in British television history.

So fascinated were the Brits with *Coronation Street* they moved it south to London and called it *EastEnders*. Hey, we're talking about a nation where the most popular actor is that tedious twit Hugh Grant, where their idea of a holiday is taking a bucket and spade to Brighton or Blackpool. We are talking about a people whose idea of risk-taking is to buy a ticket in the pools, whose idea of excitement is to join a queue.

The tirade ended with an insult that must have had Johnson and Co. quaking in their boots: 'England have historically excelled at two things – boring the fans and losing. The tradition will continue on Saturday night.' And so it went, ad nauseam.

A joke peddled by some Australians revolved around an English fan and his dog, a mongrel adorned in red and white. He takes the dog into a pub to watch England on television and when Wilkinson kicks a goal, the dog leaps onto the bar and does a high-five. 'That's incredible,' says the barman. 'What does he do when England score a try?'

'Don't know,' says the fan. 'I've only had him for three years . . .' Boom-boom.

Only a few months earlier, on 21 June 2003 under the enclosed roof of the Docklands Stadium in Melbourne, England had treated the Australians to a performance of breathtaking quality, winning the World Cup final rehearsal 25–14 through first-half tries from Ben Cohen, Mike Tindall and Will Greenwood. How strange that the Aussies should suffer from such amnesia on a national scale.

When England returned some ten weeks later for the World Cup, it was as if the Melbourne master class had never happened. Instead, they were confronted by the front page of a leading newspaper featuring a photograph of Wilkinson in goal-kicking action beneath the sneering question, 'Is that all you've got?' There were times it begged a simple answer, 'Do we need anything else?'

Wilkinson scored 20 of his team's 25 points against South Africa in Perth, 23 of the 28 against Wales in Brisbane and all 24 against France in Sydney in the semi-final. It left the Wallabies wondering what price they would have to pay for his devastating, hand-clasping, three-step penalty routine. As it turned out, it would cost them the trophy they had won in Cardiff four years earlier.

Still the youngest member of the England squad at 24, Wilkinson had done the game the mightiest of favours, never mind for Queen and country: he had rescued the tournament from being settled by the demeaning lottery of a drop-goal competition. The young fly-half had come through the most gruelling six weeks of his career when it might easily have all gone wrong. It very nearly did in catastrophic circumstances against Wales, during the quarter-final in Brisbane a fortnight earlier, when Mike Catt pulled England out of their downward spiral.

Wales, using a pick-pocket's sleight of hand to strip the meanest of defences bare, had reduced some members of what was supposedly the best team in the planet to the verge of gibbering wrecks. They rattled England into making a decisive half-time substitution; it was this intervention by the English coaching staff that ultimately prevented their wonderfully inventive neighbours from registering the mightiest hit on the Richter scale of giant-killing. Catt was brought on to play fly-half and Jonny pushed out to inside centre. Operating as Wilkinson's minder, Catt worked the touchline to perfection and secured his place in the semi-final.

In the build-up to the match Wilkinson had been asked whether his brooding introspection meant he would finish up as a 'basket case'. Grant Fox, a prolific goal kicker and World Cup winner with the All Blacks in 1987, said of Wilkinson, 'People talk of his obsessive nature. I can relate to that, but all he is trying to do is become the best he can be. Having said that, I don't think he's quite on his game. His goal kicking is still outstanding, but his running and defensive game have been a bit off. Wilkinson appears a complete fly-half. He is mentally tough and highly skilled. This guy is all class.'

Fortunately, he had the mental fortitude to ignore the doubters before the semi-final and the ability to block out the unfavourable comparisons that were being made with himself and Frédéric Michalak, who was tipped to win the game for France. On the night, he dissolved in the face of Wilkinson's eight penalties, and Michalak's withdrawal twenty minutes from time was nothing more than a humane act of mercy.

The weeks of Wilkomania that followed the tournament made him a millionaire several times over. One poll hailed him as a better role model than the England footballer David Beckham and Newcastle, Wilkinson's adopted home, gave him the freedom of the city, an honour that meant he was emulating Nelson Mandela, Alan Shearer and Jonathan Edwards.

Back in Australia, they were munching their way through a pile of humble pie about as big as Ayers Rock. Profuse apologies were being offered all round by those responsible for having been so beastly to those very nice English rugby players and their fly-half in particular. The *Sydney Morning Herald* went into the confessional in a big way. In an editorial they wrote:

> You are not too old (although we hoped you would be when the game went into extra time). You scored as many tries as we did. You kicked no more penalty goals than we did. You ran the ball as much as we did. You entertained as much as we did. You did it with one of your own as coach. You are better singers than we are.
>
> You played with class, toughness and grace. You were bloody superior and you are, for the first time in 37 years, holders of a football World Cup. We believe Twickenham is a most fitting home for Bill [the cup] though we humbly remind you that, unlike the Ashes, you have to hand it over if you don't win next time.
>
> We concede the time has come to forgive you for using Australia as a dumping ground for your poor, weak and defenceless – even if the practice continues unabated every fourth summer. We will no longer characterise your fans as beer-swilling, pot-bellied louts or knife-wielding hooligans and try to remember the sporting and enthusiastic supporters who did so much to make the final memorable.
>
> We will stop calling for the International Rugby Board to change the scoring system. In fact, if you can guarantee us a final as good as that one, maybe we'll ask them to actually increase the value of penalty and drop goals. We officially removed the 215-year-old chip(s) from our weary shoulders and encourage all Australians to be nice to any person of English persuasion they come into contact with for the rest of the week. Well, at least until the close of business today.

Sydney's *Daily Telegraph* had no option but to apologise, albeit in a roundabout way, for the voodoo doll. 'Every time we put a pin in it, Sydney was swamped by a pea-soup fog, a torrential downpour and a continual display of deadly accuracy from Wilkinson,' the paper wrote. 'Everyone at the *Daily Telegraph* says, "We give up. Jonny is unstoppable. His left foot made the World Cup un-winnable."'

Wilkinson's relish for the more physical demands of the game, invariably against much bigger opponents, came at a price and raised constant fears for his long-term future. There is a price to be paid for everything and the one he paid for a few hits too many during the World Cup removed him from the international stage for more than 18 months.

After a neck operation to save his career, Wilkinson spent the entire 2004–05 season negotiating one comeback after another. Despite having to make four in all – two from a knee injury suffered during Newcastle's European Cup tie against Perpignan – he beat the odds in time to win the forty-fifth and final place on the Lions tour of New Zealand.

Seven goals against a depleted Argentina at the Millennium Stadium left nobody in any doubt that he was back in the groove for an important piece of unfinished business. His previous Lions experience, in Australia four years before, had been a bitter-sweet one: a record-breaking start in Brisbane had made the series defeat in Sydney all the harder to bear.

The second Test in Melbourne found the Wallabies spread-eagled on the ropes. Beforehand, Joe Roff had read the jingoistic messages of good luck from Steve Waugh's cricketers, then on Ashes business in England, and wondered if this was going to be his lucky night. At half-time, he was beginning to think it might be with his team counting their blessings at being only five points behind. With 40 minutes to save the series, Roff knew Australia needed something to happen fairly quickly. That something landed in his lap like manna from heaven within 30 seconds of the re-start. The left wing's interception of Wilkinson's lofted pass and masterful one-handed finish in the corner turned the match upside down. A second, more devastating, Roff try eight minutes later, created in the rubble of a disintegrating scrum, had such a deflating effect on the Lions that they went down like the proverbial lead balloon.

One calamitous pass and one crumbling scrum scarcely explained how a series could swing so far so soon by a staggering 37 points: the difference between the Lions winning the first Test by a margin of 16 points and losing the second by 21. Worse still, Wilkinson had been carted off with a suspected broken leg. He made an almost miraculous recovery to make the final Test seven days later, only for Graham Henry's team to lose a gripping series by the inch or two that allowed the Wallaby lock Justin Harrison to steal Keith Wood's final throw and prevent Johnson's pack mauling their way over for the potentially decisive try.

Wilkinson's chance at Lions redemption came on the tour to New Zealand in June and July of 2005. It promised to be like no other Lions tour and so it proved, albeit for the wrong reasons. It would be Sir Clive Woodward's final frontier and no expense was spared in the whole operation: from assembling a squad of 45 players to shuttling them around the country in a chartered 737 complete with the Lions motif on each and every head rest.

The players wanted for nothing: they were put up in five-star luxury wherever possible and each was given a room to himself, instead of the traditional sharing. Woodward put six coaches at their disposal and found room in the twenty-nine-strong management team for that well-known Burnley Football Club enthusiast, Alastair Campbell. Even accepting Woodward's penchant for thinking outside the square, it was an extraordinary appointment and one that guaranteed that Tony Blair's spin doctor would make more headlines, directly or indirectly, than any of the players.

True to form, Wilkinson kept his head down and made the Test team, not in his customary position but at inside centre, where he had last appeared for England six years earlier. The decision to play him in tandem with Stephen Jones, Wales's Grand Slam-winning number 10, went ahead despite the fact that they had seen all of twenty minutes' action together, during the last quarter against Wellington, ten days before the opening Test in Christchurch.

It turned out to be the worst from a Lions perspective for more than 20 years, starting with the calamitous injury of captain Brian O'Driscoll in the first 45 seconds of the match. A shoulder dislocated in controversial circumstances resulted in Will Greenwood's belated entry as a Test Lion after two tours spent among the supporting cast.

Greenwood's first tour, in South Africa in 1997, almost killed him after a sickening fall on his head in a match against the Orange Free State in Bloemfontein. The second tour, to Australia in 2001, finished prematurely with a more routine injury and the third meant rolling the years back far enough to outsmart the new brigade headed by the perma-tanned Welshman Gavin Henson.

Two months after being submerged beneath the tide of Premiership relegation with Harlequins and missing the entire 2005 Six Nations because of injury, Greenwood resurfaced. O'Driscoll would have been the first to admit that the gangling northerner from Blackburn had more than paid his dues. As a Manchester City supporter, Greenwood had long been inured to the slings and arrows of outrageous fortune, which was just as well considering what awaited him on that chilling Saturday night at Lancaster Park.

When the Lions lineout collapsed in a polar storm, Wilkinson spent almost the entire match on the retreat, saving one certain early try. It was not a good omen for the rest of the series, despite his swift restoration to stand-off for the second Test in Wellington seven days later. When the All Blacks cut loose in that match, in more benign conditions, their English nemesis at the same venue two years earlier had to be helped off the field in some distress almost half an hour ahead of schedule. Two blows in rapid succession forced him to sit out what was left of the match on the touchline. If nothing else, it gave him a ringside seat at the Daniel Carter show. While one fly-half nursed the burning sensation in his neck caused by two 'stingers' in rapid succession, the other put the finishing touches to the rugby equivalent of Leonardo da Vinci painting the *Mona Lisa*.

How ironic that in his perennial search for the perfect game, Wilkinson should discover that someone else had beaten him to it, if only for one night. In proving what his rival had always maintained, that such a game did exist, Carter condemned the Lions to another losing series and Wilkinson to waiting four more years for the next opportunity to do himself full justice as part of a winning Lions squad.

Far from emulating Barry John and the Welsh superstars of the 1971 Lions in New Zealand, he trudged sadly off the pitch at Wellington with the thunderous acclaim for the All Black sorcerer ringing in his ears. Wilkinson at least has time on his side, unlike some of his compatriots for whom there will be no more such tours.

Appendix I

THE TEST LIONS OF ENGLAND

Player	Club	Tests	Tours
Aarvold, Carl	Cambridge University/ Harlequins	5	NZ, Aus 1930
Ackford, Paul	Harlequins	3	Aus 1989
Andrew, Rob	Wasps	5	Aus 1989, NZ 1993
Ashcroft, Alan	Waterloo	2	NZ, Aus 1959
Back, Neil	Leicester	5	SA 1997, Aus 2001, NZ 2005
Bainbridge, Steve	Gosforth	2	NZ 1983
Balshaw, Iain	Bath	3	Aus 2001
Bayfield, Martin	Northampton	3	NZ 1993
Beaumont, Bill	Fylde	7	NZ 1977, SA 1980
Bentley, John	Newcastle	2	SA 1997
Black, Brian	Oxford University	5	NZ, Aus 1930
Blakeway, Phil	Gloucester	1	SA 1980
Blakiston, Arthur	Blackheath	4	SA 1924
Butterfield, Jeff	Northampton	4	SA 1955
Carleton, John	Orrell	6	SA 1980, NZ 1983
Carling, Will	Harlequins	1	NZ 1993
Catt, Mike	Bath	1	SA 1997
Clarke, Ben	Bath	3	NZ 1993
Colclough, Maurice	Angoulême	8	SA 1980, NZ 1983
Corry, Martin	Leicester	6	Aus 2001, NZ 2005
Coulman, Mike	Moseley	1	SA 1968
Cove-Smith, Ronald	Old Merchant Taylors	4	SA 1924
Cueto, Mark	Sale	1	NZ 2005

Dallaglio, Lawrence	Wasps	3	SA 1997, Aus 2001, NZ 2005
Dancer, Gerry	Bedford	3	SA 1938
Davies, Phil	Harlequins	3	SA 1955
Dawson, Matt	Northampton/Wasps	7	SA 1997, Aus 2001, NZ 2005
Dodge, Paul	Leicester	2	SA 1980
Dooley, Wade	Preston Grasshoppers	2	Aus 1989
Duckham, David	Coventry	3	NZ 1971
Giles, Jimmy	Coventry	2	SA 1938
Greenwood, Will	Harlequins	3	SA 1997, Aus 2001, NZ 2005
Grewcock, Danny	Saracens	3	Aus 2001
Guscott, Jeremy	Bath	8	Aus 1989, NZ 1993, SA 1997
Harris, Stan	Blackheath	2	SA 1924
Healey, Austin	Leicester	2	SA 1997
Higgins, Reg	Liverpool	1	SA 1955
Hill, Richard	Saracens	5	SA 1997, Aus 2001, NZ 2005
Hodgson, John	Northern	2	NZ 1930
Horrocks-Taylor, Phil	Leicester	1	NZ 1959
Horton, Tony	Blackheath	3	SA 1968
Howard, William	Old Birkonians	1	SA 1938
Jackson, Peter	Coventry	5	NZ, Aus 1959
Jeeps, Dickie	Northampton	13	SA 1955, NZ, Aus 1959, SA 1962
Johnson, Martin	Leicester	8	NZ 1993, SA 1997, Aus 2001
Kay, Ben	Leicester	1	NZ 2005
Larter, Peter	Northampton	1	SA 1968
Leonard, Jason	Harlequins	4	NZ 1993, SA 1997, Aus 2001
Lewsey, Josh	Wasps	3	NZ 2005
Marques, David	Harlequins	2	NZ, Aus 1959
Maxwell, Roland	Birkenhead Park	1	SA 1924
McFadyean, Colin	Moseley	4	NZ, Aus 1966
Moody, Lewis	Leicester	2	NZ 2005
Moore, Brian	Nottingham/Harlequins	5	Aus 1989, NZ 1993
Morris, Dewi	Orrell	3	NZ 1993
Neary, Tony	Broughton Park	1	NZ 1977
Nicholson, Basil	Harlequins	1	SA 1938
Novis, Tony	Blackheath	3	NZ, Aus 1930
Patterson, Bill	Sale	1	NZ 1959
Perry, Matt	Bath	3	Aus 2001
Preece, Ivor	Coventry	1	Aus 1950
Prentice, Doug	Leicester	2	NZ 1930
Pullin, John	Bristol	7	SA 1968, NZ, Aus 1971

Ralston, Chris	Richmond	1	SA 1974
Reeve, James	Harlequins	4	NZ, Aus 1930
Regan, Mark	Bristol	1	SA 1997
Richards, Dean	Leicester	6	Aus 1989, NZ 1993
Rimmer, Gordon	Waterloo	1	NZ 1950
Risman, Bev	Manchester	4	NZ, Aus 1959
Robinson, Jason	Sale	5	Aus 2001, NZ 2005
Rodber, Tim	Northampton	2	SA 1997
Rogers, Budge	Bedford	1	SA 1962
Rowntree, Graham	Leicester	2	NZ 2005
Rutherford, Don	Gloucester	1	Aus 1966
Savage, Keith	Northampton	4	SA 1968
Sharp, Richard	Oxford University	2	SA 1962
Slemen, Mike	Liverpool	1	SA 1980
Spong, Roger	Old Millhillians	5	NZ, Aus 1930
Squires, Peter	Harrogate	1	NZ 1977
Stimpson, Tim	Newcastle	1	SA 1997
Taylor, Bob	Northampton	4	SA 1968
Teague, Mike	Gloucester	3	Aus 1989, NZ 1993
Thompson, Steve	Northampton	2	NZ 2005
Underwood, Rory	Leicester	6	Aus 1989, NZ 1993
Underwood, Tony	Newcastle	1	SA 1997
Unwin, James	Rosslyn Park	2	SA 1938
Uttley, Roger	Gosforth	4	SA 1974
Voyce, Tom	Gloucester	2	SA 1924
Wallace, William	Percy Park	1	SA 1924
Weston, Mike	Durham City	6	SA 1962, NZ, Aus 1966
Wheeler, Peter	Leicester	7	NZ 1977, SA 1980
White, Julian	Leicester	3	NZ 2005
Whitley, Herbert	Northern	3	SA 1924
Wilkinson, Jonny	Newcastle	5	Aus 2001, NZ 2005
Willcox, John	Oxford University	3	SA 1962
Winterbottom, Peter	Headingley/Harlequins	7	NZ 1983, NZ 1993
Woodward, Clive	Leicester	2	SA 1980
Young, Arthur	Cambridge University	1	SA 1924
Young, John	Harlequins	1	Aus 1959

Appendix 2

LIONS RECORDS

MOST APPEARANCES IN ALL LIONS MATCHES

68	Mike Gibson (Ireland)	28	Sandy Hinshelwood (Scotland)
67	Willie John McBride (Ireland)	27	John Pullin (England)
44	Delme Thomas (Wales)	26	Phil Bennett (Wales)
43	Syd Millar (Ireland)	26	Bobby Windsor (Wales)
42	Mike Campbell-Lamerton (Scotland)	26	J. J. Williams (Wales)
		26	Roger Young (Ireland)
42	Andy Irvine (Scotland)	26	Barry Bresnihan (Ireland)
42	Bryn Meredith (Wales)	26	Mervyn Davies (Wales)
41	Dickie Jeeps (England)	25	Fergus Slattery (Ireland)
41	Gordon Brown (Scotland)	24	Peter Wheeler (England)
39	Gareth Edwards (Wales)	24	David Hewitt (Ireland)
37	Rhys Williams (Wales)	23	Jason Leonard (England)
37	Graham Price (Wales)	23	Keith Savage (England)
36	Tony O'Reilly (Ireland)	23	Tom Kiernan (Ireland)
36	Alun Pask (Wales)	23	Colin McFadyean (England)
36	Noel Murphy (Ireland)	22	Gordon Waddell (Scotland)
34	Fran Cotton (England)	22	Maurice Colclough (England)
34	Jim Telfer (Scotland)	22	Tony Neary (England)
33	Derek Quinnell (Wales)	21	Bunner Travers (Wales)
32	Haydn Morgan (Wales)	21	Ken Scotland (Scotland)
32	Jeff Squire (Wales)	21	David Watkins (Wales)
32	Malcolm Thomas (Wales)	21	Clive Williams (Wales)
32	Dewi Bebb (Wales)	21	Stewart Wilson (Scotland)
31	Mike Weston (England)	21	John Carleton (England)
30	Bill Mulcahy (Ireland)	20	Sammy Walker (Ireland)
30	Ian McGeechan (Scotland)	20	John Taylor (Wales)
30	Ian McLauchlan (Scotland)	20	Ieuan Evans (Wales)
30	J. P. R. Williams (Wales)		
29	Ken Jones (Wales)		
28	Ken Kennedy (Ireland)		

APPENDIX 2
MOST TEST APPEARANCES

17	Willie John McBride		6	David Watkins (Wales)
13	Dickie Jeeps		6	Hugh McLeod (Scotland)
12	Mike Gibson		6	Bill Mulcahy
12	Graham Price		6	John O'Driscoll (Ireland)
10	Tony O'Reilly		6	John Carleton
10	Rhys Williams		6	Dean Richards (England)
10	Gareth Edwards		6	Gavin Hastings (Scotland)
9	Syd Millar		6	Jeff Squire
9	Andy Irvine		6	Rory Underwood (England)
8	Bryn Meredith		6	Tom Smith (Scotland)
8	Dewi Bebb		6	Martin Corry (England)
8	Mike Campbell-Lamerton		5	Carl Aarvold (England)
8	Alun Pask		5	Ivor Jones (Wales)
8	Noel Murphy		5	Jack Bassett (Wales)
8	Jim Telfer		5	George Beamish (Ireland)
8	Mervyn Davies		5	Brian Black (England)
8	Ian McLauchlan		5	Harry Bowcott (Wales)
8	J. P. R. Williams		5	Tom Clifford (Ireland)
8	Gordon Brown		5	James Farrell (Ireland)
8	Phil Bennett		5	Hugh O'Neill (Ireland)
8	Ian McGeechan		5	David Parker (Wales)
8	Maurice Colclough		5	Roger Spong (England)
8	Jeremy Guscott (England)		5	Bleddyn Williams (Wales)
8	Martin Johnson (England)		5	Malcolm Price (Wales)
7	Delme Thomas		5	John Robins (Wales)
7	John Pullin		5	Stuart Wilson (Scotland)
7	Fran Cotton		5	Peter Jackson (England)
7	Peter Wheeler		5	Ken Scotland
7	Ollie Campbell		5	Barry John (Wales)
7	J. J. Williams		5	Gerald Davies (Wales)
7	Bill Beaumont (England)		5	Denzil Williams (Wales)
7	Peter Winterbottom (England)		5	Bobby Windsor (Wales)
7	Matt Dawson (England)		5	Brian Moore
6	Jack Kyle (Ireland)		5	Rob Andrew (England)
6	Jack Matthews (Wales)		5	Jason Leonard
6	Bob Evans (Wales)		5	Keith Wood (Ireland)
6	Roy John (Wales)		5	Scott Gibbs (Wales)
6	Jim McKay (Ireland)		5	Jason Robinson (England)
6	David Hewitt		5	Jonny Wilkinson (England)
6	Ronnie Dawson (Ireland)		5	Richard Hill (England)
6	Mike Weston (England)		5	Neil Back (England)

LIONS OF ENGLAND
MOST TOURS

5	Willie John McBride	Tours – 1962, '66, '68, '71, '74
5	Mike Gibson	Tours – 1966, '68, '71, '74, '77
3	Dickie Jeeps	Tours – 1955, '59, '62
3	Bryn Meredith	Tours – 1955, '59, '62
3	Syd Millar	Tours – 1959, '62, '68
3	Delme Thomas	Tours – 1966, '68, '71
3	Gareth Edwards	Tours – 1968, '71, '74
3	Gordon Brown	Tours – 1971, '74, '77
3	Andy Irvine	Tours – 1974, '77, '80
3	Graham Price	Tours – 1977, '80, '83
3	Jeff Squire	Tours – 1977, '80, '83
3	Jeremy Guscott	Tours – 1989, '93, '97
3	David Young (Wales)	Tours – 1989, '97, 2001
3	Ieuan Evans	Tours – 1989, '93, '97
3	Scott Gibbs	Tours – 1993, '97, 2001
3	Martin Johnson (England)	Tours – 1993, '97, 2001
3	Jason Leonard	Tours – 1993, '97, 2001
3	Neil Back	Tours – 1997, 2001, '05
3	Lawrence Dallaglio (England)	Tours – 1997, 2001, '05
3	Matt Dawson	Tours – 1997, 2001, '05
3	Will Greenwood (England)	Tours – 1997, 2001, '05
3	Richard Hill	Tours – 1997, 2001, '05

MOST POINTS IN ALL LIONS MATCHES

274	Andy Irvine
228	Phil Bennett
208	Bob Hiller (England)
184	Ollie Campbell
182	Barry John
167	Gavin Hastings
152	Malcolm Thomas
142	Neil Jenkins (Wales)
119	Mike Gibson
116	Jonny Wilkinson
114	Tony O'Reilly
112	David Hewitt
111	Tim Stimpson (England)
88	Dusty Hare (England)
88	Stewart Wilson
87	Terry Davies (Wales)
84	Tom Kiernan

MOST TRIES IN ALL LIONS MATCHES

38	Tony O'Reilly
22	Mike Gibson
22	J. J. Williams
20	Andy Irvine
19	Peter Jackson
19	Sandy Hinshelwood
17	John C. Bevan (Wales)
16	Dewi Bebb
16	Gareth Edwards
16	Tony Novis (England)
16	Ken Jones
14	John Young (England)
14	Malcolm Price
13	Tom Grace (Ireland)
13	Bleddyn Williams (Wales)
13	Gerald Davies
12	John Carleton
11	David Duckham (England)
11	Elgan Rees (Wales)
11	Jason Robinson

MOST TRIES IN TESTS

6	Tony O'Reilly
5	J. J. Williams
4	Malcolm Price
3	Carl Aarvold
3	Jeff Butterfield (England)
3	Gerald Davies
2	Tony Novis
2	Jack Kyle
2	John Nelson (Wales)
2	Jim Greenwood (Scotland)
2	Peter Jackson
2	David Watkins (Wales)
2	Gordon Brown
2	Andy Irvine
2	John O'Driscoll
2	Matt Dawson
2	Jason Robinson

MOST TRIES IN A LIONS MATCH

6	David Duckham v. Wairarapa Bush, Masterton, 1971
6	J. J. Williams v. South Western Districts, Mossel Bay, 1974
5	Jason Robinson v. Queensland President's XV, Townsville, 2001
5	Shane Williams (Wales) v. Manawatu, Palmerston North, 2005

POST-WAR LIONS TEST CAPTAINS

6	Ronnie Dawson
6	Martin Johnson
4	Robin Thompson (Ireland)
4	Tom Kiernan
4	Mike Campbell-Lamerton
4	Willie John McBride
4	John Dawes (Ireland)
4	Phil Bennett
4	Bill Beaumont
4	Ciaran Fitzgerald (Ireland)
3	Karl Mullen (Ireland)
3	Arthur Smith (Scotland)
3	Finlay Calder (Scotland)
3	Gavin Hastings
2	Bleddyn Williams
2	David Watkins
2	Gareth Thomas (Wales)
1	Brian O'Driscoll (Ireland)

INDEX

INDEX